W9-DDO-202

Looking into Art

Looking
into Art

FRANK SEIBERLING

State University of Iowa

HOLT, RINEHART AND WINSTON
NEW YORK · CHICAGO · SAN FRANCISCO
TORONTO · LONDON

27799–0119
Printed in the United States of America

FORM MUST GIVE FORTH THE SPIRIT. FORM
IS THE MANNER IN WHICH THE SPIRIT IS EX-
PRESSED.

Eliel Saarinen

In Memory of
Hans and Erica Tietze

PREFACE

IN THIS ALL TOO BUSY WORLD, the individual may have more than a passing interest in and yet less than enough opportunity for things of art. This book is addressed to those who do have a little more than capsule time but a good deal less than that needed for specialization. The intelligent layman may be bewildered, amused, or outraged at contemporary art forms as often as he is captivated. He deserves an explanation which will not depreciate the respect he may have developed for earlier artists nor fail to deal seriously with his questions about those of today. It is my belief that the case for contemporary art depends in no degree on downgrading the art of the Renaissance or of any other period. Cézanne does not have to be appreciated at the expense of artists like Raphael, any more than the enjoyment of Stravinsky requires a prior conviction of his superiority to Brahms. I believe that what is important is understanding the nature of art itself. Then the rivalries among styles fall away before a larger understanding which includes a deeper insight into the nature of culture as well as of art. This is the reason for my discussing examples from so many periods.

Profound truths may often be condensed to short mathematical formulas or brief maxims. What lifts the maxim above the level of a platitude and gives meaning to the formula is a knowledge of the reasons why they came about and what went into them. The appreciation of art can be encompassed by a number of very simple statements, such as that art is expressive and unified organization, or that art is the creation of a beautiful but largely hidden symbolism. Yet such statements become meaningful only in a larger context.

I believe that the growth in enjoyment and understanding of art is essentially cumulative: like the repetition of classical music, the repetition of visual forms, or of ideas and their substance, gradually intensifies and heightens one's grasp of them. I have herein made a kind of theme and variations—in a very free sense—of the idea of art. If I have begun simply, I have also tried to develop a more challenging expression of the same ideas in depth, farther along, while remaining consistent in theme. The reader who already has some background in art may accordingly move rapidly along in the more accessible early chapters, although I have also tried hard to be as lucid as possible in my own understanding of the context in greater depth. I rely upon my intelligent, and, I trust, charitable, reader to spot the controversial aspects of what I have written, and I would be gratified if, in agreement or disagreement, he were led to his own further investigation. As an aid and encouragement to this end, a selected reading list has been appended.

Understanding destroys many of our raptures of childhood but replaces them with other satisfactions. The composer changes but does not lose his enjoyment of music because of having learned the complicated "laws" of harmony and counterpoint. As adults we may retain a portion of our childhood innocence of response, but it remains our pleasant fate to be able to respond to the world not only with feeling but with understanding—and the search for yet more understanding.

F. S.

Powell, Ohio
March 9, 1959

Acknowledgments

Among those who have read this manuscript in greater or lesser extent, and to whom I am deeply grateful for their insights, are Stanford and Eleanor Ackley, Dr. Thomas Sommer of the University of Freiburg, and Dorothy Seiberling, Assistant Editor of *Life* Magazine, who also procured the unusual photographs of the artists with their works.

Mildred Constantine, Associate Curator of Architecture at the Museum of Modern Art, made valuable suggestions about the section on architecture and helped importantly with the procurement of photographs.

As always, librarians have been generous with time and information—in this case, mostly in the securing of illustrations or of data relative to them. Most helpful have been Jacqueline Sisson, incomparable art librarian of the Ohio State University, and Olga Krill, librarian of visual art materials in the same institution. Among others assisting in the library field were Nancy Boone of the Burnham Library of the Art Institute of Chicago, E. Louise Lucas of the Fogg Art Museum, James Grote Van Derpool of the Avery Library of Columbia University, and Coman Leavenworth of The Museum of Modern Art in New York City.

By their generous loan of plates, Mr. and Mrs. J. W. Alsdorf of Winnetka, Illinois, and Peter Guille, Director of the Sterling and Francine Clark Art Institute, have contributed much-needed color to the book. The remaining illustrations in color are both of works in The Museum of Modern Art—my appreciation to Alfred H. Barr, Jr., for permission to publish.

For the general schema of Figure 11, I am indebted to Gyorgy Kepes of the Massachusetts Institute of Technology.

Thanks to a recommendation of its Committee on Research Leave, the Ohio State University granted me three months' valued time in which to gather materials and begin work on the manuscript.

Most of all I am grateful to Nancy Seiberling, who has not only endured cheerfully the semipermanent travail of being an author's wife, but who in so many ways has made smoother, more fruitful, and to the point not her own, but the author's lot and work.

Finally, I extend my appreciation, whether in memoriam or to the living person, to all the artists and architects whose works appear in these pages. No doubt my interpretation in certain ways is, or would be, at variance with their own, but the interpretation has not been made without respect or without a passion to stir the reader to his own discovery of the wonders they have wrought.

CONTENTS

Part Three: TOWARD A PERSONAL JUDGMENT OF ART

ILLUSTRATIONS

Numbers following title indicate pages on which work is mentioned.

COLOR PLATES

ILLUSTRATIONS

I. J. M. W. Turner: *Rockets and Blue Lights*. English. 1840. Williamstown, Mass.: The Sterling and Francine Clark Art Institute.

Part One

Visual Organization and Meaning

Introduction

The Nature of Form

The Nature of Content

Introduction

1-Presentation and Representation

Look, if you will, at the two scenes from the American "ring" illustrated herewith [1 and 2] and note the enormous difference in the kind of encounter represented. The one is all action, and brutal action. The other is centered in delay—that subtle polarity of action. George Bellows' painting presents the clash of savage force, a "fight," where Thomas Eakins' implies skill, a "contest."

Now it is well known that the ring has had both its butchers and its boxers, but the *plausibility* of the scene by no means guarantees its *reliability* in fact. The real "revelation" of Bellows' painting, in a sense, is not the fight at all but his awareness of sadistic behavior. He painted not so much the fight as his feelings about it. He has emphasized what would serve as visual symbols of these feelings, and it is they which contribute the driving force and real impact of the painting. We cannot even be certain that the actual fight was as savage as represented. We only know that Bellows wanted it to appear that way.

Eakins approached his subject much more coolly and selected a "cooler" incident. He reacted to it in a thinking way much more than in a feeling way. His careful and deliberate modeling of the form and of the space is as appropriate to his scene's atmosphere of knowing skill as Bellows' slashing brush strokes are to an atmosphere of impetuous force. In fact the contrasting painterly approaches by the artists contribute to the highly different effect of the two paintings as much as does the choice of different types of encounter.

Thus the sad or the bright truth—depending on how we look at it— is that we are obliged to see these fighters and the crowds watching them in a way altered by the concerns of the individual artist and by

1. George Bellows: *Both Members of This Club.* 1909. Washington: National Gallery of Art, Chester Dale Collection.*

whatever interpretation our own experience may add. The two paintings stand for *reactions* to the ring. The original scene has become enriched—or if that is a presumption, then at least modified—by the artist's viewpoint. And this raises the disturbing thought that at a maximum the "reality" of the original scene might be entirely different from what you or I may have interpreted.

And yet the vividness of art, as in each of these works, almost convinces us that each presents the truth about the subject depicted. Many millions of people, in fact, are innocent victims of this aspect of art, and herein lies its great propagandistic power. Actually, as we shall see more clearly in the course of these pages, the truth about art is the truth about the artist and his world and about the observer and his. Even apparent documentation of the visible world and of events in it is subject to the inevitable altering influence of the artist's feelings and outlook. And the observer's reaction—yours and mine—creates in turn further dilution or enrichment, depending on our time and personal development.

We tend to associate *presenting* with the direct, firsthand appearance of something. The toastmaster presents the speaker of the evening; the dean presents a diploma—hands the physical object—to the graduating

* Unless otherwise noted in the captions, illustrations are of works by American artists, and paintings are in oil. Where no artist is listed, name is unknown.

2. Thomas Eakins: *Taking the Count.* 1898. New Haven, Conn.: Yale University Art Gallery, The Whitney Collections of Sporting Art.

senior. Even when something abstract is presented—an idea, for example —we still associate it with directness. We do not represent our own view at a meeting, we present it. *Representing* has the implication of indirection and of an intermediary. We speak of a representative of the State Department or of a corporation, meaning that the person so designated is serving as an agent.

Now the artist cannot, at last, produce his subject in person nor in its natural state. He is forced to remain a *representative* of nature and the social world. He can create a certain illusion of presentation but—one of

3. Jean-Baptiste Greuze: *The Return of the Prodigal Son.* French. 1778. Paris: Louvre.

its charms—it is still a sleight of hand. For all his realism, Eakins could not even represent, let alone present, the sounds of the arena, the heat of the lights, the smell of the air. He could be faithful only to many visual elements and thus enter into the spirit of presenting at least the visual aspect of the scene.

For Bellows, on the other hand, the actuality of the scene was not a vivid sense of cannily attuned physical bodies in space, but of activated passion and violence. Because of his emotional involvement, he is farther removed from the more presentational objectivity of Eakins. Bellows' figures, at the actual fight, were of course bodies in the round and in three-dimensional space. Eakins felt it important to recreate this illusion, where Bellows rendered only a shallow space and a hasty modeling of the bodies. In other words, the degree of presentational interest may vary with the artist. Other elements, emotional, didactic, or esthetic, may become the artist's preoccupation to a point where the original subject is scarcely discernible and, finally, may be left out altogether.

All art is representational in the sense of standing for something outside itself, even if this something be no more than a fancy, a whim, or an

4. Rembrandt van Rijn: *The Return of the Prodigal Son.* Dutch. *c.* 1665. Leningrad: Hermitage.

impulse of the artist. One of the most liberating awarenesses about art is to realize this, and to see that in art true presentation is impossible. After the master of ceremonies sits down, his part is over. The speaker continues on his own. But the artist always leaves the continuing mark of his presence, no matter how dispassionately he tries to present his subject. Art may have its presentational tendencies, but it can never entirely liberate the subject from the artist's vision and understanding. In the end, it is representational. While we have to take the representation of the subject, therefore, with a grain of salt, the mark of the thinking, feeling, visually sensitive artist *may* invest the whole with a far greater impact and significance than an actual presentation would possess. The representation as a whole may be casual or informed, limited in scope or broad, superficial or profound, descriptive or interpretive, of passing or lasting concern, detailed or generalized—all depending on what kind of person is making the observation and how deeply he is involved in the thing observed.

Consider the accompanying two versions of the Return of the Prodigal Son. The one by Greuze [3] emphasizes, in a grandiloquent way, the fruits of filial disobedience: a crippling blow to the father, a devastating remorse for the son, a state of self-conscious horror for the family. In Rembrandt's version [4] the emphasis is not upon the heinousness and frightening consequences of the act but upon the healing power of love and forgiveness. The artificial gestures and empty exaggeration of Greuze's work are as reflective of his limited concept as the moving radiance of Rembrandt's is of his humanity.

Is this judgment unfair to Greuze? After all, he did not look disparagingly on his own work. Others of his day and perhaps the reader today might well disagree with such an interpretation. What is involved here?

Each of these two artists' views about the prodigal son sprang from a set of values, the artist's sense of the nature of right and wrong, his sense of the significant in life. A qualitative comparison of these attitudes inevitably requires a standard of one's own against which a perception can be formed. Thus, judgments on human endeavor are fundamentally—and perhaps fundamentally no more than—a statement and comparison of values.

Clearly understood values, of course, are not necessarily "good." Some of the worst tyrants of history have had a very clear conception of and belief in their own standards of right and wrong. In the case of Rembrandt and Greuze the question of relative quality, in any event, is a matter of the standards of reference against which the comparison is made. We shall return later to the problem of relative quality, but for our present discussion it is essential to recognize that art has the power to represent not only the *appearance* of the world but *values concerning it*. These values, of course, are not represented directly; they are implicit only. They are *symbolized* in the way the external illusion is created.

What else does art have the power to symbolize? If it can symbolize personal values it follows that it must be able to symbolize group and

5. *Madonna and Child.* French. Late 12th century. Polychromed wood. New York: Metropolitan Museum of Art, Gift of J. Pierpont Morgan.

cultural values, too, for the simple reason that personal values may be shared by others, and are generally rooted in the culture around them.

The majestic figure of Mary and Jesus carved in wood in the twelfth century [5] symbolized a concept of the Madonna as dignified and human—yet also awesome and a little aloof. This concept was gradually to shift and the approach to Mary to become more informal. Thus, in the fourteenth century she was frequently shown as a young, even pretty girl, playing with her child, although still capable of a certain aristocracy or "queenliness" of gesture and carriage [6].

Each of these concepts was widely followed in its time and stood for a group or cultural attitude. Whether the change from an emphasis on reverence to one of shared experience is a retrogression or a growth depends, again, on the values against which the change is measured. In any case, we may add that art has the power to symbolize both personal and *group* values.

But what of those influences on human behavior which are antecedent to values? The nature of one's physical health, for example, can greatly influence his personality development and have an important

6. *Madonna and Child*. French. 14th century. Ivory. Cincinnati, O.: Taft Museum.

influence on outlook. The weighting and intensity of one's emotional-intellectual drive, whether in the intellectual or emotional direction, is not a value in itself but is of strong influence on the personality and on the kind of values one establishes. Finally, the moods one experiences, whether joyful or melancholy, constitute no principle of behavior, yet take their part in the coloration of the total behavior pattern. These aspects of human behavior are generally grouped together as *temperament*, or *personality traits*. As we shall see, they, too, find expression in art.

Indeed, in the first two works we have considered, the fight scenes, even the casual observer is likely to sense strikingly different temperaments: Eakins, analytical; Bellows, emotional. Our reaction in each case, naturally, must be very tentative, tempered by the knowledge that it is based on one creative work only. But the important thing at this point is not the ultimate truth of the impression, but that such traits can be indicated at all. The fact that our impressions must frequently be held in abeyance as to verification does not invalidate them at the very outset.

The power of even entirely abstract symbols to evoke the personality is illustrated in the accompanying works by Kandinsky and Mondrian

7. Wassily Kandinsky: *Composition.* Russian. 1914. New York: The Solomon R. Guggenheim Museum.

8. Piet Mondrian: *Composition*. Dutch. 1936. Philadelphia: The Philadelphia Museum of Art, Arensberg Collection.

[7 and 8]. You may observe that the orderly and firm rectangles of Mondrian create the impression of calm calculation, while the other design, if no less visually whole, suggests a more volatile, improvisational impulse. This is no less true because Kandinsky, too, on other occasions, made more static, geometric compositions. That would merely reflect the variability or development of his personality.

These interpretations are necessarily subjective, which means that you and I might draw diametrically opposite conclusions about the symbolic character of the same thing. But this need not disturb our thesis. The difference might result from an opposition or contrast of our values and temperaments. All subjective conclusions are necessarily tentative. They are deeply involved in the variability of the human being's complex nature.

We can never know from his art alone that Rembrandt really believed in the redeeming power of love. The effect created by his *Return of the Prodigal Son* could have been a hoax of Rembrandt's, or our interpretation could be in error because of psychological blindness created by personality or cultural differences. And yet, even while remaining alert to such possibilities, we are likely to say from what we know of human behavior that evidentially, if not categorically, Rembrandt's *Prodigal Son* is not a hoax but indeed reveals an expressive belief in the redeeming power of love and forgiveness.

It may be safer to take no stand in such matters, to take refuge in the imponderables and exceptions that often can be invoked. Willingness to take a stand and to make a judgment as to esthetic quality or as to meaning is partly a matter of being informed but is also basically related to the individual's temperament and personality. A good thing about art is that, except in matters of sale or purchase, no penalty is attached to erroneous judgments. In financial dealings and in personal relationships, for example, the possibility of error has to be more carefully considered to avoid negative repercussions. Art thus supplies an area—a kind of testing ground—for the expression of viewpoints or insights *without penalty*. This frees it to experiment and to illumine, often to lead the way.

Nevertheless, many people have felt that because interpretations of art are so often different they are therefore without point. How can there be truth—the argument runs—in the midst of so much disagreement? This same argument can be applied equally well to religion, politics, philosophy, and social theories. If in none of these areas it is maintained that the search for the truth is without value because of disagreement, why should it be so for art? As in many other fields, sound judgments here are an expression of the underlying premises of the culture, as well as of the self-confidence, awareness from experience, weighting of the factors involved, and willingness to consider new evidence on the part of an individual. Only the genius can establish new premises, although lesser creative talents can help develop the way.

The artist has suffered the same restraints as other people under dictatorship or other forms of oppression. The power of art to contain more than appears on the surface has made it, in spite of such restraints, an intimate symbol of his spirit, aspirations, and culture. In its intelligent interpretation lies a larger understanding not only of the other man—the artist and his society—but of ourselves and our society. For the answers to this to be pat or universally accepted, however, life itself would have to be pat and uniform. The complexity of art is a direct reflection of the complexity of life. And instead of this being a liability, it is one of the glories of art, as it is of life. Art forever holds before us, in varyingly beautiful and revealing symbols, the quality and nature of man and his times.

To summarize, the important thing is not that symbolic interpretation of art is difficult or subject to differing conclusions, but that the representative, symbolic nature of art is there at all. Without it, art would only appeal to the visual sense of order or stand as a dry imitation. At best it would be reduced to the level of wallpaper design. It would no longer speak to the heart or contribute to our mutual understanding. The human side of art, symbolically revealed, is fascinating, complex, moving, for the very reason that its source is man, and so ourselves.

The Nature of Form

2-Strictly Visual

Let us look again at the twelfth-century *Madonna and Child* [5]. Notice the regularity of the folds of the dress in the Madonna's gown. On the shoulder and upper sleeve, this consists of a series of U-shaped arches, as also—in reverse—on the lower gown to indicate the falling of the material from the knee. These "arches" appear again on the right arm of the Christ Child and, in reversed form, on his garment both below and at the chest. Elsewhere on the Madonna's robe the folds are straighter and more sweeping, but they are spaced about as far apart as those on the sleeve. The fingers, too, have the same regularity of spacing and insistent continuity.

Now the regularity of this system of folds is such that it appears highly disciplined, controlled, almost severe in comparison with the sweeping softness of the folds of the later work [6]. The shallowness of the folds in the earlier work, moreover, together with their frequency of occurrence, create a consistent unity of texture. The regularity here, the rather severe, yet simple orderliness, contributes to the psychological effect of austerity. The type of design becomes a part of the symbolization of these qualities. That is what we talked about in the first chapter. *But the folds are also—for strictly visual reasons—attention-catching; they produce a unified total effect.*

The arches constitute visual *motifs* which, constantly repeated, form a *pattern* over the figures. All this catches the eye because these motifs are employed in such a way as to create *a wholeness of effect in a rhythmic and balanced way.* The upsweep on the arms is countered by the downsweep on neck and chest. Thus, in the shoulders, the rhythmic repetition of the arch motif is clear, contrasting pleasantly with the rhythmic repetition of the sweeping motif in the gown and headpiece. An *orderly opposition* is also created by the intriguing contrasts of finger direction. These contrasts balance one another and contribute to a *system* of orderly arrangement of the surface design.

15

While all this is basically simple and easy to describe, it is the very simplicity in this work which offers us visual pleasure. It is just varied enough to provide some richness and yet it is consistent enough to create a wholeness of effect. This is the sign of an *artist* (here as sculptor) at work, of the unifying, visual power he exerts, of the delight this visual reordering of nature can create.

We have already noticed that the folds of the twelfth-century Madonna's gown are rather shallow in projection. This makes the garment appear to cling to the body. We are kept very conscious of solid form. Now you will note that the approach of the sculptor to this treatment of the solidity of his subject is characterized by the same regularity and simplicity that he employed in treating the drapery. He keeps both figures looking straight ahead and with their shoulders in the same plane as the hip. The faces are modeled with broad cheeks, large noses, clearly defined and firm lips.

The symmetry of the pose, its uncompromising frontality, the simplicity, yet massiveness, of the modeling of the heads and faces, the solidity of the bodies—these contribute, again, to the effect of stability and dignity, becoming additional symbols of this characteristic noted in the first chapter.

But these elements, too, are a pleasure just to see. They are a pleasure because they express a reordering of natural, three-dimensional form to a new and convincing simplicity. The artist seems to have caught what we sense to be the purity and elemental strength of solidity. "The Lord is my rock," says the Scripture, and in the firmness and easy balance of this group we find a subjective outpouring of this insight, as well as a visual delight in the simple unities wrought by the sculptor.

The later Madonna was carved with a greater emphasis on the visual appeal of drapery and the flowing lines it may establish. You will notice that the contour of the cape and head cover leads the eye down and then back up again to the Child. This serves visually to help hold the Child within a single design conception. The Madonna's right hand repeats the tying effect of the drapery, which is reinforced by the reciprocal movement of the Child's arm towards her. These movements evoke a rhythmic response in us. We see them as movement and countermovement, as sweeping flow, all establishing a coherent visual effect.

Note how the V-shaped folds in the gown repeat the down-and-up rhythm of the garment falling from the shoulder and make an easy visual connection between the upper and lower part of the sculpture. The curving lines of the Madonna's blouse are repeated in kind in the folds that fall from the waist. Thus we have a rich interplay of rhythmic elements, both horizontal and vertical, to provide us with a visual effect which is harmonious and unified.

In neither of these sculptures is the drapery entirely realistic, though we know beyond doubt that it is drapery. Something has been added, and this is the sculptor's desire to make the drapery *visually significant.* We enjoy it not because it is drapery but because it is presented to us in a way to stimulate our sense of what is visually interesting and harmonious. These two sculptors have approached the same problem—posing and rendering in three-dimensional form the draped figures of a mother and child—and have made a convincing and attractive result in seemingly divergent ways. This is the magic of art.

Thus, art has two interlocking aspects: that related to external description and to human moods, insights, beliefs, values—the *content* of art; and that related to visual order and effect—its *form*. This latter aspect, which is the concern of this chapter, provides a sensuous satisfaction, a delight for the eye, while it simultaneously creates a psychological symbolism.

The above uses of the words *form* and *content* are specific to this book and will be enlarged upon as we go along. But a reasonable query should be anticipated here first: Why isn't form a part of the total content? Answer: It is, if content is used in its broadest sense. In such usage our terms *content* and *form* would become, respectively, *nonformal content* and *formal content*. In certain circumstances these alternatives are indeed clarifying and will be discussed later on. But ordinarily it will be clearer to use *content* in its nonformal application and *form* in its application as visual organization. The interlocking of the two is seen in the fact that the content is at least partially created or evoked by the character of the form. Thus, the form could be regarded alone for its visual (esthetic) appeal, or for its content (meaning), or for both.

Here is another reasonable query: Isn't it doing violence to the art work's unity to isolate its various aspects? Answer: Not if by so doing we finally have a richer, more unified grasp of it. And that is exactly what we are setting out to achieve.

3-The Elements of Form

Please look, now, at the shapes shown in Figure 9. The first thing likely to strike you about them is that, irregular though they are, you "see" them as the same. It is obvious that the eye does not do this alone. The eye is only a lens attached to nerve cells which transmit an optical image to the brain. While this is in itself remarkable enough and is not yet entirely understood, even more remarkable is the fact that your seeing was combined with a judgment. You saw not just two shapes, but two similar shapes. Some kind of "computer" in your brain sized up and compared these shapes and gave you an awareness of their similarity.

This is a very simple example of a marvelous faculty possessed by human beings everywhere. Evidently some deep tendency in us exists to make *purely visual* observations, observations which are not necessarily utilitarian in any way or directly translatable into human actions. To be sure, not all people have equally refined visual discrimination, but it is normally refined to an astonishing degree. And there is no doubt that it can be improved through practice. The important thing here, to repeat, is that the mind is capable of drawing a kind of *visual* conclusion, based on visual relationships. This is essential to our study of art, for it reveals that the artist may make use of relationships which are partly or altogether of a strictly visual sort.

His problem is to find or create relationships which will be intriguing to the beholder, starting with himself. Ultimately a particular choice of relationships, through being especially satisfying to the artist, will become his own particular complex. They will then move over into the field of meaning and symbol and, while remaining visually significant, will also have a relationship to the personality—to the artist's moods, feelings,

18

9. Shape comparison.

ideas, experiences. Thus the artist's problem ultimately is not to discover relationships, but to discover significant relationships.

Before taking up the important problem of what is significant in relationships, let us look more extensively at what the "eye" observes. We have already seen how the eye picks up *similarity of shape.* But not only can we distinguish irregular shapes which are identical [9], we can distinguish basic community or unity among variants. For example, we can recognize an apple tree almost any time we see one, because all apple trees have enough in common to establish a basic unity of appearance. Yet this basic unity is an abstraction only, a kind of composite awareness in the mind. Nor is it necessary consciously to work out the "apple tree quality" by a point-to-point analysis—although analysis would ultimately show just what the constants are. The exciting fact is that the mysterious "computer" in our minds stores up the impressions of apple trees we have seen and then formulates a composite for us without our trying. While this perception of relationships can undoubtedly be sharpened by study and observation, it is basically automatic.

And it is wonderful how refined is our perception of these visual unities and contrasts. Not only can we recognize an apple tree on sight, we can discern that, because of a storm, it has evidently lost a main branch, or that it has been heavily pruned, or that it is unusually tall for an apple tree.

If you look at both parts of Figure 10 in rapid alternation, you can readily see that the shaded bars are about the same length. This appears so in spite of the size disparity of their respective companion bars, for you still have a basis of comparison. Now cover the right part with your hand. The other dark bar now looks quite short; and when you cover the left part, the other dark bar looks quite large. This is the result of our "computer" establishing a *norm* of size *from the total data supplied.*

The same faculty enables us to recognize close similarities in color —or hue, as it is technically called—while at the same time permitting "total data norms" that *alter the effect of the part.* As we shall see, size and color and even shape are *relative to the total situation in which they are found.* Clearly this has fundamental implications for the artist, who creates within a framework of his own determining. So, when we speak of shape, size, and color discrimination, we speak of relative discrimina-

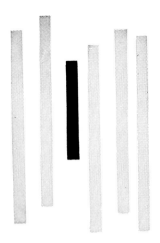

10. Size comparison.

tion: of discrimination through relationships, for who shall say what is "big," "round," or even "red" without a basis of comparison? True, we can define color exactly by spectroscopic analysis, but art depends on human observation, with all its marvelous inexactness and subjectivity. It is here that the impression is so dependent on the role of the part in its immediate and total situation.

The eye is sensitive to a limited range of wavelengths of energy which we see as white light. This is the light from the sun. If only a portion of this range is seen—because of the remainder being absorbed, rather than reflected, by some object—that portion appears as a color or hue. For reasons which need not concern us here, the physicist regards red, green, and blue as the basic hues. The artist has traditionally selected red, yellow, and blue, which are primary to him because they cannot be produced by mixing other hues together.

If there is a high concentration of substance reflecting a particular hue, an effect of intense color is produced. This is often called high saturation, or intensity. If such a concentration is in the form of pigment from a tube of color, it may be lightened in effect (raised in value) by the addition of white, or darkened (lowered in value) by the addition of black. The value of a color, then, in this technical sense, is its degree of lightness or darkness. High values are light to the eye and low values dark, black and white being the extremes.

Pablo Picasso's *Girl before a Mirror* [II] will illustrate some of these points. Notice the violet color on the breast of the figure at the left and on the arm extending across the mirror. This violet is interrupted by a violet of lower value, and a violet of yet lower value appears above the wrist. At the same time, this lower value shows a higher intensity, or saturation, of the violet hue. It has more concentration of color than the brighter color of the arm. While *brightness* is a function of both intensity and value, high value plays the leading role. Picasso's painting makes use in general of a high intensity of color. This is augmented by

II. Pablo Picasso: *Girl before a Mirror*. French. 1932. New York: The Museum of Modern Art, Gift of Mrs. Simon Guggenheim.

the presence of both white and black which, lacking or nearly lacking all color, make the rest more colorful by comparison. If you notice the greens in the lower left and upper middle you will again see differences both of value and of intensity. The lack of brightness in the upper green is compensated by its higher intensity.

One more technical matter: certain hues when mixed absorb almost all white light, producing an effect of near black. These _complementary pairs_ are red and green, orange and blue, violet and yellow. When unmixed, however, and placed side by side, the colors of each pair produce a vibrant, even clashing, effect. In general, women are more alert to this than are men, because of their more colorful dress. Few women wear red blouses with green skirts, for example, preferring to use one of these colors only as an accent to the other, or to use them in combination with other colors. This is what Picasso has done in his painting. All the complementary colors will be found here, and this is another reason why the black and white are so important. They provide visual relief in an ensemble which the complementary associations make very lively and even pleasantly clashing. The black and white also serve to allow the individual hues some independence.

The basic elements we have dealt with so far—shape, size, and hue—can be distinguished to a lesser extent by the animal world. Even rats have a limited shape and size discrimination and many animals have some color discrimination, but there are two other visual phenomena basic to art which, although employed by animals in their physical activity, are too abstract for them to "recognize." These visual elements are _balance_ and _rhythm,_ and they are at the very core of the art process. Even though they are not necessarily employed consciously by the artist, they describe basic aspects of the higher unity the artist achieves.

Balance is the equilibrium achieved by equal opposition of forces. Balance implies a resolution of tensions, a holding-steady of dynamic elements. There is a good deal of evidence that visual balance is related to our sense of physical balance. Living things usually bear an axial relationship to the earth, either in its plane, like the turtle, or perpendicular to it, like a tree. At rest and active, mankind occupies either relationship, and we know from the laws of mechanics that a balanced relationship with the earth's plane is maintained by the human being or animal even in bending over. The two dominant positions experienced by all of us, however, are the horizontal and vertical.

In art these are repeated in the typical rectangular shape of paintings and very probably are the basis for the overwhelming preponderance of the rectangular format in art. This is so despite the fact that the circular field of vision of our eye presents to us a concentric view of things, as Cézanne observed. When we do see a round painting, like the Italian _tondo,_ it appears exceptional, a tour de force. The great majority of paintings, moreover, not only have a rectangular format but have within them a strong use of horizontal or vertical shapes, or both.

The first equilibrium, then, the first great balance, is the simple and

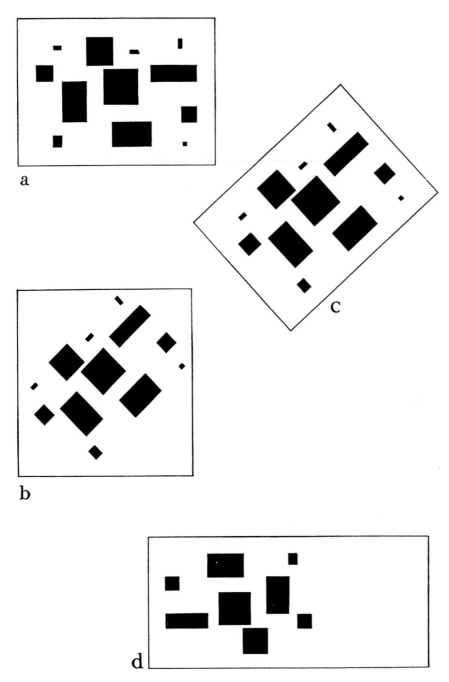

11. Shape and field relations.

instinctive harmonization with the force of gravity. Even the nonobjective painting, the total abstraction, generally has a top and bottom.

Now, the boundaries of a painting, whether rectangular, oval, or other, establish its visual frame of reference. This frame of reference is a flat surface having a particular shape and size. In art parlance, it is variously called the *picture plane,* the *field,* or the *ground.* The three words are used interchangeably. The last two have overtones of meaning relating to Gestalt psychology which need not concern us here but will be taken up later on. For the present, let us think of the "field" and "ground" as referring to the particular flat surface on which the artist must develop his visual organization. It is important to see that the shape and size of this plane create a kind of *visual situation* which interacts with, and to a certain extent dominates, whatever goes into it.

This is shown in a simplified way in Figure 11. Whereas in *a* the shapes seem quite stable and visually organized because their boundaries and axes are parallel to the boundaries and axes of their rectangular ground or field, in *b* they seem to be floating, although they bear the same stable relationship among themselves. The basic importance of the "field" is indicated again in *c*, where the small shapes no longer seem "floating" because they are visually organized in it. Here it is the whole thing that is on edge, a disturbance, again, of our sense of physical balance. In *d*, the shapes are oriented so as to relate to the boundaries of their field but are not *placed* in it to achieve equilibrium. The group of shapes appears too far to the left: a tension exists, a visual tension, between the shapes and their field.

Thus we see the basic principle that *the size and shape of the ground sets up a visual precondition to which subsequent shapes within must relate,* if an effect of planar unity is to be achieved. *Balance,* here, implies balance of part with part and of part with whole. Not all art, to be sure, has pushed balance to this refinement. Nevertheless, even artists who have seemingly destroyed the "field," in the sense of its being a plane, have usually handled their subject matter in a way to re-establish it at least partially.

In Eakins' fight scene [2], for example, there is a definite illusion of depth which breaks through the plane of the canvas and creates the sense of a hollow space beyond. The frame, instead of being the boundary of a flat plane, is the boundary of a "window" or "keyhole" through which we look at a scene in three-dimensional space. Thus, in a sense, Eakins "denies" the picture plane—in fact, dissolves it. Nevertheless, in a number of ways he has instinctively or by intent honored it. Both fighters are turned so that the exposed portion of their bodies is relatively at right angles to our line of vision—that is, *parallel to the plane of the picture.* Although the referee is turned away from this plane at the shoulders, the light on his head, dress shirt, and hand squares considerably with the picture plane, as does the dark silhouette of his suit; and as do the hanging advertisements in the right background. In brief, Eakins in some ways accepts the ruling force of the picture plane and in some ways denies it. It is like a stage scene in which the actors are placed in depth yet relate themselves to the plane of the proscenium or avoid creating diagonal planes vis-à-vis the audience. Even Bellows' free-wheeling scene [1], as you may observe, is to a considerable degree squared away with the picture plane.

Many artists in the past have arranged their subjects in this field-parallel way or made them dominantly so. We find it in Egyptian wall and in Greek vase painting, and it was common during the Renaissance. During the following eras of Mannerism and Baroque, artists began to concentrate more on a vivid illusion of space beyond the plane, but many of them continued to define or imply a picture plane of sorts.

The spectator of art, in other words, often is required to look at a painting in two ways. On the one hand, he sees as though he were looking into a hollow space; on the other, he sees what appears to be a flat design.

From the foregoing it should be clear that balance in painting refers primarily to *balance in or on the picture plane.* The fact that objects may appear to be in front or back of others and that the painting may convey the illusion of space is immaterial to the strong sense of plane which is created by the definite boundaries of the painting and by its literal, physical flatness. The painting has two visual worlds—one two-dimensional, the other, three-dimensional. They exist simultaneously and they may be simultaneously apprehended, despite a certain contradiction inherent in seeing flatly and in depth.

Finally, the field proportions create a basic visual situation to which the total shape structure within is usually accommodated. Bellows did not entirely do this with his fight scene, as you may prove to yourself. Place your hand along the right side of the illustration of his painting [1] so as to cut off the section to the right of a line running vertically through the highlight on the Negro fighter's calf. You will notice that the shapes of the two fighters are now related to, or visually locked in, their field more tightly. This is so because the central, vertical axis of the field now occurs approximately between the two fighters. Their shapes are hence more symmetrically balanced in the picture plane.

You will notice, also, that the more balanced organization has the curious effect of freezing the action, in spite of its apparent violence. The reason is that an effect has been set up which is related purely to visual matters, to organization of form in the abstract, and which could as well apply to nonrealistic shapes as to the shapes of fighters. The fighters' shapes, in fact, have taken on certain attributes of the abstract not evident in the looser composition actually painted by Bellows. As he designed it, the painting has more space than it needs to relate to the existing subject matter. The eye can wander off the picture at the upper right, because the field has been thought of by Bellows as hollow space rather than as a flat design area.

Eakins prevented this in his scene by placing the two placards above the kneeling figure. A more recent artist would probably not have hesitated to brighten the tone of these placards, for he would be less concerned about their appearance of aerial depth. Eakins, nevertheless, applies the principle of a *closed composition,* in contrast to the more diffuse, *open composition* of Bellows. Eakins' painting may be taken as an example of an uncomplicated, basically symmetrical, balanced composition. It has three main elements, which makes it easy to place the "odd" one—in this case the referee—along the central axis of the picture plane. The other two elements are balanced on either side.

Bellows' use of only two main elements is looser in tendency, harder to organize. The "openness" of Bellows' composition, while militating against the esthetic unity achieved by visually unifying the picture plane, is helpful to a vivid sense of the passing moment. It is as though we were looking at the scene through the viewfinder of a moving camera which crowds the subjects a little at the top but includes a little more than needed at the side. We can imagine that the "camera" has been pointed to something over at the right and has not swung quite all the way back to the incident taking place. This effect psychologically approaches the shifting sensations we experience as mobile observers in the vast world around us.

Balance is something the artist brings to nature or extracts from it in a simplified, humanized version. If nature itself has balance, it is on a scale at once too vast and too minute for the artist's brush. Certainly our ordinary experience of nature is not one of visual order but of vast complexity. The looser, freer approach in the painting by Bellows is thus closer to common experience, where the more studied composition of Eakins introduces that simplifying discipline which is the artist's creative tool, *the organized visual effect—Form.*

If balance is the first great organizing principle, rhythm is the second. Rhythm is so universally discernible in the world of nature—and indeed in the life of man—that it is no wonder to find it a driving force in art. Indeed, rhythm may so far supplant balance in the artist's sense of form as to become the primary organizing element, although *equilibrium* —that *balance of tensions*—must still be achieved.

Among the arts, music is one which is inseparable from rhythm. To be sure, music makes use of harmony, tone color, dynamics, and other devices; but without rhythm it would be inchoate. Rhythm is music's most basic organizing and unifying element. If a one-year-old child beats on a drum, it does so aimlessly and without rhythm, unless accidentally. By the age of two, the child can do "pattycake" with a fairly regular beat and by three can clap hands in time to a simple song. Rhythm is one of the very first, if not the first, organizing mediums to which we respond. Distinguishing the rhythmic response from the earlier aimless whamming is the presence of order, of pattern. *Rhythm is orderly repetition.*

Does an alarm clock in action have rhythm? By the above definition it does, but, if so, it is rhythm of a low order; it lacks form, is rhythmically boring, monotonous. A simple waltz likewise has a regular beat, but with the all-important difference of having every third beat accented. This immediately brings the rhythm into a comprehensible pattern, to which the theme of the waltz, however varied, must conform. In a sonata or other more complex form, the rhythm of the theme or themes may be so complex as to conceal the underlying and basic unit of measure. Nevertheless, and although a few contemporary composers have eliminated the measure entirely, the vast preponderance of music has a definite rhythmic unit based on 2, 3, 4, or 6 beats, with accent on the first. This basic rhythm forms the continuous and orderly plane—to borrow a visual arts term—within which the rest of the music has a related place. To emphasize the distinction between the rhythm of music and of the alarm clock, we may define rhythm more subjectively as *unified and significant repetition*. Rhythm in music has interval, beat, and accent. And because it is a continuing thing, it has flow. All these characteristics are found in the visual arts.

In the mosaic of two birds [12] by Gino Novello we see several examples of flowing rhythms. The contour of both birds is marked by a definite dark line which sweeps around their bodies; the wings, too, are so defined. These lines have the quality of rhythm because they have flow, repetition, accent. The flow of the contour of the bird at the right, for example, is clear. Notice the way the line seems to sweep continuously from head around rump and back again in a curve which changes from flat to sharp and which reverses from convex to concave along the back. This is a flowing rhythm. It is continuous but varied. It is consistent without being monotonous. To observe these effects requires a projected awareness on your part. But the awareness is stimulated by what you see, and very probably was also felt by the artist.

Notice, for example, how the contours of the other bird complement the one on the right. The left bird's back has a convex curve and its breast a concave—the opposite of the other. The upper contour of his wings is mainly concave, where the other's are mainly convex. But note how in each instance enough curve is employed to establish a quality of curve, a consistency, and so a unified visual rhythm. Although there is the effect of flow, the balance of up against down, of concave against convex creates a kind of rhythmic equilibrium. The eye sweeps easily from one bird to the other: up the back of the bird on the left, down the back of the bird on the right, around, and back again. It does not matter where you begin or whether your eye happens to sweep from right to left or vice versa. Notice how the wings make subrhythms with the bodies, repeating with variations the curves of the bodies or contrasting with them. And played against these curving forms are the straight lines of the flower stems and the rectangular rhythms of the dark border.

Now it is interesting and important to note that these contours can also be regarded as defining various flat shapes. First of all comes the rectangular shape of the whole work. Next comes the irregular shape of the white field in which the birds appear. This white field assumes considerable independence from the over-all rectangle; yet all its angles are right angles and in a general way it conforms to the total rectangular format. This irregular white field has the function of loosening up the severity of the over-all rectangle and of preparing the way for the curving shapes of the birds. The ups and downs of this white field at once enliven the whole work and create a dancelike effect entirely harmonious

12. Gino Novello: *Two Birds*. Italian. 1953. Mosaic. Private collection.

to the dance of the birds. If you imagine this field a straight rectangle, extending out to the borders, you will see how much more static the design would become. As it is, the birds seem much freer in their field, while remaining in balanced opposition. Here, then, is a *dynamic equilibrium*, and one which we may regard in terms either of rhythmic contours or of related shapes, or—best of all—in both respects. While the parallel is not exact, seeing this dynamic equilibrium is akin to hearing the simultaneous use of different themes in a musical fugue.

The sweeping rhythms used by artist Novello in his mosaic are a natural organizing means for the sculptor also. Although some contemporary sculptors have deliberately avoided a continuous silhouette, the existence of the sculpture in space tends naturally to call attention to its boundaries, its contour. Henry Moore's *Recumbent Figure* and the Greek *Theseus* from the Parthenon [13 and 14] are nearly 2500 years apart in the making, yet each artist made use of varied undulation of contour as a means of visual intensification. In both works the modeling is simplified so that the eye can easily grasp masses wholly. No doubt of their being sculpture, something solid and three-dimensional.

Another good example—both of the rhythmic use of contours and of the simplification of form—is seen in Egon Weiner's *Figure* [15]. By eliminating head and legs, the sculptor forces attention upon the esthetic components of his design.

So far we have considered rhythm only in its application to shape contours, where it appears usually in a sweeping or undulating way. An-

13. Henry Moore: *Recumbent Figure*. English. 1938. Green Hornton stone. London: Tate Gallery.

other important use of rhythm is in the *repetition of motif or shape*. Consider, for example, the huge abstract canvas by Sam Francis partially seen in the background of Figure 16. You will notice a giant dark shape in the form of a kind of hollow rectangle. Both this dark shape and the lighter ground on which it is painted are composed of irregular shapes of about the same size. The repetition of this sameness of size creates a unifying rhythm—a kind of beat—which underlies the huge scale of the major shape and gives it energy.

Picasso's *Girl before a Mirror* [II] shows a rhythmic repetition of diamond shapes, circles, and parallel bars, as well as having curvilinear, flowing rhythms. Here, too, color is used to repeat the beat or to accent the sweep of the painting's shapes.

Closely related to the rhythmic repetition of shape is the use of *texture*. Texture is tied to our sense of touch and refers to the *apparent quality of surface*. In Novello's mosaic [12] the individual tesserae or pieces of mosaic are allowed to show clearly. They impart a peculiar and characteristic texture to the whole. The consistency of this texture creates an added unifying element. In Weiner's *Figure* [15] the stone has been

14. *Theseus,* from the Parthenon East Gable. Greek. 5th century B.C. Marble.
London: British Museum.

smoothed only to the point of having a uniform rough grain which is consistent throughout. The stony look of this texture is set off by the more
roughly chiseled base, but beyond this contrast of rough with relatively
smooth, there is no attempt to suggest the look of skin.

On the other hand, a material may be made to assume several textures not associated with it, as seen in the illustrated detail from the famous wooden altar at Breisach on the Rhine [17]. Here the smooth texture of the skin is contrasted with the richly indented and curling textures of beard and crown. Dating from the early sixteenth century, this
is the work of a virtuoso at wood carving who expands his material beyond common appearance and gives it new textural brilliance. Whether
the material is exploited to have the look of several textures, as in the
Breisach altar, or whether it is kept close to its original is a matter of
swinging taste. But with either approach artists have noted and used the
distinctness of texture as an end in itself.

In painting, artists have also made a consistent use of texture as a
means to visual intensification. In some periods this has been accomplished by illusionistically emphasizing the varying textures of the things

THE ELEMENTS OF FORM   29

15. Egon Weiner: *Figure*. 1945. Stone. Private collection. (Dave West photo)

painted, as in the lovely textural contrasts of the Madonna by Jan van Eyck [18]. In more recent times there has been a trend towards using the texture of the *medium* as a unifying element. Where the surface of the painting of the van Eyck Madonna has very little look of paint, Rembrandt frankly emphasizes it in his later painting. In the detail illustrated [19] from his *Saul and David,* we see that the texture of the harp, the cloth, and the skin are closely similar. Although the reference to the texture of the actual objects is not entirely lacking, we are constantly reminded of the oil pigment used in rendering them.

In the nineteenth century, artists like Delacroix and Manet paved the way for the complete abandonment of the texture of the object and the substitution of the texture of the pigment and of the brush stroke. The Impressionists, although basically realistic in intent, did achieve a high degree of textural abstraction through applying their paint in small dabs or clearly visible strokes. This gave their canvases a characteristic independence of texture which their followers exploited still more.

16. Sam Francis and painting. (John Sadovy photo, courtesy TIME Magazine)

In analyzing most of the works illustrated in this chapter we have noted balance and rhythm applying within the work, often to relatively small parts. Let us not forget that the artist, whatever his attention to detail, still has or had a total work to complete. He is unlikely to be satisfied with his finished achievement if it is a mere composite of parts, organized within themselves, perhaps, but unrelated to the whole or total effect. Not always, but almost always the artist has directed a definite effort toward the composition in its broadest sense, striving for a larger unity of the whole.

A frequent solution to this problem consists in arranging the subject matter so that it forms equally balancing parts on either side of an emphasized central section. Memling's *Madonna and Saints* [120] is a good example. It is noteworthy here that, in addition to his balanced grouping of the figures, the artist has strongly repeated the vertical lines of the format in the recurring columns. The lower line of the rug exactly paral-

17. *Christ Enthroned,* detail from the Altar at Breisach on the Rhine. German. 1526. Wood.

18. Jan van Eyck: *Madonna and Child*, detail from the *Madonna of Canon van der Paele*. Flemish. 1436. Bruges, Belgium: City Museum.

19. Rembrandt van Rijn: *David*, detail from *Saul and David*. Dutch. *c.* 1665. The Hague: Mauritshuis.

lels the lower line of the frame, and the curtained top of the canopy, the upper. The women and angels are arranged so that there is a rising curve from them to the Madonna, just as the line from the inner shoulder of the male saints leads towards the Christ child. It is not necessary to the appreciation of the painting to see these mechanics of its organization in detail. They are noted here merely to show that despite his carefully constructed illusion of space, the artist was yet aware of his picture plane.

During the Baroque period, the seventeenth century, the compositions loosened up markedly, but even in an "open" composition such as Claude Lorrain's *Wedding of Isaac and Rebecca* [20], with its asymmetrical emphasis towards the right side, there is a feeling for the plane of the picture and the limiting effect of its borders. Shadows and highlights in the foreground generally parallel the frame, as do the trees and clouds their respective sides. And incidentally, where light in Memling's painting largely defines form, here it flickers through the painting and is of more interest for its own sake. There is a definite feeling of the concentric to the arrangement, with the lake becoming the pivotal or focal

20. Claude Lorrain: *Wedding of Isaac and Rebecca*. French. 17th century. London: National Gallery.

point. Thus the composition at once adheres to the rectilinear boundaries and breaks away from them towards another form. These two examples, drawn from the earlier masters, show the artist's concern for creating a total effect.

In modern times this objective has become intensified, as the interest in subject matter for itself has decreased and the interest in expression through form has increased. In Kandinsky's *Composition* [7] the field and the irregular shapes on it flow together so that the distinction between the two becomes indefinite. This is evident again in the Mondrian [8], where the lighter areas between the lines may be regarded either as individual shapes or as part of a general field, or both. Picasso's painting [Plate II] is integrated by a balance of color intensity, of figure against figure, of flowing line, and of repeating shape and hue. Yet its parts do not dominate the effect but unite in a brilliant ensemble. It was the central achievement of Cézanne at his best to keep the part related to the whole field so that the part retained interest of its own and yet contributed inconspicuously to the totality.

And indeed, it is this totality which remains one of the tests of the artist's accomplishment and also of our capacity to perceive and understand a work of art. The psychiatrist's step-by-step analysis of a personality is useless unless it fits together, at last, into a meaningful total. The composer of a fugue must know its intricate rules, but the test is in the total composition, which has to have more than rules well applied. The art work, generally, must be greater than the sum of its parts. Analysis provides us a basis for enriching our background of understanding. It comes to our help in probing a difficult or subtle work; but mainly it should serve to increase the awareness which is the prelude to instant grasp and sensitivity to an art work's qualities. In viewing art we should be like the good sight-reader of music, who must learn not to read every note. Appreciation of such great organizing principles as rhythm and balance, after a little training in their use, can become quite unconscious in application, permitting instant and effortless awareness and enjoyment.

The Nature of Content

4-Projective Perception

In the 1930's a famous villain of the cinema, Erich von Stroheim, was billed as "the man you love to hate." This clever press agentry, undoubtedly good public relations for the movie star, had a sound foundation in his smooth and villainous effectiveness. Yet only the very most naive thought von Stroheim actually was hateful. The rest, certainly the majority, although hating him enthusiastically, knew he was hateful only on the screen.

Thus do we keep touch with both fantasy and reality. The response we get from projecting ourselves into a situation that we know is not real (or that is real but not ours) and yet *experience as real* is called *empathy*. People had an empathic response of hatred for the suave and dastardly von Stroheim. The capacity to know all the time that he was just a player—*to retain a normal sense of reality* as a balance to fantasy —is called *psychical distance*. These terms express a very important aspect of our responsive powers as human beings.

Most of us have heard tales of active audience participation in nineteenth-century melodramas, particularly in the West, where the villain was hissed and even challenged from the floor by an occasional cowpuncher. This is the confusion of fantasy with reality. It is the loss of all psychical distance. When the cowpuncher stood up in the audience and shouted at the villain on the stage he had achieved "total empathic involvement."

On the other hand, when a later, sophisticated audience "revived" the Western melodrama and hissed the villain *for fun*—as was actually done—there was no empathic response to the play but only to the situation. Great psychical distance from the play was a precondition to the audience's commonly felt and very knowing spirit of burlesque. The audience was having fun at the expense of another generation's credulity, but by joining in the fun the audience was creating a new fantasy and having an empathic response from it.

It is entirely possible, moreover, for an informed audience to become inwardly very excited at a chess match, although chess is a game which depends almost entirely on the powers of visualization and reason. Even here the empathic response is a matter of the feelings, but it can have its stimulus, its origin, in something quite intellectual. The reverse also happens, and the success of many a cause depends upon arousing an intellectual commitment through emotional means, so that the intellectual reaction becomes a rationalization that satisfies an emotional stimulus or cause. Indeed, a great many more of our "rational" acts than we realize have at least a toe hold in fantasy, so that the problem of balance between fantasy and reality, which is the balance between empathy and psychical distance, is as real in life as in the arts.

Playwrights and producers have long recognized the desirability of both elements in audience appeal. In the cinema, the actors are almost never permitted to look at the camera, since this destroys the fantasy and "lowers" the effect to one of immediate reality. And it is true that we obtain a richer experience for this not happening. We *feel* ourselves part of the situation in a play (that is our empathic response), laugh as if we were in the situation of humor and suffer with the principals of a tragedy; but the continuing contact with reality maintained in the background by our psychical distance enables us to see more broadly. We not only experience the play by involving ourselves in its fantasy; we see it in at least some perspective. Being outside the drama we have the detachment to see it inside. Psychical distance, not only with respect to a play but with respect to life itself, is a powerful contributor to breadth of understanding and insight. By its condensation and intensity, the play distills the essence that, in the real life situation, can be found only with greater effort or superior powers of synthesis and perception. Indeed, this is what distinguishes the great play from the lesser.

Thus fantasy, if not precisely better than the real thing, makes the real thing more vivid, helps us leap across the maze of reality's complexity, extraneousness, and compartmentalization.

A problem confronting us all is the balance we strike between empathy and psychical distance. The child's response, of course, is largely empathic. I remember seeing a puppet show conducted by a very perceptive puppeteer who so captivated the watching children that he was able to incorporate them into the play, the children and puppets conversing together freely. At the opposite extreme is the jaded sophisticate who finds it so hard to become empathically involved that only the most intense or richest dramas can arouse him.

Dramatists have experimented with different levels of psychical distance. In Thornton Wilder's *Our Town,* for example, the stage manager addresses the audience directly, while the rest of the players act without seeming awareness of the audience. This device has the effect of increasing the psychical distance of the play proper, because it is approached in part through an intermediary. This is a variation on the "play within the play." All such devices—and there are many—depend on the retention both of empathic response and of psychical distance, for we no longer have a sense of drama if we are identified too closely with an occurrence or, on the contrary, if we are not identified at all.

When the historian or biographer treats a contemporary subject he often thinks of himself as "too close" to it for sound understanding. We lack psychical distance from our own times and experiences. Quite possibly, this was one reason why Mr. Wilder introduced the stage manager into *Our Town*, for he thus gave us a little more distance from the everyday happenings in the rest of the play. *Our Town* makes a moving drama of that which is ordinarily too close to us to appear significant.

The theater provides clear examples of the working out of these concepts, but they are equally applicable to other forms. There can be little doubt that the artist's degree of empathic involvement in his subject or in his painting affects his product. Consider the problem, for example, of Bellows' attitude towards his fight scene [1]. It is reasonably evident that this is a highly charged scene emotionally, but what was Bellows' own attitude towards it? The clue may lie in his treatment of the crowd. Notice the expressions on the faces of the crowd on the opposite side of the ring. There is an exaggeration here, a tendency almost to caricature, that implies neither objective reporting nor whole-hearted rapport. For all its apparent realism, the painting goes far beyond straight reporting and represents a mixture of amusement and hostility on Bellows' part towards the sadism of the crowd. The painting is certainly a successful means of evoking in us at least some of the empathic sense of ring violence. The catch is that this is *Bellows'* sense of ring violence. We are simultaneously in touch with the incident and with the artist's personality, but in the end it is the personality, the intent of the artist that comes through.

J. M. W. Turner's *Rockets and Blue Lights* [I], painted in 1840, was at least a generation ahead of its time and in some respects looks contemporary even today. It was misunderstood for the very reason that the artist was guided by the fire of his esthetic experience more than by the capacity for detailed visual reporting which he had once exhibited. As the wave emerged beneath his brush, he saw not only water, but a scintillating intermingling of blue and white which, in a rapture, he continued to build upon until it glowed in a rich scumble of pigment. In the smoke of the steamers he saw not only smoke, but soft grays unfolding in appealing related tones. And pervading all he saw not just the light of the rockets and sky, but their wonderful combination on his canvas, which he fervently allowed to invade each area, spreading a lyrical tenderness or calm. To be sure, this picture is suggestive of a stormy sea at night, but more, it is an emotional experience, a work of the heart in which the canvas became its own expressive area for an experience *esthetically* evoked.

Your own subjective reaction to Turner's painting may be somewhat different from the above and both may be somewhat different from Turner's, but we must not allow the need for an openness of interpretation to discourage us from attempting it at all. Communication among human beings—and art is unquestionably a form of communication—would be even more tenuous without effort. Art provides a means of probing our response to a great wealth and depth of human expression. When we "respond" to an art work, we are responding to a commingling of the artist and reality. The difference between the art work and the real life situation it represents results from the artist's personality standing between us and the life situation. Our own personalities intervene additionally. Hopefully these "interventions" may prove enlightening. If the artist is a man of insight, he may intensify that life situation, eliminating nonessentials and making it clearer to us; but in any case, and through the vehicle of his handling of form and of the subject, he conveys the empathy of his own response and the imprint of his personality. The play or the painting become new incidents while also remaining old incidents, and it is the form of the new incident which largely gives it its quality.

5-Varying Conceptions
of Content

Since our empathic response to art may be to both its form and its content, or to either, it may be well here to distinguish content types, since content is an area related to art which has been greatly misunderstood. The moral and didactic approach to art in the nineteenth century was by no means universal, but it was universal enough to create a violent reaction on the part of the more progressive artists and critics. This led to their devaluation of content as a legitimate concern in art, with the gradual substitution of the concept of "art for art's sake." We have already seen—and will explore further—what many of the progressives overlooked: that content contains elements beyond subject.[1] This may be suggested in degree by the following sequence:

1. Content inherent in subject
2. Content resulting from interaction of artist and subject
3. Content independent of subject
4. Content where there is no subject except form

The first of these involves the aspect of content which, most of all, bothered the progressive critics. If a "beautiful" woman is no more than realistically portrayed, their argument ran, the resulting "beauty" had little if anything to do with art, for it was originally, and so remained, an attribute of subject. While the painting might be attractive because of its subject's loveliness, the artist's only credit was that of being a good technician, a kind of reporter of the brush.

[1] Theoretically *subject* is the broad term and *subject matter* the specific; if the subject of a painting is the Last Supper, the apostles, the table, etc., are the subject matter. In practice the terms frequently are used interchangeably, which has the advantage that either term does double duty, except where context reveals otherwise. *Subject* here is used as applying to both.

On the other hand, it is possible for such a painting to have art qualities, qualities of form. The background and dress could be integrated into a design; consideration could be given to the design-possibilities of flesh tones, to placement of the figure, to rhythmic contour, and so on. But even then—and one thinks of Renoir's lovely subjects—the artist is receiving help from a favorable visual factor, the content inherently evoked by the subject.

It is easy to see how, as a result, some artists would be tempted by the still life, by commonplace or even unattractive subject matter, and, finally, by total abstraction. Such subjects reduce the extent to which the painting's success rests on the effect of subject, rather than on the esthetic capabilities of the artist.

It might be argued that such a viewpoint would only indicate insecurity on the part of the artist: that if the subject happened to be attractive on its own, this was no more than a pleasant visual dividend which the artist should be glad to pass along. Many artists, including, again, Renoir, have accepted the subject's inherent contribution quite frankly and yet have given it a setting having visual form.

Many others, particularly in more recent times, have apparently felt that the recording of interesting or attractive subject matter could be made best by the camera, and that the subject, if it becomes a matter of independent interest, actually competes with the central artistic purpose. Still others have felt that while the subject does not have to be attractive, *any* recognizable subject matter introduces an element extraneous to the esthetic concern. Hence the need for total abstraction.

It is hard to know when, historically, the artist first sensed in subject matter a rival rather than an ally. Primitive man put the esthetic first quite naturally. It was only when realism developed that the problem arose. Certainly the first man to paint a still life, whoever he was, demonstrated the desire to give a greater independence to the artistic effort.

To summarize: the content of the subject, if related solely to its appearance or association, has nothing to do with art quality but may stimulate a strong empathic response from the observer. Buyers of art through the ages have often been attracted by "extraneous" content factors. Many critics praised paintings solely on this basis, a fact which any artist worthy of the name could not but regard as an oversight of his own contribution. The artist, therefore, very gradually came to look upon subject matter as a crutch, if not actually as an inanimate rival, and began to distort it deliberately in an effort to reassert the primacy of his esthetic vision. Psychologically, this may have been linked to a dissatisfaction with the external world and to a new sense of its nature, growing out of life in a scientific age.

The emphasis on subject matter which was created—or was served—by realism in art contained within it an inevitable tension between content and form. Where the artist capitulated most to appearance, form and art were losers. The failure of the public to see the distinction between art as imitation and art as esthetic vision aggravated the tension and helped to drive the artist away from realism and appearances. But before this happened, the artist turned to the second kind of content.

Using nature or life as his subject, the artist may give us a direct report, *or the mark of his personal insight,* created through changes or alterations of what he sees. The great advantage of the artist, indeed, is that he can control the solution—present his vision—as freely as his desire and imagination will permit. One might say that it is his *business* to be freely individual. While some few artists have succeeded remarkably in keeping interpretation out of their works, others have normally indulged willingly in interpretation, either through purposeful treatment of externals or through the formal organization of the subject matter, or through both.

For example, in Claude Lorrain's *Wedding of Isaac and Rebecca* [20], the artist has used such elements as the dancing couple and the relaxed onlookers, or the evidence of sumptuous food and drink, as external suggestions of a secure and tranquil scene. Other such external suggestions are the calmness of the water, the billowing softness of the trees, the dappled light in the foreground.

The formal organization of the painting is dependent partly on its broad balance of light and dark, but the artist has handled this so as to create a simultaneous effect of content. The framing of the sky and river by the dark trees and foreground intensifies the relative brightness of the distance and renders more restful and cool the subjective effect of the darkened foreground. This is an example of formal balance being used to produce content-evoking results. By such devices, both external and internal, and others in the painting which you may discover for yourself, Claude Lorrain stimulates in us an empathic feeling of security and serenity. His is a spacious and also an orderly world. In his painting, the content and form are linked together in a mutual contribution.

But—coming to the third category—what if inner content has no connection with the apparent content? What of content independent of subject? In the altar at Breisach [17], the external content, the subject, is that of Christ enthroned. There is also an unintended "inner" content which is simultaneous, *growing entirely out of the form.* This is the marvelously vital rhythms of the drapery and the exciting contrasts of texture which set them off. These have nothing to do with the Biblical theme and serve to confuse those who think only in terms of subject. This inner content almost certainly springs from an energetic and vital human being, the artist; and his creation puts us subjectively in touch with his spirit.

We have to respond empathically to make the contact. The subject is undoubtedly of interest to the devout, but anyone who has the perception can thrill to the presence of a creative and vital spirit which fairly bursts from this great work. Thus there are two distinct content stimuli here—that related to the subject, and that related to the artist and revealed only through form.

It follows—fourth, and finally—that in works without any external references the entire content of the work of art must be hidden within its form. We may think of the example of music, for music can move us as deeply as a play or a great painting. Music may bring tears to our eyes, cause laughter, exaltation, depression, nostalgia, yearning, and countless other feelings. Yet these feelings are aroused through an abstract, or, better, a *nonobjective* medium. We are swept up by the music and become empathically involved in it without being able to explain why. And indeed, we listen to the music in order to achieve such involvement. This is the real mystery of art: how it manages to take possession of us, to invoke in us any of a wide range of feelings without any effort on our own part.

Nor do these feelings have to be translatable into words to be satisfying. They are not verbal to begin with and do not need to become so. Subsequent verbal reflections may be interesting in themselves or throw a new light on what we felt, but the first reaction is likely to be more intense if it is direct and nonreflective. When this happens, we have responded empathically to form in music or, as the case may be, in any other art. We have let go our own identities enough to become feelingly aware of another. We have established a kind of psychic rapport with the artist through the esthetic experience of his work. We experience with him and share his feelings. This is empathy in art.

Toward this end, to recapitulate, the subject may contribute variously. It may be quite independent, an extra factor; it may retain some of its inherent interest along with a specific reaction to it by the artist; it may be strongly minimized, overwhelmed by the force of the artist's esthetic drive; it may be eliminated entirely, in which case the subject becomes form itself.

The combination of instant intellectual comprehension and of a feeling response is the mark of maturest art appreciation. For even as we become involved in art empathically, we retain a subtle perspective on our experience through our sense of reality, our psychical distance, and we are thus enabled to use art to enrich our awareness and experience of life.

6-Subjectivity, Symbol, and Meaning

Consider the sky at eventide as we see it from across an open field or from the quiet shore of a lake. We enjoy the varied and brilliant orange shapes of the clouds against the darkening blue of the sky. The gathering shroud of night rests peacefully about us and heightens the glow to the west. The tension between day and night seems momentarily in abeyance—as if to allow us to enjoy them both.

Or consider the more exciting spectacle of a broken gas main afire, shooting a roaring torch a hundred feet into the sky. It was a brilliant display in the failing light of an early winter evening. Someone remarked jokingly that this was the original "flaming sunset." And indeed, the red orange of the flame was akin to the very colors appearing in the sky at that moment. But how different their effect! The sunset was like that described at the outset and which we have all seen in variation. The horizontal, spacious, "slow" shapes of its clouds, in their suggestive effect, were at polarities with the vertical, energetic, dashing flame. The one evoked a mood of calm and peace, where the other was stimulating, exciting.

To be sure, all this is a projection into the scene, and other thoughts might have been brought to mind, but the point is that things external to us, *mere shapes and colors to the eye*, can evoke in us feelings and moods. For they are shapes and colors *in a context*, a context partly of our associations.

The artist, in turn, creates his *own* variants of shape, color, line, texture, and so on, which, in their totality, *comprise a context representative of him*. They evoke a feeling of satisfaction in him and "represent" him subjectively. Or on his conscious plane they may express a particular feeling

47

or mood or a complex of feelings and moods. They may also evoke a similar or a widely different range of feelings in us.

This is at once the fortune and the misfortune of the artist. On one hand, he is able to communicate with us through our common ability to respond to visual contexts. On the other, differences of personality and experience may cause the artist's context to affect us differently than it does him. It is understandable that many an artist should be annoyed by this, particularly if an interpretation is published which is at variance with his own feelings about his painting. And yet, however regrettable this may be, it represents no more than a normal difficulty among human beings communicating on the level of inner understanding. Moreover, if the person with the "erroneous" interpretation has been favorably stimulated by the art work at all, it shows that he has something in common with the creator of the work; and his interpretation may actually throw new light on it. Every composer has had the experience of hearing new things brought out in his music by others. No, differences of interpretation are not to be condemned; they are a part of the rich and varied matrix of human understanding. Yet this is not to say—and more of this later—that all interpretations are equally good.

Most of us like to think that we see life objectively, although simple logic makes it obvious that we cannot possibly know all the variables or every aspect of an issue. Objectivity involves the marshaling of all relevant facts, the weighing of their evidence, the avoidance of prejudging, and the openness to evidence, regardless of outcome. Objectivity implies complete impartiality and freedom from bias. It is centered in things external, is observant, reasoned.

Now all this sounds highly desirable and undoubtedly is, yet it represents only one direction of man's potential of action. The other is his subjectivity. This is as personal to him as objectivity is impersonal. Subjectivity has its inception in feelings, moods, hunches, impulses. Because the degree and character of a person's subjectivity is individual to him, it is a very characteristic aspect of his personality. The degree of objectivity of which he is capable will vary with the incident and with the extent to which subjective factors may interfere. Extreme subjectivity tends towards the introspective, as extreme objectivity ignores the feelings. Every human being is governed in his actions by a complex of these elements, and however desirable objectivity may be, there are perceptions and understandings of a subjective sort which greatly illumine and enrich life. Religions, particularly those of the East, depend heavily upon subjectivity for their approach to truth, and everywhere man's subjective nature may contribute a delicacy and subtlety to his perceptions that go beyond the objective. Even if we could objectively know what all the facets of a problem are, we would still require wisdom to do the right thing about them. Free selection among multiple choices of human action ultimately requires a philosophical and moral basis. We need principles as well as alternatives.

Both our objective and subjective experiences may be symbolized in various ways. *A symbol is that which stands for something beyond itself.*

Simple enough, you say, but what of the corollary: Is everything which stands for something beyond itself a symbol? Step on a dog's toe and he will squeal loudly—definitely a different sound from his bark. This "stands for" the dog's pain and, moreover, is a specific or near-specific sound for it. But is it a symbol? Most people who have thought about this kind of problem would say no, that the pain and the squeal have a one-to-one relation which is not truly symbolic.

Then what is it? It has been called a *sign* of the dog's pain—a useful distinction—and we might also term it an *unconscious symbol*. If the dog could make the squeal without having his toe stepped on or without experiencing sharp pain—if he were thus capable of perpetrating a canine hoax and of *knowing* it—he would have lifted his squeal to a conscious level and have made it into language. The power to symbolize consciously is perhaps the key mark—symbol, in fact—of man's superiority to beast.

However, the reason for stressing the element of unconscious symbol is that man, too, expresses it. Suppose an artist who is desperately lonely paints city scenes in which he unconsciously expresses his loneliness by painting the streets empty of people. The empty streets would then be an unconscious symbol of his loneliness. On the other hand, if he were aware of this and deliberately made the streets empty, he would be making of an empty street a conscious symbol.

Is self-consciousness or awareness in this latter case an advantage or a disadvantage? The answer is not clear-cut, but the self-consciousness may well be an advantage. Unconscious symbols may be powerfully affecting, but a conscious symbol has a potential for enlargement that greatly increases the range of its expressiveness. For example, if the artist realizes that the empty street evokes loneliness, he can heighten this effect by, say, making the street unusually broad; by bringing it forcefully into the immediate foreground so that we feel ourselves more strongly included in its emptiness; by extending it out to the horizon, so that we feel that its emptiness has no end; and so forth. It is, of course, also possible that he might do all these things subconsciously.

The hazard of conscious symbolism is that it may merely invoke awareness without feeling. We may accept the idea that a painting is attempting to symbolize loneliness, but unless we are affected by it and share the feeling, the symbol is partly wasted. The spontaneous, unconscious reactions are safer because they are automatically related to the experience, but they are also limited by not going beyond it. They may not evoke a level of awareness beyond the recognition of fact.

Because it is possible to develop symbolic meaning consciously, it does not mean that conscious symbolism is necessarily any clearer than unconscious. In fact, *hidden meaning is necessary to the true symbol*. The Crucifixion apparently shows only a man nailed to a cross. It *symbolizes* the redemption of man by the self-sacrifice of Christ, which is not *apparent* at all.

In the case of the crucifix the symbolic intent is more important than the thing outwardly revealed. The figure of Christ is often left off entirely, and the cross alone used in a variety of ways, as in a pendant to hang from the neck or as the topping of a cathedral spire. Indeed, the figure of Christ may actually detract from the symbolic aspect of the Crucifixion by throwing emphasis on the event rather than on its meaning.

The nature of the symbol requires it to include that which is not directly revealed but only hinted at or, perhaps, is dependent only on convention. The fish referring to Christ is an Early Christian example of a symbol having no apparent resemblance, even remote, to its reference.

But let us suppose someone had made a life mask of Jesus and that it had survived to our time. Would this be a symbol of Him? If people attached to it a reverential and larger significance, which they undoubtedly would, then even this objective phenomenon would take on a larger significance having hidden overtones—symbolism. The point is that symbolic significance is bestowed on something *from outside*. The symbol itself may, therefore, be highly realistic or highly abstract, but it tends to be more effective when it leans towards the abstract because the imagination is thereby given freer play and there is less distraction from "extraneous" —that is, nonsymbolic—factors.

Suppose we represent a flagellation in a very realistic way which vividly portrays the physical torture of a beaten man. Is this a *symbol* of the flagellation of Christ? It would be, if we and others attached this meaning to it, but as a realistic portrayal it would also have a nonsymbolic potential. All its factual data could simply be regarded *as such* and referred to no one in particular. Thus, while realism may be accorded symbolic significance, it tends to distract by its very realism. Symbolism is oblique and does not really need realism.

You can also see from this discussion that there are many levels of symbolism. A flagellation scene may be construed as symbolizing only the physical mortification of Christ. It may also symbolize the doctrine of passive resistance or, again, that of the total love of God. It is clear that the more realistic the symbol, the "lower" its evocative tendency, the more the distractions placed in the way of an imaginative or abstract symbolic level.

It will be apparent that it is the subjective experiences and perceptions which are most closely related to rendering unconscious symbols. Furthermore, these are the very experiences which are sometimes so complex, so moving, so subtle or unclear that ordinary, reasoned communication breaks down or is inadequate. The artist himself might not be able to clarify such an experience verbally, but if his work of art created under the spell of the experience satisfies him, the chances are good that he has transposed his experience into an unconscious symbolism. The painting then becomes a hidden cry, a many-colored rejoicing, or any other affective statement, depending on how the artist felt. It might be possible for the artist consciously to heighten the subjective effect, and many undoubtedly do, but it is not necessary. Form may be the *automatic* vehicle for affective expression.

One of the chief impediments to an understanding of symbol and of meaning in art—indeed it may be the chief impediment—is that a given symbol may be differently interpreted by different people. "How do I know the empty street isn't supposed to indicate delight and happiness?" The answer is that maybe it could. By a choice of gay colors, architectural charm, and other effects the artist might completely alter the meaning of the symbol. It is also possible that someone might think a work gay which another thought sad. But this has nothing to do with the *presence* of symbolism, either intended or unintended. It merely means that circumstances cause the same symbol to evoke opposite results. This constantly happens in life and there is no reason whatever why it should not also happen in art.

The Japanese make of white a symbol of death; we do the same with black. This in no way invalidates the power of black or white to symbolize death. If an empty street in a painting evokes the feeling of loneliness in us, we would be Caspar Milquetoasts indeed to repudiate this because someone else had a contrary notion. In the event of such a contradiction, our only obligation is to examine the basis for the opposite view, if any, so as further to corroborate, or to reverse, our own view. Let us make an end once and for all to the notion that without unity of interpretation, interpretation itself is invalid. Nor is esthetic validity determined by counting noses. Such a procedure can no more than establish the existence of a fashion or taste.

The use of black or white to symbolize death may go back, in each case, to a remote occurrence which was repeated and then became ritualized. But in both instances we are now dealing with a consciously recognized or adopted symbol. Many other symbols spring so naturally from the expression of man that he may be quite unaware of them. Fra Angelico would not have to represent a religious subject to reveal his gentle piety. It is implicit in his choice of color, in his choice of scale, in the delicacy of his modeling, and in other ways. Delacroix did not have to try to paint like an early nineteenth-century romantic. He naturally painted this way, and we later recognize the psychological place of his painting in the sweep of art. For all his individuality, Botticelli still painted like a fifteenth-century Florentine *as a matter of course*. Unconscious symbols are built into and are integral with the esthetic expression.

These facts explain further why the artist is often annoyed at the efforts of others to find meaning in his art, for at first thought it might seem humiliating to have meaning revealed of which one was not aware and did not consciously intend. The meaning is there, nevertheless, although it may be many years before conditions are right for its revelation. It required many years before it was even realized that the Baroque was a distinct style and not just an elaboration or deterioration of the Renaissance. The psychological identity of the Baroque world—its deep concern with the inner man, its introspection, the tension between its worldliness and rather Gothic yearning for the infinite, its passion for the moment in time—such aspects of a new world outlook may now be seen as hidden symbols within that style.

If the artist will in any case create unconscious symbols, it is when he tries to create them consciously that he is sorely tried. The terror of night, for example, cannot be suggested simply by painting a dark landscape. The artist would have to find form or subject symbols to evoke not just the night, but the *feeling*. The darkness, originally, was merely a trigger for an emotional response, the reality of the situation was not the darkness, but the reaction. It is in these very areas where description is inadequate that the symbolism of art—poetic, visual, or musical—is at its best. And is it not clear that this symbolism would have to have an abstract basis? The objective description is not enough because it is the *subjective reaction to the objective that we are really after*. A means of communication, a symbolism, is required which will evoke in us or in others what has only been felt.

The nearly *objective* phases of human perception and activity can be expressed through verbal analysis and discussion or, in the sciences, through mathematical, chemical, or other scientific symbols. Countless activities, as varied as bookkeeping, tree surgery, or watch repairing, are relatively impersonal, precise, objective. The solutions to their problems lie almost entirely, though not entirely, outside the influence of personality.

The location of a pinion within the works of a watch predetermines the order in which it will have to be taken out or inserted. This is a factor *within the nature of the problem* and is entirely independent of the personality of the repair man. On the other hand, the man who designs the case for the watch can go part way into the more subjective area of art. It is only part way, because he is still limited by restrictions inherent in size and shape requirements, but beyond that the possibility for self-expression is there. The works of a lady's watch of a hundred years ago are almost identical with those of today. The watch cases, however, are very different in appearance because the esthetic impulse behind their creation—over this hundred-year period—has become invested with a different symbolical character.

The more objective activities consequently limit the expression of individuality. In an industrial society, where many thousands of workers are obliged to adapt themselves daily to the requirements of machine work, this becomes a serious impediment to self-expression. Incidentally, for such people the study or practice of art may be one effective way of opening new vistas and opportunities for acting in a personal way.

Countless other areas of perception and activity permit a more personal approach. The teacher, the businessman, the homemaker, while dealing with well-defined problems the solutions of which are often cut and dried, still have the opportunity over a period of time to influence the character of that solution so that it becomes *theirs*. The nature of the solution is no longer so predetermined by the nature of the problem but is partly within the individuality of the solver. That portion of the solution which shows his personal influence *becomes his symbol and also his style*. *Style* is simply characteristic form, a typical esthetic "way" which may apply to a whole epoch as well as to an individual. It is intimately related to symbol making. Every businessman can spot the deal that "has the ear-mark of so-and-so." Every age has its distinctive flavor, suffused throughout its creative expression. This imparting of the individual imprint to activity is closely allied to art.

A prime symbol maker at any time is the artist, for it is through his symbols, concealed in an esthetic framework, that many of the deepest intuitions and sensibilities of the age are expressed. This is made possible by the freedom which is inherent in art. As we have seen, some activities leave practically no room for individuality of expression, are severely limited by functional requirements. Even the executive is limited by the hazard involved in making mistakes and by the usual necessity of consultation. Only the artist can experiment without penalty, although he does have to pay for this privilege a price which some would consider a penalty: misunderstanding by much of the public and, usually, an insufficient income from his art. Occupationally, the artist is the opposite of the adding-machine operator or of any doer of routine work, however skilled. The latter frequently serves *society* well but at the expense of his own personal growth through his occupation. The former, the artist, serves *himself* well through freedom in and devotion to his art, but in so doing he also serves society, although the contribution to society has to be on a "take it or leave it" basis. This applies to the fine artist of our times, of course. In the medieval period the artist was completely integrated in his society and his products were as normal to his society as are those of the commercial artist today.

To summarize: Human perception may be at the logical, objective, descriptive level, and much of it is; other phases of human perception, however, are only intuited or felt, though they may be felt very deeply and keenly. Description does not best serve the communication of such perceptions. They need to be *evoked*, and symbols are then the most effective intermediary between the communicator and the communicant, for the very reason that symbols function obliquely. The symbol is only a catalyst, evoking an awareness beyond itself. To succeed, it must call forth the higher or more subtle perception needed to reach the complex feeling or perception for which it stands as representative. *The creation of such symbolism is one of the prime functions of art.* This is true of any art form, be it poetry, music, painting, or some other.

It is important to remember that the symbolism of art may be only partly a conscious symbolism. The artist *is* consciously creating a unity which we call form, but this unity also has a particular character which is symbolic. We may be refreshed by the esthetic unity, and no more; again, the nature of this unity may evoke other awarenesses or feelings. Then the art work is functioning in the oblique, evocative way characteristic of the symbol. It awakes something beyond itself. What it awakes may be only a feeling or a complex feeling. Or it may be an understanding.

Finally, it is my thesis that the artist, on the whole, is none the worse for dealing partly or largely in unconscious symbols. In this way there are placed in symbolic storage, so to speak, meanings which might be too personal or revealing but which may be significant for a later age or for the most penetrating perceptions. And in so far as the artist may employ symbols consciously, he still has the protection against bare revelation afforded by the subtle screen of nonverbal expression. He can "say" what he wants without being open except to himself, and perhaps a few initiates. For others the contribution of the work can rest on its esthetic appeal. Symbolic interpretation is therefore a kind of dividend to the esthetic equity, but a very rich one.

We shall now begin to investigate these general principles more specifically so that we can test them in operation and, hopefully, build them into a vehicle for a larger understanding of art.

Part Two

Special Problems

The Influence of Medium

Levels of Approach to Art

The Influence of Medium

7-Space, Function, and Design in Church Architecture

Was architecture born at that moment in the dim past when man first constructed a shelter to keep out the rain or otherwise protect himself? The answer is a matter of definition, and let ours be that that first shelter was not architecture but only primitive engineering, *unless some thought, instinctive or conscious, was given to its form.* This must be emphasized at the outset, for much that appears in these pages on architecture—particularly on the domestic house—will deal with its practical aspects.

Whenever its beginning, architecture revealed man's power of imagination as well as reason and became another important evidence of his "superiority" to other animals. Through the millennia it has grown to be, in the view of many, the noblest of the arts.

Dimensionally larger than man, yet under his control, it demonstrates his ability to invest the practical with beauty, to shape and use the materials of the earth, and, more recently, to create entirely new materials for building. It serves most of his activities, is deliberately shaped to fit his private life, his social and political organization, his practical pursuits, and his religious and cultural aspirations.

Where architecture departs most from the other arts is in the multiplicity of its aspects and in the consequent range of professional talents it requires. The architect must be not only an artist, in the sense of creating form through his work, but also something of an engineer, sociologist, psychologist, historian, and business man. His talents frequently extend to the allied fields of landscape design, furniture design, and even painting and sculpture. Architects have often had a scientific as well as artistic bent, and they have been more prolific as writers than any others practicing in the visual arts. The relative permanence of their creation and its constant presence before the eyes of all of us helps to dignify cultural tradition and provides visible evidence both of the continuity of human patterns and of their slow change.

In terms of design, architecture involves many of the same basic elements, such as volume, texture, shape, and color, that are employed in the other visual arts and the same organizing principles of rhythm and balance. To these, as we shall see, must be added the important concepts of space organization, proportion, and functional design.

The ancient Egyptians thought of space as a continuous extension rather than as a unity and developed no great esthetic feeling for it. The Greeks were even less concerned about space, being more interested in the sculptural refinement of detail and in the mass and proportions of their temples than in the interiors. It remained for the Arabian, Roman, and Gothic worlds to develop the first great spatial architecture of the West. We have been their heirs.

When we enter a large interior, such as that of a cathedral, we not only have an immediate sense of the vast proportions of the space in relation to our human scale, but we are able to move about in it and absorb it both gradually and as a whole. The photograph not only reduces all this to a pitifully small, two-dimensional abstraction but forces a fixed view. It will require more imagination on our part to achieve our empathic response from photographs of architecture than it has of paintings, but let us see what can be done.

If you can visualize yourself standing in either the interior of the ancient church of Santa Sabina in Rome [21] or the modern church of St. Anne at Duren [22], you can vicariously experience one of the simplest and most direct spatial volumes: the continuous, longitudinal space. In both interiors you feel the space *as a whole*. It is true that the Roman church's arcaded treatment of the first story is visually rather demanding, but the arches rhythmically continue the horizontal movement—as does the horizontal band above them. And more important, the total space is so vast that it nearly overpowers the visually delaying effect of the arcade's detail. The arcade therefore becomes essentially decorative, an embellishment of the boundaries, leaving *space* the most essential, architecturally created element.

The same is true of the German church [22]. Here, a delaying action is created by the pattern in the ceiling and by the strongly framed vertical panels in the windows. The continuous brick wall at our right is therefore an important element in re-emphasizing the basic longitudinal thrust of the space; and again, the sheer magnitude of the space is enough to take esthetic command and to prevent the subdivisions from assuming the lead.

One might raise this question: What would the German church be like

21. Santa Sabina, nave. 5th century. Rome. (Alinari photo)

if it omitted the zigzag or diamond pattern in the ceiling, employing a plain surface there? Why did the architect insert this prominent ceiling pattern? The answer is that he wanted to turn the structural members of the ceiling to account also as design. This makes it easier for us to define the total space, but without detracting from it. Not only does the zigzag of the ceiling lead us down the length of the space, but the "diamonds" and triangles it forms define stages along the way. This involves the same principle as the arcades in Santa Sabina, but is more boldly executed. Indeed, if the columns and capitals of Santa Sabina appear too numerous and a bit too "fussy" for the majesty of the architectural space, the ceiling in St. Anne's may be a bit too bold. However, the brick wall, there, works wonders in simplifying the spatial effect.

Next consider the effect created by the side aisles, one in Germany and two in Rome. You will notice that both architects have kept this space —in terms of relative volume—quite inconspicuous and subordinate to that of the nave. The aisle is a spatial relief to the main theme and does not rob that theme of any of its glory. While it very slightly broadens out the main space in its lower portion, the dominant rectilinear feeling is enhanced rather than weakened.

Photographs, again, are inadequate and even deceptive, but judging from the photographs what do you notice about the over-all *proportion* of these two interiors? The German church seems somewhat narrower in

22. Church of St. Anne,
nave.   Contemporary.
Düren, Germany.

proportion to its length; the Roman church appears broader, an effect enhanced by its double aisle. As a result, S. Sabina produces a more relaxed
and gracious subjective effect and appears more noble, despite its over-
elaboration of columnar detail. The German church is stunning and powerful, and in its comparative attenuation of space is more tense.

These are highly subjective reactions, of course, and others may not be
in agreement, but we must be aware that spatial proportion does evoke
differing subjective effects. And please note again that the fundamental
architectural element in both these interiors is not the walls, ceiling, or
floors but the *space they create*.

Now let us look at some spatial organizations that are more complex.
In the Cathedral of Regensburg in Germany [23] the side aisles are not
treated as mere embellishments or accents of the main space but achieve
independent spatial importance. In contrast to the darkness of the aisles
in the previously discussed churches, the aisles here receive enough light

23. Cathedral, side aisle and nave from crossing. Late 13th century. Regensburg, Germany.

24. Cathedral, nave. 13th century. Chartres, France.

from their own windows to define their structural elements. They do not simply borrow light from the nave. Their four-part vaulting in each bay,[1] a repetition in reduced scale of that in the nave, although opening out freely into the nave, also has surfaces related only to the aisle and helping to give the aisle's space independent importance. Moreover, the substantial width of the aisles in relation to their height—and for that matter, their height alone, of approximately forty feet—gives spaciousness, dignity, and emphasis to the aisles. Regensburg Cathedral is thus an assemblage of contiguous space-volumes each contributing to the total effect but also having its independent character.

This is further emphasized by the difference in proportion of the nave, which is higher in relation to width than are the aisles. Proportionately

[1] Vaulting is arched or curved roofing, sometimes supported, as here, on stone ribs. A bay is the area bounded by a group of structural members. Usually it is a three-dimensional space but the term may also be applied to a façade or wall having a series of distinct divisions and hence to each of these divisions.

25. Cathedral, nave. Late 15th century. Munich, Germany. (Photo taken during postwar restoration)

considered, the aisle is more than a miniature of the nave. In moving from aisle to nave we go not just from the large to larger, but from a spatial proportion having breadth, simplicity, and a closer relation to human scale to one having a much more emotional, soaring, and beyond-human scale. Broad though the nave may be, its relative narrowness in relation to height—and the accent on height created by its continuous ribs—evokes a certain emotional, straining effect that is very characteristic of the High Gothic. This period had begun in France by the early thirteenth century and was marked in engineering by the successful support and balancing of enormously high stone vaults and by the substantial increase of window space in place of walls [24].

Finally, the richness of the treatment of the pier surface and the elaboration of small elements in the upper (triforium) gallery and in the tracery of the windows at Regensburg give greater emphasis to *structure* than is seen in the other two churches, although space is still the dominant element.

In the cathedral at Munich, the famous Frauenkirche [25], the side aisles are as high as the nave. This is the so-called hall-type church. (If

26. Church of the Fourteen Saints, nave. 1743–1772. Near Bamberg, Germany.

you look above the pulpit and to the right in the illustration you will see
the vaulting in one of the aisles.) The piers now become elements *inside* a
total space, thereby emphasizing its vastness.

This treatment must have seemed very plain to the French of that day,
whose taste was more flamboyant and whose more elegant churches [24]
dated back over two hundred years, but to modern taste the simplicity of
the spatial organization at Munich and the unadorned mass of the piers is
strikingly beautiful. The rich ceiling treatment is the right complement to
the general simplicity of the interior.

Now look at the extraordinary church interior illustrated in Figure 26.
This is the famous pilgrimage Church of the Fourteen Saints, near Bamberg in Germany, one of the greatest churches of the Rococo, that mid-
eighteenth-century period of lavish design, exuberant ornament, and
ingenious engineering. Your first reaction is likely to be a feeling of
complexity. And no wonder! For in place of the simple, rectilinear organization of space which we have seen, with variation, in the other churches,
here is a space *simultaneously* rectilinear and curvilinear. If you look at

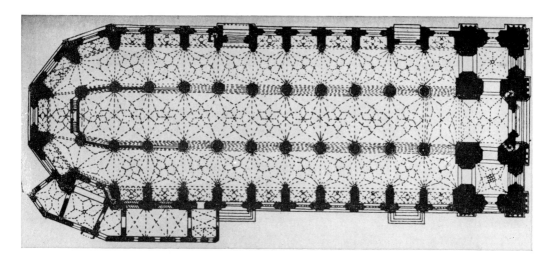

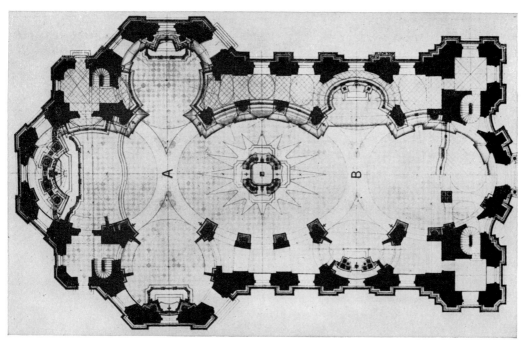

27 (*above*). Cathedral of Munich, floor plan. 28 (*below*). Church of the Fourteen Saints, floor plan.

the line of the balcony or mezzanine balustrade at the right, you will see how it juts out sharply into the nave, then evidently turns back, runs straight ahead, comes out again, then turns back at the crossing, or transept. Compare the floor plan with that of the Cathedral at Munich [27 and 28]. The curving effect of the interior walls of the Church of the Fourteen Saints is clear. The piers at Munich define orderly, straight lanes toward the altar, while in the other church the altar is approached through interlocking oval spaces which are nevertheless within the larger rectilinear shape of the whole building. This makes a more elaborate total effect which is more difficult to grasp. The rococo church is *architecturally less accessible*. That is, its structure and space organization—the essence of architecture—are complex and shifting, rather than clear and consistent, as at Regensburg. The rococo church is therefore harder to "understand" at first sight.

Consider the lighting. If you look at the first two interiors [21 and 22], you will note that the light fills them evenly, defining their wall planes clearly. In the Church of the Fourteen Saints, the light not only appears around and behind architectural members; it flickers before us, producing a shifting, dazzling effect. The back of the columns may be more brilliantly lighted than the front, and the walls appear both stable and unstable. Moreover, the aisles are not so independent as at Regensburg [23]. In the rococo church the emphasis is on a complex total effect.

Nevertheless, different though these churches undoubtedly are, a knowledge of their spatial nature helps to reveal their dynamic quality as architecture. What the rococo churches lack in solemnity they replace with a gracious opening up of their space, with flowing movement, with vibrant decoration (notice the flaming capitals of the columns), and above all with the opening up of the walls to a flood of dancing clear light. If the Church of the Fourteen Saints is complex, sophisticated, and elegant, it is also magnificent.

All this indicates differing approaches to the same Roman Catholic faith. Life, again, imposes its pattern on art—here on architecture—and even man's approach to space reflects his ever-changing answers to the fundamental problem. The Fourteen Saints Church reflects as clearly the joyous, rational, aristocratic spirit of the eighteenth century as the Munich Cathedral does the exalted faith of the fifteenth, even though both periods had other contradictory elements. Indeed, this is one of the most moving experiences of architecture, the discovery of its deep relationship to differing outlooks upon the world. As Frank Lloyd Wright, American architectural genius and originator of the "organic" conception of building says: "Architecture is life itself taking form." Medieval mysticism found expression amid the lights and shadows and the soaring, even straining, verticality of the Gothic church [24], just as Renaissance humanism was at home in an architecture of more human scale, of clarity of light and readily comprehensible, "reasonable" space [29]. Architecture, in short, like the other arts, is functional to its culture and symbolically represents it.

And even as it does so in this broad way, so it reflects more specific, practical factors. Thus the Roman Catholic service centers around the altar, and the axial thrust of the nave logically culminates in it. Moreover, the cathedral was used for the clergy, the resident monastic order, and the people. It was thus operationally functional to have a small section of the church, the choir, for the clergy and a longer nave for the more numerous lay worshippers. Attempts to depart from this scheme via a square or circular plan never took firm hold, despite experimentation by some of the best architects.

29. Pazzi Chapel, in Cloister of S. Croce. 1429. Florence, Italy.
(Alinari photo)

The church aisles, too, were structurally functional—their outer walls
increasing the resistance to the lateral thrust of the nave vaulting—and
socially functional, in facilitating a better circulation of traffic. To this may
be added a subjective function of the aisles (equally, if less intentionally,
important) of making the spatial interior more varied and mysterious, so
that the interior of a cathedral like that of Munich [25] has the aspect almost of a great forest. Or again, the decoration may serve better to define
the wall, as in the Renaissance Pazzi Chapel [29] producing a subjective
effect of clarity, reserve, and poise. Or the structure itself may be decorative—that is, may assume independent design interest—along with its

30. Church in der Wies, detail of nave. 18th century. Near Munich, Germany.

applied decoration, as in the rococo church In der Wies [30]. Here the effect is energetic, joyous, ecstatic.

In brief, there may be many functional aspects and points of view with reference to an architectural monument. And inevitably some of these will come into conflict. A high nave may be functional to subjective feelings of spiritual exaltation, but it is unfunctional to heat in the winter; again, the building of a large cathedral was functional to the religious or spiritual ambitions and aspirations of the community but was not always functional to its general economic welfare, since the finished cathedral was economically unproductive. By these examples, which could be greatly multiplied, we may realize how very complex the question of functionalism may become and how untenable, or at any rate oversimplified, any general statement of it is likely to be. The most succinct version—"form follows function"—was proposed by Louis Sullivan, one of the great pioneers of the modern movement. Yet his definition is subject to all sorts of qualifications in practice.

Suppose, for example, that we were commissioned to set down principles for the functional design of the façade of the Church of the Fourteen Saints. It is a fairly safe assumption that our actual design should follow the working out of the interior conception.

Indeed, in Italy the façade was often left for a later architectural competition which an entirely new architect might win; or the façade might never be finished at all. Northern cathedrals were often begun at the choir end. Thus there is at least some traditional support for regarding the façade as secondary to the interior. In terms of functional principle this would mean that in appearance the façade must not be more prepossessing than the interior. The interior must be the climax; yet the external appearance—we may reason—should still pave the way for the kind of interior we are to see. A three-aisled church, for example, might logically have a corresponding tripartite division of the façade; and the vertical divisions might also be made to correspond.

But the façade is also an *external* phenomenon which may often be seen at some distance and in the neighborhood of other buildings. Thus it must also be functional to an external situation! This can make for a virtually insoluble conflict of functions. The Church of the Fourteen Saints is situated in the country on a high prominence having a view of the valley. It has no large surrounding buildings. In thinking of its façade as functional to its site, we might reasonably decide that it should be structurally imposing because of its commanding position in the countryside, yet that it should blend with a natural setting. Also, as a pilgrimage church it should be monumental enough to encourage the distant pilgrim as he approaches, effectively promising a thrilling conclusion to his journey.

Since the interior of the church is already designed in a system of curving spaces and of dancing lights and darks, we may reasonably think of the façade functionally as having a curving *mass* and shadow-casting projections, so as to be stylistically comparable to the interior.

Now let us look at the actual design [31] to see how the architect, Balthasar Neumann, solved the problem. As you see, it is basically a four-story wall with flanking towers at the angles and a broad pediment over the central section. There are also four horizontal divisions. Notice that the corner angle of the tower is beveled all the way up, producing a rounded transition from front to side. The entire central wall above the entry is curved convexly. The sections between this tall central "bay" and the towers are curved the other way, concavely, as may be seen in the illustration by looking at the line of the cornice, or horizontal molding, that runs along above the second-story window. Thus the flowing treatment of *space* inside is here reflected in *mass*.

The swelling and contracting of the building's surfaces create advancing surfaces, which catch the light and retarding surfaces, which are shadowed. These produce an over-all flickering effect of light across the façade, harmoniously related to the contrasts of light in the interior. Moreover, the

31. Church of the Fourteen Saints, façade.

textures of the surface of the façade are varied. Note the rougher masonry of the first two stories and the varying textures of moldings and capitals. The decorative effect of the pilasters and applied columns is also evident. They define the boundaries of their respective areas of the façade and, by their projection, add to the light-catching dazzle. The changing silhouette of the topping of the towers is particularly effective against the sky, carrying out again, in the mass, the spirit of movement and countermovement so excitingly brought to a climax in the interior. The sculptures above the central section are likewise not entirely self-contained but reveal movement by their projecting arms or equipment, and so form a connection with their surrounding space. Indeed, the entire façade is vibrant with movement, is proud and soaring, affirmative.

And yet in at least one respect this façade is a functional anomaly. The photograph does not reveal the setting, but in your mind's eye picture this building all by itself in the country. Its highly organized, sophisticated, almost regal look seems to be more appropriate to an architectural, rather than a bucolic, environment. It cries out for a great public square or for appropriately monumental flanking architecture.

One way the architect, Neumann, could have altered this effect would have been by eliminating the windows, or at least radically reducing their number. With an increased amount of revealed wall surface, the mass of the structure would be more strongly emphasized and its then more simple, monumental appeal would substitute for the decorative surface of the executed design. But to remove the windows would eliminate interior rooms needed for administrative and other purposes. Another conflict of functions!

Or again, the architect could have achieved an effect appropriate to the rustic setting by radically reducing the richness of detail, greatly simplifying the complex topping of the towers, the elaborateness of the capitals, broken pediments, and so forth. But the resulting façade might then serve as inadequate preparation for the richness and magnificence of the interior.

The foregoing discussion will help to suggest the complexities of the functional problem. Architecture has always been functional to the aims of its builders, and if it is possible for us to see conflicting functions and unrealized solutions in the architecture of the past, let us remember that, like us, they chose the result they most wanted. The effect may still be moving, magnificent, and consistent in its way, even though a succeeding age may recognize anomalies. May later ages be as charitable with us!

These things are noteworthy because one of the greatest blocks to the enjoyment of architecture and art can be the insistence, so to speak, on black or white. Art is not perfect, and as an expression of human culture and personality it cannot be. If Diogenes looked in vain for an honest man, how much more futile the search for a flawless art, since art springs from a base which includes so much more than ethical virtues. We need not close our eyes to the deficiencies of a work of art, which are often illuminating,

32. Saarinen, Saarinen and Associates, architects: Tabernacle Church of Christ, front elevation. 1940. Columbus, Ind. (Hedrich-Blessing photo)

but certainly it would be a loss to allow them to blind us to any present excellence. Put another way, by basing our appraisal of architecture on broad principles such as suitability to purpose, relatedness to site, unity of conception, effective use of materials, expressiveness of design, and consistency of execution, we find that strongly contrasting designs may each be understandable and "good."

Where, for example, the Church of the Fourteen Saints depends for its success on its magnificent spatial complexity and its richness of detail, and on its unified expression of these, the modern Tabernacle Church of Christ

33. Tabernacle Church of Christ, nave.

in Columbus, Indiana [32 and 33], achieves its compelling effect through the emphasis of extreme simplicity of structure and space and the utmost reserve in the use of ornament. This truly magnificent achievement of Eliel Saarinen, which deserves to be more generally known, demonstrates the effectiveness of clarity of form, elegance in the use of materials, and subtlety of placement. (Note how much more interesting both crosses are in their present placement than they would be if centered in their respective planes.)

In Saarinen's church you can only imagine what is also a superb use of color; the interior is a delicate buff and white with one richly-hued contrast in the choir in the form of a large, specially woven tapestry. In its spatial proportion, this church is a modern refinement of what we saw in Santa Sabina [21].

A final spatial type to be noted is that employing the dome. The dome was a development of the ancient Near East and in recent times has had something of a revival in synagogues. In the monumental and dignified Park Synagogue [34] at Cleveland, Ohio, Eric Mendelsohn brings the advantages of modern materials and engineering to this ancient form. Thus the Cleveland dome, one hundred feet across and over sixty feet high inside, is supported in part by boldly upcurving flat piers. This permits the astonishing impression of a drum of glass having divisions of very handsome proportion and achieving, with the piers, a wonderful effect of lightness and strength. The great protective encirclement of the dome not only

34. Eric Mendelsohn, architect: Park Synagogue. 1946–1950. Cleveland, O.

produces a remarkably unified space, but is peculiarly adapted to the Jewish religion, with its emphasis upon the importance of the community and of individual worship within it.

More recently, the central plan has had a superlative treatment in the little chapel at the Massachusetts Institute of Technology, designed by Eero Saarinen, the son of Eliel [35–37]. The keynotes here are simplicity, economy of means, fastidious use of material, and sensitivity of proportion. Where the Park Synagogne is sumptuous in its appointments and mighty in scale, the M.I.T. Chapel is reticent and intimate. Its interior is architecturally unified by its uninterrupted cylindrical shape and simple continuous brick texture. The straight, ladder-back chairs reflect this architectural spareness, and indeed the one sumptuous note is the altar, a rectangular form faced with richly veined marble and raised on a circular stage of three steps. Back of the altar is a magnificent screen, designed and made by Harry Bertoia, of flat pieces of brass suspended from the circular screened opening above. These floating bits of golden light contribute to an atmosphere of exalted and suspended calm. The plainness of the brick wall makes an extremely effective setting for these features, as for the decorative openness of the organ pipes [36]. The exterior [37] is

35. Eero Saarinen, architect: Kresge Chapel at Massachusetts Institute of Technology, interior with altar. Screen by Harry Bertoia. Cambridge, Mass. (J. W. Molitor photo)

36. Kresge Chapel, organ.
(J. W. Molitor photo)

surrounded by a shallow moat of water as if symbolically to isolate it from the surrounding world. It is kept severely simple in design, its esthetic effect depending upon the purity of its geometrical form and the unity of its texture. Its only decorative feature is the aluminum topping by Theodore Roszak.

While the Park Synagogue makes effective use of reinforced concrete in its dome, it is a relatively conservative instance of modern engineering. And in its shape it reflects an ancient type. In contrast, a few architects have used new techniques of concrete construction—of which more in the next chapter—and new structural shapes to produce creative new spatial effects. One of the most interesting of these shapes is the *hyperbolic paraboloid,* shown in Figure 38. A section cut vertically through AB and FE on the curved surface AFBE will be parabolic in contour, while a horizontal section—as through MH or LJ—will be hyperbolic. This is a geometric oddity, but the most amazing—and architecturally useful— feature is that despite the very complex curve of this surface, two, and only two, *straight* lines may be drawn through every point on it. This is the way the building is constructed on the actual site and is worked out

37. Kresge Chapel, exterior. (Robert D. Harvey photo)

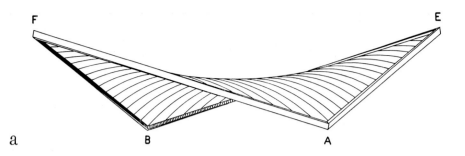

a

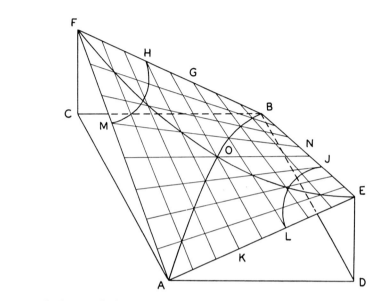

b

38. Hyperbolic paraboloids. *a*. Free variation in perspective. *b*. Geometrical construction.

first, geometrically.[1] The hyperbolic paraboloid unites the strength of a curved surface with the ease of work with straight wooden members or—in concrete—straight reinforcing rods. Concrete given these shapes not only is so strong that it can be made extremely thin in section, but esthetically it produces very rich and flowing effects, as if the space surrounding it were molded. This is seen in La Virgen Milagrosa [39 and 40], the Virgin of Miracles, by Felix Candela, one of Mexico's brilliant

[1] ACBD is a square plane from which equal vertical extensions are constructed at C and D. Connecting lines are extended to A and B. Equidistant connecting lines are drawn between them and could be drawn between any *equivalently* located points on their lengths—that is, KL = GH, AM = EN. Through these straight lines is passed a surface (AFBE) which will be complexly curving throughout its course despite the fact that it traverses intersecting straight lines at every point. The parabolic curve may be seen clearly in Figure 38b from F to E, and a hyperbola may be seen from M to H and L to J. AB is also a parabola, this time convex, but it does not show well in perspective. An almost uncanny, but geometrically demonstrable feature of this construction is that no matter how high FC and ED are extended, the point O automatically assumes the proper distance from the plane below, which is the directrix of the construction, to assure that the curves will remain geometrically true. The hyperbolic paraboloid in domestic usage is illustrated in Figure 180.

39. Felix Candela, architect: La Virgen Milagrosa—The Virgin of Miracles. 1956. Colonia Narvarte, a suburb of Mexico City. (Erwin Lang photo)

contemporary architects. The interior of this church is a complex of curves [40]. It is dynamic in appeal, vital and pulsing. The curving wall carries through to the outside, where it may be seen in the roofs over the side chapels and in the main roof itself [39].

40. La Virgen Milagrosa, nave toward entry. (Erwin Lang photo)

Subjectively, some people will prefer calmer, more stable space shapes, as in the two Saarinen churches; others will prefer the more ebullient, emotional flow of the Candela. In any case, concrete has been handled in the latter with a plasticity and virtuosity that is as exciting to the layman as to the engineer. We have here an imaginative approach to space and shape design, employing advanced knowledge of engineering principles— a stirring blend of structural dynamics with an awareness of its emotional potential. The new space has grown out of new structural discoveries.

Now we have reached a point in our architectural study where a summary might be helpful.

1. Through the medium of church architecture we have seen examples of the long Western tradition of spatial emphasis.

2. We have seen how the approach to designing space may vary from creation of a single, static form to one of space which flows into other space and the boundaries of which may be curving or indefinite.

3. We have seen how the proportions and handling of space stimulates differing subjective effects.

4. We have seen how the design and decoration of walls may create formal organization through the use of texture, balance, and rhythm, and

also of color, in a way paralleling the creation of form in sculpture and painting.

5. We have seen how decoration may apply to the rhythmic and plastic handling of structure, as well as to the applied ornament on it. Hence, space, too, is made decorative.

6. We have seen how functional problems affecting design rise from site and use, as well as from the psychological or spiritual attitudes towards the building.

7. We have seen evidence that architecture, no less than the other arts, is a rich symbol of the culture and personalities which produced it.

The thoughtful reader will have deduced from this discussion an additional point, that within architecture there may easily be a tension between the aims of engineering and those of art. In this potential conflict between the practical and the ideal, the artist—that is, the architect as artist—has sometimes been the laggard. He has applied old forms to new conceptions of building, as in the nineteenth century, when iron construction, a thrilling new potential, was cast into classical columns, or when the skyscraper was treated like a classical temple. On the other hand, the engineer may take command, producing buildings which lack all adornment or quality of form. It is the challenge of the architect, well understood by the most creative, to make these diverging tendencies into mutually supporting forces. Inventive structural engineering, as we shall see, still requires the spiritual touch of form to achieve greatness as architecture.

8-New Directions in Secular Architecture

If you hold a sheet of writing paper by the edge, it will immediately fold towards the floor; but if you make a tube of it, it will become quite stiff and will even resist a small amount of pressure before bending. This is a simple illustration of the well-known fact that certain *shapes* are inherently stronger than others. We have seen an experimental instance of this in the hyperbolic paraboloids of Felix Candela; yet this building is exceptional. The whole dynamics of shape and material is still highly experimental, despite the phenomenal advances made since the development, in the late nineteenth century, of inexpensive steel, reinforced concrete, and the I-beam, as well as of the hollow steel column, which actually is stronger than the solid.

Among the now classic structures using the new developments is the suspension bridge, of which that spanning the Straits of Mackinac is a dramatic example [41]. The continuous, sweeping cables, firmly anchored on either end, make possible the amazing lightness of the great central span. This is an illustration of the principle of equal opposition of tensions. The cascading vertical cables evenly support the weight of the roadbed and understructure, but the weight of the central span pulls, at the top of the towers, against the cable anchored near the shore. The pressure on the towers is thus directed downward, rather than laterally, which makes possible their relative slenderness. The understructure functions chiefly as a

41. Bridge across Straits of Mackinac. 1957. (Al Fenn photo, courtesy LIFE Magazine)

stiffening brace against any tendency of high winds or traffic to cause oscillation in the roadbed.

Since its first major development in the Brooklyn Bridge, the suspension bridge has had esthetic appeal. Advances in engineering techniques have made possible the lighter, more soaring appearance of the vastly larger bridge at the Straits; but the same satisfying effect comes from the rhythmic sweep of the *catenary curve* of the main cables meeting the delicate curve of the roadbed, and from the shower of wire that drops from the main cables to the bridge below. Finally, the basic simplicity of the bridge's over-all shape, and its great height, assure an effect of monumentality and, for some, of nobility. Amazing spans of reinforced concrete have been built for static bridges, particularly in Switzerland, but the suspension bridge remains the queen of them all.

By itself, concrete has tremendous resistance to compression but relatively less to any lateral bending. Continuous steel rods and a steel mesh, placed inside, stiffen the cement to produce the familiar *reinforced concrete*. It is amazingly strong and, as we have already seen, can be formed into curving walls. Since the concrete—a mixture of sand, gravel, and ce-

42. Annibale Vitellozzi, architect; Pier Luigi Nervi, engineer: Small Sports Arena. 1958. Rome. (Wide World photo)

ment—is fluid to begin with, it has to be contained by *forms*, usually of wood, built to follow the exact contours of the desired slab. The construction of forms for a curving surface is likely to involve a very high labor cost. It is principally for this reason that the most daring concrete structures have been built outside the United States, where lengthy form building would be prohibitively expensive.

Among the most brilliant builders with reinforced concrete is the Italian engineer Pier Luigi Nervi. He has developed a new type of reinforcing which he calls *ferrocement*, made with sandwiched layers of fine steel mesh. When reinforced with steel rods, it makes the strongest thin slabs ever produced. The flexibility of the mesh permits curving surfaces, and its fineness works like lathing to plaster, reducing the construction of forms to a minimum. Nervi has also experimented extensively with *prestressed concrete*. Here the steel reinforcing is artificially placed under a tension which reverses in direction the future load-bearing strain. The concrete is then poured around the prestressed reinforcing. When it hardens the tension is released and the resistance to load is thereby permanently increased. Notable advances in strength of slab have been achieved in this way.

Another modern technique applied to concrete work is *prefabrication*. Standard slabs, made with reusable molds, can be moved by truck to the

42a. Small Sports Arena, interior. (Wide World photo)

construction site and there fitted into a preconstructed frame, thus saving
expensive forming. Prefabrication has also been applied to concrete beams
made with four reinforcing rods prestressed around a hollow center. A
collapsible mold is used to produce this weight-saving space. Valuable
time is also gained in concrete prefabrication by steam-curing the poured
concrete, which then hardens without cracking in approximately a quarter
of the time it would in the open air. The result of these various developments has been to increase vastly the potential of concrete as a building
material and to make possible daring architectural effects never before
achieved.

Working with Annibale Vitellozzi as architect, Nervi designed a sports
arena for the 1960 Olympic Games at Rome [42]. Its huge dome, nearly
200 feet in diameter, appears to rest lightly on its Y-shaped structural
members. The dome was built of prefabricated concrete coffers held in
place by a metal *centering* (an arch supported from the floor) until sealed
together with poured concrete. The finished dome is only 4 inches thick
and from the inside appears marvelously to be floating.

The versatility of the concrete medium is seen again in a distinguished
architectural landmark on which Nervi collaborated with Marcel Breuer
and Bernard Fehrfuss, the UNESCO Headquarters in Paris. It consists of
a Y-shaped office building (Secretariat) and a separate Conference-Assembly Building tied to the Secretariat by a large entrance lobby [43 and
44]. The Secretariat has eyebrows (eaves) of pierced concrete at each
story to provide shade. Between these are vertical concrete frames which
break the horizontal sweep into more intimate compartments. The combined effect is emphasized and given visual variety by alternate placing

43. Marcel Breuer and Bernard Fehrfuss, architects; Pier Luigi Nervi, engineer: UNESCO Headquarters. 1958. Paris. *Left,* Conference-Assembly Building. *Right,* Secretariat.

of the slabs so that they do not tie vertically with those of the next story.

It is the Conference-Assembly Building, however, which is structurally most interesting and imposing. Its huge front wall of concrete is corrugated and folds at the top into a slanting roof. This roof slopes down to its principal supports in the main corridor and then up again to the top of the auditorium. The building is monolithic in appearance, but because of its curving or slanting surfaces, it still appears remarkably light. It is undoubtedly one of the great achievements of modern concrete construction.

A dramatic example of concrete work in this country is the University of South Carolina dormitories by G. Thomas Harmon and Edward D. Stone [45]. The functional purpose of the concrete screen is to provide privacy and a shield from the hot southern sun, while allowing adequate daylight. The design preserves and emphasizes the simple mass of the building, and the perforations give it a rich texture. The concrete screen costs no more per square foot than Venetian blinds and reduces the air-conditioning load by one third.

Another exciting example of concrete work—also employing exterior screens and again by Stone—is the factory, in Pasadena, California, of the Stuart Company, manufacturers of vitamins and antibiotics [46 and 47]. In the Stuart plant the screen extends not only across the whole 400 feet of the façade but also over the balconied executive offices, which are cantilevered over a long fountain pool dotted with islands of greenery. The

44. UNESCO Headquarters, wall and ceiling construction in Auditorium.

sumptuous entrance lobby, adjacent to a meeting room and employees cafeteria, also has planting.

Concrete as a building material may be central and functional not only to daring structural achievements or to broad decorative effects, but also to a general effect of sculptural plasticity. The UNESCO auditorium and the church by Candela were instances of this, and we see it emphasized in Frank Lloyd Wright's Guggenheim Museum [48]. Even if by some legerdemain the sloping sides of this building could be erected in brick, the present effect of the smooth continuity of concrete would be decreased. Here is a building absolutely functional to its material and also to its use, but esthetically it is best seen as a large abstract sculpture. Its shape relates to the idea of a museum with curving walls (thereby limiting the number of works of art visible at any one time), with a slowly declining ramp (thereby easing the visitor's walk), and with a pleasant open garden-court inside (thereby providing eye-relief without including acres of pictures). To these requirements the plasticity of concrete provided a natural fulfillment. Concrete is used here with a knowing respect for its effectiveness in displaying the interplay of large masses and for its adaptability to sloping or curving angles. This museum widens at the top to open up the interior garden to more outside light and to create a space psychologically pleasant and "un-tunnel-like."

If concrete is the most promising structural material of the twentieth century, the skyscraper is its most characteristic new building type, at

45. G. Thomas Harmon and Edward D. Stone, architects: University of South Carolina Dormitory. 1958. Columbia, S. C.

least in this country, where it was first developed. The structural principle of the skyscraper is that *the steel framework carries the entire weight,* the walls being merely a screen to provide insulation against the elements. The fact that this simple and apparently obvious idea was not conceived until the 1880's illustrates how a variety of discoveries need to be integrated in order to produce a major change, and also how the medium, again, fundamentally affects the product.

First, there had to be a desire for taller buildings, stimulated partly by the rise of land values in downtown Chicago and New York and partly by the convenience of the physical proximity of related services. The tall building promoted the existence of a *community* of business and increased its effectiveness, including the psychological assurances derived from the propinquity of a broad variety of commercial, professional, and managerial enterprises.

Second, given the underlying social and economic purpose, many technical discoveries were required to make the tall building possible. Without elevators, for example, and particularly without the automatic protection

46. Edward D. Stone, architect: The Stuart Company, detail of exterior. 1958. Pasadena, Calif. (Julius Shulman photo)

against a broken cable—developed by Elisha Otis—building heights would have remained limited to the endurance level of the stair climber. A way had to be found to produce steel much more cheaply—the Bessemer open-hearth process—and, where bedrock lay too deep, to support the enormous weight of tall buildings without the danger of settling—the spread-foot caisson.

The skyscraper was thus a sociotechnical phenomenon involving a complex of simultaneously developing factors. With the exception of Louis Sullivan, architects at first lagged behind engineers in finding creative solutions to the new problems. And the finished building which we today attribute to the architect is still the fruit of thousands of contributing discoveries of nonesthetic, yet creative, distinction. The skyscraper is truly the manifestation of a highly developed civilization and of the complexity of cooperating talents and specialties implied by that word. Such being the case, it is interesting that, in the end, it is for its esthetic effect that the skyscraper comes to be admired. The power of form still is required to

47. The Stuart Company, lobby. (Julius Shulman photo)

give a visual synthesis to the tall building; form enhances and controls its mighty size and gives a unified appearance to what in the early years was but a jumble of monotonously piled-up stories.

The Seagram Building [49] in New York is the world's only large, bronzefaced building, and it is also the ultimate in the tall buildings of Miës van der Rohe and Johnson. It pushes the conception of the soaring block-mass to its purest expression to date. The only decoration consists in the recessing of the horizontal floor line of each story behind continuous vertical shafts. The top of the building has a two-story section without any horizontal division, which creates an effective cap to the design. The scale of the design is made more impressive by relating the main tower to two adjacent and much lower blocks.

The visual effectiveness of the Seagram Building derives from its handsome material and from the soaring texture of its surface, but mostly from the purity and proportion of its masses. This is Mondrian in the third dimension or—to state it a little differently—useful nonobjectivity. And it is exactly this feature—the combination of usefulness with an almost ascetic

48. Frank Lloyd Wright, architect: The Solomon R. Guggenheim Museum. 1959.
New York. (William Short photo)

economy and purity of form—that makes this building so significant. It reveals how the design principles of abstract art have penetrated to the public domain. This is true, of course, of most progressive contemporary architecture, but the Seagram Building is perhaps its most decisive statement.

In contrast with the above is Frank Lloyd Wright's Price Tower in Bartlesville, Oklahoma [50]. Note the combination of vertical and horizontal elements, the varieties of surface texture and tone, and the interplay of secondary masses with the main block throughout its reach. Subjectively, we might feel that this is a romantic conception having a certain warmth missing from the essentially intellectual and classic reserve of the Seagram Building. Take your pick. Each is a splendid contemporary expression. The effect of warmth in the Price Tower, incidentally, is enhanced at closer range by the applied decoration of an abstract design in low relief on copper squares [51]. These squares—about 3 feet on a side—are placed along the parapet above the ground floor and on alternate balcony facings.

49. Miës van der Rohe and Philip Johnson, architects: Seagram Building. 1957.
New York. (Ezra Stoller photo)

50. Frank Lloyd Wright, architect: Price Tower (H. C. Price Company). 1953–1956. Bartlesville, Okla.

Although architects will continue to develop new solutions to the problems of the skyscraper, it has certainly reached maturity as a type. Structural and design theorizing are now being applied to other facets of building; recall, for example, the curving shapes of concrete previously mentioned. Some of the most exciting theoretical and experimental work is in the field of *geodesics*. This is the study of the nearest and farthest distances between points—simple enough on a plane surface but complex in the third dimension and even more complex when dealing with bodies in motion.

Geodesics has already yielded important practical discoveries in architecture and engineering. Pioneering in the field is R. Buckminster Fuller, an engineer, designer, philosopher. His general goal is "maximum gain of advantage from minimum energy output," an engineering ideal which has only lately been combined with considerations of form. His best-known development is the *geodesic dome* [52]. There is no single structural solution to the problems this form presents, but Fuller has had great success with a system based on the angular relations of the tetrahedron (four-sided solid). When shaped to approximate a demisphere—that is, a dome—such a structure is phenomenally strong for its weight. The reason is that outside pressure applied at any point is distributed throughout the

51. Price Tower, detail of façade.

52. R. Buckminster Fuller, designer: Geodesic dome. 1956. Kabul, Afghanistan.

structure. The bars of the polygons form connecting parts of a network of great circles around the sphere.

Figure 52 shows a demountable dome of aluminum tubing with an envelope of nylon suspended inside. It has a diameter of 100 feet (covering 8000 square feet of floor) and weighs only 5 tons. The nylon cover provides a pleasant general diffusion of light. This dome was flown to Kabul, Afghanistan, in a single cargo plane, in 1956, and was assembled in a week end by four men, only one of whom was a technician. It there became the pavilion of the United States at an International Fair. The geodesic pavilion was the architectural sensation of the exhibition and has since been flown to eight other such trade fairs.

In 1953 Fuller constructed the dome for the rotunda at Ford's Dearborn Village. A continuous cage of connecting tetrahedrons, it spans 95 feet and weighs only 9 tons. The dome of the American Society of Metals Building in Cleveland is 275 feet in diameter and 100 feet high. It makes use of arched trusses and two geodesic domes. To Michelangelo or Christopher Wren, builders of great domes in the past, such a structure would have been one of the wonders of the world. Smaller, but still spacious, is the paperboard dome, built upon a very light geodesic matrix, which can be lifted by a helicopter and transported as a ready-made shelter. It measures 35 feet in diameter and has been adopted as a type by the U. S. Marine Corps.

Firmly anchored to the ground and with a waterproof covering, the geodesic dome has remarkable resistance to snow and is hurricane-proof. It can be mass-produced for a fraction of the wall cost of a modern house. Given a large enough radius, the dome is psychologically a pleasant interior space for most people. Hence, Fuller's principle may well have an application in domestic housing.

The group of contemporary buildings and experiments discussed above are representative of a tremendous ferment that is making our time perhaps the most exciting ever in architecture. In this development, the architect may combine in himself a working knowledge of several professional fields, or he may serve as part of a team. In either case, the complex, interlocking problems of planning, financing, engineering, designing, constructing, and supervising call for an initial *comprehensive design*. The connecting role of all contributing services must be preplanned and then coordinated in action.

Since new relationships and problems arise from the bringing together of people and from discoveries which may previously have had a different purpose, comprehensive design calls for an openness to unexpected possibilities in the interaction of forces. The resulting behavior of the whole system may be different from what is predictable through a knowledge of its subsystems. This leads to *synergy*, the study of aggregates in relation to the function of their parts. And is this not what the abstract artist, intuitively proceeding, is exploring on his canvas or with his construction in metal? The complexities of modern life call for new levels of synthesis in all the arts.

9-The Domestic House

The principles underlying the design of the large public monuments we have just discussed are as broad and encompassing as architecture itself and may be applied to the smallest private dwelling. Architecture is all of, by, and for man and no basic gulf except in function separates one aspect of it from another. The functional difference, however, is a reason why we need not expect the domestic house to resemble *in appearance* the public building, a point that has not always been appreciated by architects. In recent times, however, more conscious attention than ever before has been given to the relationship of design to use. It was inevitable that appearance would be governed less by fixed conceptions or tradition, such as a columned porch—handsome though it might be—and more by a natural development resulting from immediate, functional considerations.

An example will be found in the home designed by Brooks and Coddington for Mr. and Mr. Ben C. Morse of Lithopolis, Ohio. Located at the foot of a gentle slope in the wood lot of a large farm, the site was chosen for the protection from hot summer sun offered by the trees and for the view sweeping up to open sky that the situation afforded. There was ample ground on which to place the house, and it would have been simple to construct it along a single axis, to produce a typical "ranch" house. The hillside location, however, made possible a more interesting solution [53]. The house was placed at a point where the land begins to drop off more rapidly, and a bedroom wing was run out over the fall, permitting a lighted basement area beneath. This removed the bedroom area from frontal association with the house, giving it the privacy of a new building axis. Not only is it placed well to the left of the entry, but the entrance hall terminates, at the west end, not on a doorway, but on the sliding panels of two closets. They give the effect of an end wall. The true entry to the bedroom wing is through an inconspicuous opening in the north wall. The privacy of the bedroom wing is further insured by

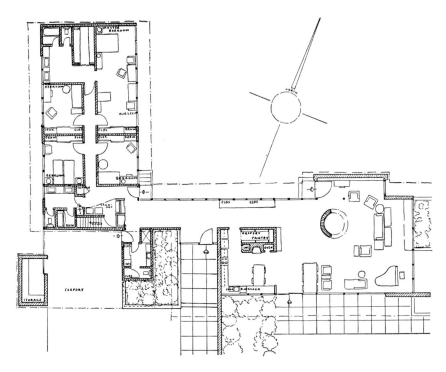

53. Brooks and Coddington, architects: Mr. and Mrs. Ben Morse III residence, plan. 1955. Near Lithopolis, O.

windows above eye level along the north side of the living room wing and by the location of the garage, which hides the bedroom wing from the outside.

As a means of visually isolating the living area, the architects wished to raise the exterior wall at the entry (at the extreme left in Figure 54) above eye level, thus tending to separate the two masses of the house from external view. The owners cut this wall down in height, fearing that in the summer it might interfere with the prevailing southwest breeze. In short, sound modern design calls for the most careful evaluation of site and for integration of the planning with its special features.

Inside, in spite of inviting glimpses of the living room area from the hall, the living room is enough to one side to constitute a new experience as one enters it [55]. Here we see immediately how the architects have made a creative advantage of the house's location at the foot of a rising slope (partly visible through the window). They have designed the roof to curve up towards the hill, suggesting the upsweep of the exterior setting. This assures that the view will include the hill's crest and some sky. The characteristic of the rising ground thus became the means to a uniquely successful organization of the interior space, a fine example of the harmonious union of function and design.

The upsweep of the ceiling is made simple and forceful by the powerful but widely spaced beams, laminated and supported on brick and small steel posts. The whole ceiling appears lighter because of the beams'

54. Morse residence, exterior.

tapering ends. The ceiling appears almost as light as a lattice, yet actually is made of 2 by 4 boards which act as lateral bracing and structurally support the tar and gravel weatherproofing outside. This effected a substantial saving in cost by doing away with the usual double sheathing of wood, and the ceiling is attractive in appearance besides.

Notice the brick wall at the end of the room back of the piano [53 and 55]. This serves to brace the roof (and so the building) against lateral thrust and by contrast emphasizes the transparent, screenlike nature of the glassed-in south and east "walls." Indeed, we see how inadequate the term "wall" is for such a design; its inadequacy is a measure of the revolution in architecture which sees the house as a subdivision of the space outside and screens off that space against the elements while remaining on intimate terms with it visually.

Now let us step into the living room [56]. The semicircular brick wall back of the iron fire hood has no structural function and therefore is kept short of the ceiling. It serves both as an interesting shape and as a screen, helping to define a subarea of the living room but without destroying the room's spaciousness as a whole. The handsome iron hood and its screen create a simple and virile effect for this country house. The same is true of the storage area at the west end of the room, a brick enclosure lightened only by a plain white molding around its top.

Notice how appealingly the sun streams in through the south window on this winter day. The outside overhang [53 and 54] is calculated to shade the sun in the summer, when its direct rays would be unwanted.

The kitchen is at the west end of the main living area. In the north wall, between two built-in ovens, is a rotary spit. All shelves are within easy reach and there is ample counter space. The refrigerator is partially concealed behind the brick storage and oven area and is out of sight from most of the living room. Indeed, the kitchen's presence is unobtrusive, and yet the room is immediately accessible to the dining area, offering the wife of the household an efficient and delightful place in which to work. A folding screen can be used to shield the kitchen if a formal occasion demands.

From the foregoing discussion, it is clear that space in the Morse house is not compartmentalized except where necessary—in the bedroom wing. The living-room area [53 and 56] can be conceived of either as a single large space—very useful for a large reception or party—or as a series of interlocking spaces for such everyday requirements as cooking, dining, and relaxation around the fire. By the avoidance of walls separating these areas, each of them is given a greater spaciousness through proximity to the others, although subtly set off by the fireplace wall and the storage room. Here space is conceived as flowing and flexible in use. This is the *open plan*.

A view of the master bedroom, even in plan, reveals again the intimate association of interior and exterior. Of functional interest in this area are the huge master closet and bathroom, the latter doubling as a capacious dressing room.

Looking again at the façade [54], notice how the varying horizontals of the window mullions harmonize with the irregular branching of the trees. It would have been easy to design the window divisions in a continuous horizontal line, but the resulting chicness would have been less appropriate to an Ohio farm house in the woods.

Most of us have such a stereotyped picture of houses that it is difficult for us to think of the Morse's as a farm house. Yet the architects, together with the owners, have achieved complete freedom from the needless blocks created by such conventions. The Morse house is spacious and even elegant in a restrained way, yet it retains a basic simplicity and ruggedness appropriate to its rustic setting and to its function as the principal dwelling on a large farm. It is an example of creative planning in which the needs of the family, the peculiarities of the site, the possibilities of local and modern materials (brick and glass) and of new structural developments (laminated wood on steel supports) all have been combined to control space in a practical and attractive way. This is functionalism at its best.

The beauty of an architecture which grows out of and expresses its special situation is that it is *endlessly rich in design possibilities*. Consider, for example, the house built by Frank Lloyd Wright for his son David [57–59]. The site is in the Arizona desert adjacent to a great orange grove. Frank Lloyd Wright conceived the idea of raising the whole house in the air, both to get away from the hot desert floor and to achieve enough elevation to see over the tops of the orange trees. The orange grove thus becomes a new and gorgeous "lawn" beyond which mountains enclose the horizon.

55 (*right*). Morse residence, living room from entry.

56 (*below*). Morse residence, living room.

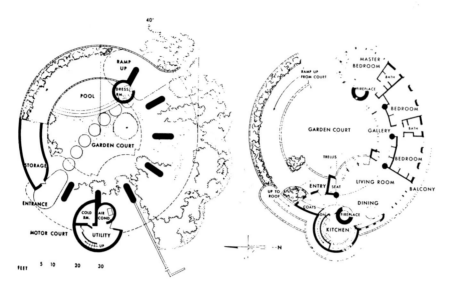

57. Frank Lloyd Wright, architect: David Wright residence, plan. 1952. Near Phoenix, Ariz.

To suggest the circling nature of the plain and the circumferential beauty of the view, Wright based the entire design upon a circle. The approach is up a gently ascending ramp, lined with flowers, which completes the half circle made by the house itself. The material is concrete block, which can be machine-moulded into a variety of shapes and which here blends in color with the desert floor. The severe appearance of the concrete surface is lightened by climbing vines and by a decorative border at floor level which runs all the way around the building. This border is composed of interlocking circles, thereby carrying out the basic circular theme even in an embellishment; it is also designed as a water drip to minimize discoloration of the block from rain. While the illustration does not reveal this decorative border in detail, note how very important it is in giving lightness and charm to the ensemble. It is not only in basic new conceptions but in small touches such as this that the genius of Wright is revealed.

The living room has almost no right-angle corners to suggest a rigid cubical space. The mahogany ceiling is a rich smooth brown against the texture of the concrete and delightfully follows the curving character of the plan. Here is spaciousness and elegance where it counts—the room is about 22 by 28 feet—while the bedrooms are ample but compact. The master bedroom, with its marvelous curving glass wall and private fireplace is unusually ingenious. A glassed-in corridor leads along the bedroom area of the building and the open balcony extending around the outside of both bedrooms and living room. French doors open out onto this balcony from all the rooms, inviting in the desert air in pleasant weather. There is sufficient projection, as in the Morse house, to keep the summer sun out of the interior.

58. David Wright residence, exterior. (P. E. Guerrero photo)

59. David Wright residence, living room. (P. E. Guerrero photo)

The David Wright house, although a small one, is an eloquent statement of the amazing possibilities open to "organic" design, to an approach which draws its form from roots deep in its own situation. It is thus an architectural expression of the belief in the inevitability of change and of the desire to make the most of it while still benefiting from the contributory best of the past. Stating this idea another way, we may say that form grows out of content as well as out of form itself, and, indeed, this has been true of all the great art and architecture of the past. Only recently, however, and in the field of architecture has the functional, organic conception been given the status of a guiding, pervasive principle.

The two houses discussed so far were isolated from a community and were therefore not functional to a local architectural situation. What happens when houses are adjacent? There is little doubt that they create a mutual effect which is a part of the architectural content of any community. Along a street such as we see in Figure 60 the houses vary greatly in age but still have similarities which produce an agreeable community of effect. They are basically of the same material; they are all two stories high, and their designs are all characterized by irregularities of surface in the form of porch projections, gables, or wings. Moreover, the street landscaping makes a contribution of its own through the stately trees. The ensemble blends into that old-fashioned, comfortable look which graced certain middle-class suburbs from the late nineteenth century through the 1920's. One can see that dwellings do not have to be

60 (*above*). Residences. Worthington, O. 61 (*below*). Suburban street. Columbus, O.

closely similar to achieve a harmonious community of appearance; they need only have certain generic resemblances and some individual character. Also implicit is the enormous advantage of town landscaping, planning, and zoning. A filling station at the corner here would spread its slick commercial pall invisibly but in no less deadly a fashion along the street, spoiling its charm.

The fashionable suburbs of many American cities frequently adopt the alternative solution of every house having its own period style. Sometimes two of a kind are neighbors, but often not. The result [61] can be very disjointed, vitiating any pleasing community of architecture. In the illustration you see a contemporary "split-level" house between a "Cotswold cottage" at the left and a "modern Tudor" house at the right. These

62. Suburban street. Columbus, O.   63. Suburban street. Columbus, O.

expensive architectural neighbors have no neighborliness of appearance. This does not result from deliberate antineighborliness, we may assume, but from a simple failure to appreciate the esthetic potential of at least a modicum of architectural relatedness in the area.

A planned relatedness, on the other hand, is not always appealing. Suburban developments with a modernized version of the Cape Cod cottage—now to be found in many eastern parts of the United States—are trim and orderly but generally lacking in distinction [62]. The lots are too narrow (55 feet) to provide any restful interval between architectural masses, and all too seldom is provision made for the enriching potential of intelligent landscaping. However, such limitations, if corrected, would still not result in a distinguished architectural area. The modernized Cape Cod house, lacking the simple craftsmanly qualities of its prototype, has no dynamic quality in its design, no expressiveness. It is a stamped-out adaptation, a commercial package without distinction of shape, trim, or use of materials. It may be argued that the need for building at low cost is the reason for this condition, but all of us have seen developments having much more expensive homes, as in Figure 63, which are equally

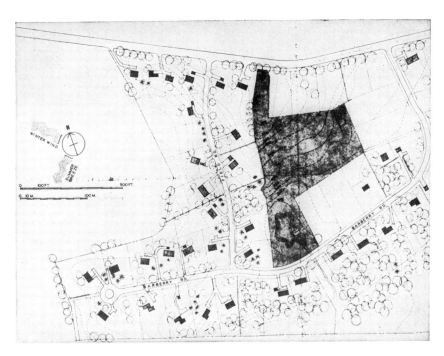

64. Architects Collaborative: Five Fields, residential development, plot plan. 1950 and after. Lexington, Mass.

undistinguished. The reasons are the same in both instances—lack of quality in the design of both the individual house and the area site.

It takes more than architectural propinquity or conformity of style to produce a worthy community architecture. It takes, first of all, the appropriate level of architectural taste, then a concern for the area's architectural appearance and a determination to do something about it.

But what hope is there for a better domestic architecture in the light of present building trends? Prefabrication and mass production have made very slow gains, yet they undoubtedly hold the potential for very substantial savings. The day may not be too distant when a person would no more think of buying an individually designed house than he would of having a special design for the body of his automobile. He might like the idea in both cases but not be able to afford it. Already the large sub-division offers more square footage for the dollar than a person can obtain by building for himself.

It is encouraging to know that a few developments have been successfully completed, mostly by cooperative groups, which demonstrate that a residential subdivision *can* provide interesting situations and designs at a relatively modest cost. For example, there is the development by Architects Collaborative, a group headed by Walter Gropius. Former dean of the Harvard School of Architecture, Gropius was founder, in 1919, of the famous Bauhaus in Germany—that pioneer school in cooperation among the arts, in fostering better commercial art, and in developing the International School of architecture. Architects Collaborative

65. Lexington development residence, split-level type.

sought to provide the client with a choice among several related types of plans and construction, each of which would cost between $15,000 and $20,000 on previously acquired land. That was in 1950 and the price would be proportionately higher today, but still a bargain in terms of current values.

The houses, wherever possible, were oriented to any topographical advantages of the particular lot and were placed so as to minimize the presence of neighboring houses [64]. The split-level design [65 and 66] in each case is oriented for the most favorable view and exposure. It offers many of the other features basic to the structurally and spatially more lavish houses first discussed. The interiors [67 and 68] ingeniously vary the basic plan. The functional principles of interlocking space, the

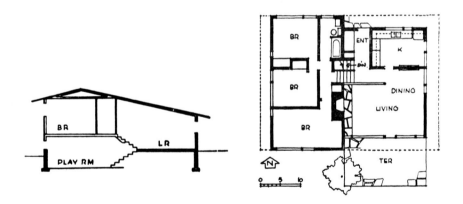

66. Lexington development residence, plan.

screen wall, planning for use, creative employment of modern materials and the appropriateness to site—all these can be developed to a degree even in the modest home, as has been achieved here.

The basic design is adaptable to enlargement or reduction of the bedroom area, depending on needs. The large semibasement area marked playroom [66] can also be developed alternatively as a second living

67 and 68. Lexington development residences, interiors.

69.   Cooperative Client Group Project. 1949–1950. Ardsley, N. Y. Lionel Freedman residence. (Lionel Freedman photo)

room, guest room, or utility room; and the basic design permits one- and two-level variants, as well as the split-level design illustrated. The Architects Collaborative project thus shows that moderate cost, community interests, and a degree of individual flexibility can all be served with thoughtful planning. Incidentally, in the 80-acre tract of this development, 20 acres, including a small lake, were set aside for the common welfare—further evidence of the enlightened approach of the developers.

While there is no immediate prospect of the unorganized house builder bringing group pressure to bear for better development planning and housing, there is nothing to prevent smaller groups of potential home owners from forming cooperative enterprises of their own for the same purpose. "Cooperative Client Group," an Ardsley, New York, corporation, is such an organization. It developed a businesslike approach to the development of thirteen lots on 21 acres. A competent board of architects had complete control of building but made every effort to adapt its savings—in the form of a standard frame and materials and mass buying—to the individual needs of the participating families. In spite of the adaptations thus accepted, building costs were held to an average of less than $20,000 per home.

The homes, in a hilly and wooded area, were located for maximum

70 (*right*). Cooperative Client Group Project, Dr. Montague Ullman residence. (Lionel Freedman photo) 71 (*below*). Ullman residence, interior toward porch. (Lionel Freedman photo)

72. Cooperative Client Group Project, F. M. Ginsbern residence at night. (Lionel Freedman photo)

privacy and best possible view [69 and 70]. The basic rectangular shape was varied to suit individual requirements and sites. For example, the Ullman house was enlarged beyond the basic design simply by adding a lean-to to the main block. In the interiors [71 and 72] the basic structure has been left exposed and with a plain finish. Good workmanship and clean designing yield a modest and attractive result. Both interiors are broadly oriented to the out-of-doors. In the view of the Ginsbern house you may observe how the open planning separates dining and living areas by using the chimney as a screen wall, and how the natural textures of the building materials give visual variety.

While the above incursion into development building may seem a long digression between the David Wright house and the special features of houses to be discussed, it serves to make clear that we must frankly recognize the exceptional status of a house like Wright's: that it not only required genius to conceive, but more money to build than the average man can afford. The houses illustrated in most modern books on architecture are quite beyond the means of most people, yet many of them are well worth studying. Features in which they pioneer can often be adapted to a more modest situation and the latitude provided the architect in such houses offers the best opportunity for experimentation.

We must also speak briefly of the *International Style* of architecture, which has been almost as influential in this country as in Europe. It had its beginnings before World War I but achieved its full development and

73. Marcel Breuer, architect: Vassar College, Dwight Ferry, Jr., Cooperative House. 1949. Poughkeepsie, N. Y.

international character in the 1920's and after. Its most brilliant spokesman is undoubtedly the great Swiss architect Le Corbusier, but Miës van der Rohe, Walter Gropius, and others have contributed importantly to the movement.

In its break with the past, which was very probably influenced by the modern movement in painting, the International Style was most violent in its early years, so that people who have only a nodding acquaintance with it associate the style with its early and severely rectangular plans, asymmetrical wall penetrations, white concrete surfaces, flat roofs, bare interiors with tubular furniture, and a rather sterilized look. Actually the aims of the movement were more laudable than most scoffers realized. It sought to return architecture to "fundamentals" linking modern engineering and materials in a house of planned usefulness having esthetic clarity and simplicity of design. Reinforced concrete, the glass wall, and the open plan are developments, if not discoveries, of the movement, and its emphasis upon the beauty of simple geometric shapes and of the natural texture of materials has had a healthy effect in scourging architecture of excesses of ornament and overelaborateness of structure.

Among the pioneers of the movement, then identified chiefly with interior design, was Marcel Breuer, who taught at the Bauhaus and later,

74. Philip Johnson, architect: Philip Johnson residence. 1949. New Canaan, Conn. (Wayne Andrews photo)

in this country, worked as an architect with Walter Gropius. Now working independently, he has continued the International Style with a flavor that is his own. The Dwight Ferry, Jr., Cooperative House [73], student living quarters at Vassar College, is an American example of Breuer's use of the style and shows most of the characteristics mentioned. Of interest is the regular division of the wall into rectangular units by the use of vertical rods which support the sun shades and of alternating glassed and wood-paneled shapes. The wall design is thus given clarity, yet with the variety provided by a change of texture. The sun shades are corrugated asbestos sheets laid on a simple metal frame. They add yet another texture, and their spacing is such as to admit the shifting rays of the sun along the wall without overheating the rooms. Light and shadow are found here in a pleasant blending of utility and design. Typically functional is the stilting of the dormitory portion of the building, assuring privacy, while leaving the lounge and eating area accessible at ground level.

The home that Philip Johnson designed for himself [74] also exemplifies the International Style in its geometric clarity of shape, in the directness and simplicity of use of material, and in the avoidance of ornament. It is American in its more emphatic relation to the out-of-doors, achieved all but totally by means of a glass wall. Although the windows have pandanus curtains which may be shifted according to the protection needed, obviously a house so exposed is functional only in a site having complete privacy.

75. Philip Johnson, architect: Wiley residence. 1953. New Canaan, Conn. (Ezra Stoller photo)

These two specialized buildings introduce the American version of the International Style and its unities of appearance under different situations. Depending on one's taste, a limitation or asset of the International Style is its self-sufficient look: an almost ostentatious contrast in appearance with its setting. Abstract visual purity is emphasized at the expense of developing any visual relatedness with the more varied or irregular materials, contours, shapes, and colors in the surrounding environment. In its subjective appeal, the International Style is self-contained, aloof, aristocratic. This is true not only of its private buildings but of large public monuments such as the Seagram Building [49].

Now let us turn to some special features of contemporary domestic architecture, particularly to the use of materials, structure, and site. The Philip Johnson house is a spectacular example of the enormous increase in the use of *glass*. Glass is without structural strength and always has to be placed between self-supporting frames, but its clarity, resistance to scratch, and good insulation when double-paned make it an excellent medium for a screen wall where transparency is desired. It is unlikely to be replaced by newer synthetics, except where curving surfaces and greater strength are needed. For those who can acquire the necessary

76. Wiley residence, upper living room.

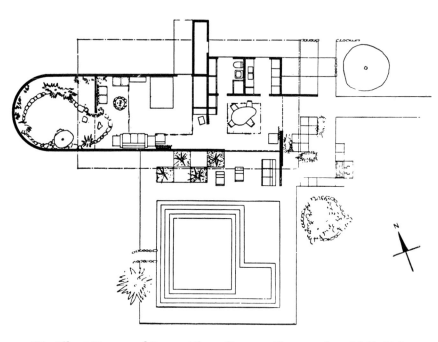

77. Albert Frey, architect: Albert Frey residence, plan. 1941. Palm Springs, Calif.

78. Frey residence, exterior. (Julius Shulman photo)

spatial privacy, glass makes possible a living situation in which nature visually replaces the wall, the glass serving chiefly as a screen against the elements.

Glass is so used at the Wiley residence [75 and 76] in New Canaan, Connecticut, also designed by Philip Johnson. Structurally, it is a two-story wooden cage with glass panels. In the ordinary frame house, the studs and posts which support the wall are no more than 16 or 18 inches apart. Johnson widened this division, using only eight very strong posts, placed on facing walls; two may be seen at both left and right in Figure 76. The interior ceiling is hung underneath the connecting laminated beams, which brace the posts and support the roof. The main structural strength of the building is in these eight supports, which relieve the load from the outer wall and make possible the much wider window divisions.

You will notice that the framework of the glass wall is comprised of similar units, except for a fractional unit at the angles. A particular unit so used as a measure and wall division is called a *module*. Orthodox modular division runs from corner to corner; the "irregularity" at the angles, here, keeps the feeling of wall division more interesting and varied. Modular division of the wall is frequently found in contemporary architecture and is particularly functional to designs which make use of prefabricated panels for wall insulation or screening.

79. Frey residence, interior toward screen wall. (Julius Shulman photo) 80. Frey residence, bed-sitting room. (Julius Shulman photo)

81. Richard Neutra, architect: W. D. Tremaine residence. 1948. Santa Barbara, Calif. (Wayne Andrews photo)

While the glass wall in the Wiley house makes possible a virtually unobstructed view of the wooded setting, the feeling of an architectural, vertical plane is maintained by the framing. A similar effect of sheer plane is seen at floor level, created by the large amount of floor space in proportion to furniture and by the metal-legged furniture, under which the floor's continuing plane is readily seen. Rugs are kept to a minimum, further enhancing this architectural purity of effect. In contrast, notice how the potted plants contribute to the sense of the immediate presence of nature, providing a soft, opulent texture as a foil for the refinement and geometric austerity of the architecture.

The remaining living quarters of this house are entirely contained in the stone section under the glass pavilion, which serves only as an upstairs living room and place for entertaining. The key to this arrangement is a double kitchen, one behind the area showing in Figure 76 and one downstairs in the family living quarters. This makes it possible for meals to be served the children downstairs while the parents entertain above, and on occasion—no doubt—vice versa. In short, the presence of guests need not affect the activities of any but those most directly concerned—a luxurious solution to one of the aspects of independence within the family.

At Palm Springs, California, Albert Frey has built a house [77–80] which likewise breaks down the indoor-outdoor separation created by the more usual opaque wall. By carrying the wall out through the window

82. Edward Stone & Associates, architects: William Rayburn residence, corner of living room and bedroom wing. 1949. White Plains, N. Y. (Lionel Freedman photo)

83. Rayburn residence, view across dining room to living room. (Lionel Freedman photo)

[79], the architect emphasizes the wall's planar, screenlike nature and helps further to destroy the psychological feeling of the interior as cubical or bounded by limiting junctures. On the other hand, privacy and a feeling for defined space are achieved in the marvelously conceived bed-sitting room [80], the west end of which opens out into a charming walled-off garden and pool. This pool is also partially brought through the "wall" into the bedroom itself (see also on the plan, Figure 77). The structure here is of *corrugated sheet iron, aluminum, plywood,* and an *asbestos sheet roofing* covered with reflective aluminum sheeting—modern materials all.

The Freys live in a broad valley and command distant views, but the screen wall can be equally delightful in a more intimate setting, as in Richard Neutra's house for Mr. W. D. Tremaine in Santa Barbara [81]. Here the glass "wall" slides, permitting complete freedom of circulation in good weather. Note how the plane of the floor continues right outside, inviting our presence in either area.

Traditional materials, wood and stone, are delightfully employed by Edward Stone and Associates, architects, in the William Rayburn house [82 and 83], White Plains, New York. Here is openly revealed one of the simplest types of construction—the double beam, bolted on either side of a post. Neat and skilled workmanship, a pleasant contrast of wood and stone textures, and an emphasis on simplicity make this conservative

THE DOMESTIC HOUSE 121

84. Harwell H. Harris, architect: Weston Havens residence. 1941. Berkeley, Calif. (Wayne Andrews photo)

modern design a deeply satisfying one. The house is located on sloping land, and the architect has taken advantage of this by dropping the living room down five steps from the other portion of the house. This gives greater height and spaciousness to the living room, neatly separates it from the dining area on the upper level, and yet permits the eye to sweep past the fireplace on either side, thus giving an effect of much greater total space. The exterior reveals the same thoughtful planning and care in the use of materials. The upturned eave is a jaunty touch, and the location of the sleeping area above and at the back gives added privacy and allows the living-room area, through its projection, to have more glass and a sweeping vista.

Contemporary designers of houses are also making effective use of the *cantilever*, where sharply dropping land or a dramatic view make over-hang desirable. The idea of the cantilever is simply that one weight is offset by another, as in a scale; a firmly anchored "fulcrum" thus makes possible the broad extension of the "arms." The Weston Havens house [84], Harwell H. Harris, architect, and the George Sturges house [85], Frank Lloyd Wright, architect, provide examples. Often utilizing the

85. Frank Lloyd Wright, architect: George Sturges residence. 1939. Brentwood Heights, Calif. (Wayne Andrews photo)

strength of steel and reinforced concrete, the cantilever makes possible exciting effects of suspension, "defying" gravity and achieving a look of soaring and lightness. The Sturges house [85] further reveals the use of a very inexpensive traditional wall treatment—the *board and batten,* a narrow exterior strip nailed across the cracks between parallel boards. This produces a texture in contrast to the brick and directs the eye horizontally, making the overhang seem to shoot out more dramatically into space. The effect is implemented by the similar sweep of the eaves. The Havens house [84] makes use of an equally venerable type of wall surface —the *clapboard,* overlapped edges. In the sections shown, the boards are ingeniously fitted to repeat the triangular shape of the structure.

In all of the houses discussed, the architects have taken special consideration of the *site,* in orientation to available light, sun, and view, in the advantage taken of unusual topographical features, and in the choice of harmonizing materials and construction. Adaptability to site, in fact, often makes possible the successful use of a narrow or otherwise unpromising area and results in solutions which may be more unusual than and just as attractive and useful as homes on larger plots. Such a dwell-

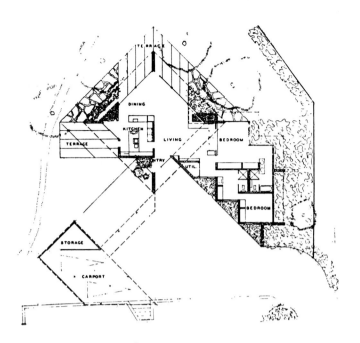

86. Honnold and Rex, archi
tects: Arch Ekdale residence
plan. 1950. San Pedro, Calif.

87. Ekdale residence, exterior. (Julius Shulman photo)

ing is the Arch Ekdale house [86–89] at San Pedro, California, Honnold and Rex, architects. The site is a narrow knoll having a view on three sides. The architect's solution, an unusual square plan, is worth careful study. Parking space and carport are adequate but kept completely at the back, while the living room and kitchen are pushed forward toward the edge of the hill and the good view. Only a screen wall separates kitchen and living area, yet this gives to each of the interlocking areas an interesting shape within the total space. What might be the severity of the square is further alleviated by making an alcove at the entry to the bedroom wing, which opens a vista beyond and under the line of the living-room ceiling. Beautifully finished woodwork gives luster and sheerness to the wall and ceiling planes, and contrasts pleasantly with the textures of curtain and stone. In part the glass is a wall, sweeping almost without interruption from floor to ceiling. In part it is an upper level, making a *clerestory*—a wall, usually fenestrated, above a lower roof line. Finally, on the outside, terrace and planting are integrated to extend the living area outwards in good weather and to make a more intimate and pleasing connection between house and site.

To summarize typical applications of the insights, analyses, and bits of information given above, we find that in a functional modern house:

1. *Plan and construction are adapted to intended use.* The size and individual interests of the family, the aids to housekeeping in a society lacking servants, the need for flexibility of use on different types of occasion, the realistic appraisal of initial cost and probable maintenance— instead of adapting these things to a conventional plan and construction, the plan and construction are adapted to them.

89 Ekdale residence, view across kitchen. (Julius Shulman photo)

2. *The potential of the given climate and site are carefully considered in relation to the original planning.* Thoughtful functional design does not have a large "picture window" fronting a busy street, but on the garden side, where it may even be extended to the floor. Northern houses are oriented to maximize interior sunshine, except in summer, and southern to afford maximum cross-ventilation. If at all possible, the principal living area is oriented towards the best view, and the house is planned to take interesting and beneficial advantage of peculiarities of terrain, climate, and natural landscape features.

3. Consistent with necessary economies, *native and other building materials are exploited for their inherent beauty and their contribution to the planned uses of the house.* Wood and stone in New England, brick in large parts of the Middle West, wood in the Northwest—such readily available or indigenously produced materials contribute to a regional homogeneity of appearance and harmony with landscape. Materials are used so as to reveal their own properties of strength, texture, color, or workability. Modern materials, synthetics, and metals are employed if appropriate to basic purpose and for beauty of design.

4. *Exterior design is a contribution to the architecture of its area.* A house has a community architectural function; it is a monument among other monuments. A concrete house on stilts—to cite an extreme hypothetical example—no matter how handsome as an isolated design, would be a jarring architectural note in close association with a group of Cape Cod cottages. Any general departure from a previously established architectural norm in the area calls for the secluding tact of heavy landscaping or of a large and private land plot. While there is leadership in architecture, there is also architectural responsibility to the community.

5. *Interior space, in general, is flexibly conceived, using an open plan where feasible.* Areas are frequently set off from each other by furniture, removable screens, change of axis, or by different floor levels, rather than by permanent and space-enclosing walls. The exterior landscape, if attractive, is incorporated as an extension of the interior. Walls are conceived as screens rather than as enclosures of static areas. Space is mobile, flowing, adaptable to changing uses.

6. *Finally, all of these features are outwardly expressed in a compelling and unified visual ensemble.* It is the genius of the great architect to give "significant" form to the building which yet fulfills all these practical and functional requirements.

This discussion of the domestic house has avoided the exclusive consideration of form and emphasized factors of content because the best modern houses should be functional to living in the broadest sense. They should contribute to fuller living in general, as also to the needs of the individual. A glass house may be esthetically captivating, but it is not worth the steel supporting its roof if it does not express the living needs and the spirit of its inhabitants. While all art is related to life and becomes effete or confused in departing from it, architecture is especially affronted by formal pretense. Successful architecture bridges the gap between man and nature and between beauty and usefulness more broadly than does any other art form.

Architecture is also more nearly the product of a creative group than is any other art form, and this gives it a broader base in its culture. Today, the product designer, metallurgist, lighting engineer, acoustical engineer, structural engineer, interior designer, cabinetmaker, and landscape architect may all contribute to a building, where the architect himself does not absorb their duties. Without the slightest derogation of the many practical contributions involved, however, we must remember that the designs given contemporary buildings do reflect, more strongly than ever before, the importance of form in creating a vital and pleasing unity in the appearance of the building and as an expression of our culture. In this process, the experimental painter and sculptor are helping to create the new *kinds* of form which in principle will be remanifest in buildings such as those we have just observed.

10-Functionalism and the Graphic Arts

If architecture is the most monumental, public, and possibly noblest of the arts, the various graphic media are contrastingly small in dimension, intimate in appeal, and modest in intent. Yet the graphic arts have often been likened to chamber music as a choice of the connoisseur, and examples of them have for centuries been sought by discriminating collectors.

The graphic arts are broadly identified with drawing, and on this basis the term has been applied to practically every art form appearing on a flat surface. Even the usual exclusion of painting is arbitrary and merely a convention, since the use of a brush and of pigment by no means eliminates drawing, even in the restricted sense of producing fine lines. In many of the accepted graphic arts a brush is employed; moreover, the effect of many examples closely resembles what we ordinarily think of as painting. The overlapping of usage is suggested by the apparent interchangeability of the terms water-color *painting* and water-color *drawing*. As we shall see, even if a brush is not used and the color is monochromatic, the effect may still be "painterly."

Is there, then, no useful distinction to be made between drawing and painting? A distinction is appropriate only in the very broad sense that drawing, most characteristically, has a linear emphasis, while painting builds with tones. By this definition, a work like Guercino's *Aurora* [90], with its combination of washed tones and of sharply defined contours, would be a combination of drawing and painting. Even so do countless other works, in various media, show a combination of draftsmanly and painterly effects.

Other distinctions worth mentioning are that the conventional "graphic

129

90. Guercino (Giovanni Francesco Barbieri): *Aurora*. Italian. *c.* 1615. Pen, bister, and bister wash. Cleveland, O.: The Cleveland Museum of Art, The Dudley P. Allen Collection.

work" generally is smaller in format than the painting, is done on paper rather than on wood or canvas, and is even more closely associated with the touch of the artist's hand. This smallness of size and direct sense of the movement of a particular hand together impart such characteristic intimacy to the graphic arts. If you imagine the Guercino in its original dimensions of 10 by 15 inches, you will see a small work in which every brush stroke or pen line may be regarded *as such*. The lightly washed-in area above the figure, for example, may be seen as a distant cloud, as a balancing tone across the light ground at the top, or *as a simple brush mark*, the physical evidence of contact by a particular hand. Of course, all three of the above reactions may commingle in the total impression. But the direct evidence of the artist's hand, even to the point of allowing correcting lines to show, constantly suggests a sense of the artist at work and of the warmth of a particular human touch.

Another characteristic of the graphic arts is the use of the ground—usually paper, as noted—as a part of the design. In the *Aurora* you will observe that half or more of the ground is left untouched. Paintings so treated (for occasionally an artist will reveal substantial portions of bare canvas) tend to look like sketches—that is, more draftsmanly. Conversely, if a drawing largely covers up its ground, it approaches more closely the look of a painting, as in Corot's *Forest of Coubron* [91]. Again, it is clear that drawing and painting are no respecters of media. A charcoal

91. Camille Corot: *The Forest of Coubron.* French. *c.* 1872. Charcoal. Cambridge, Mass.: The Fogg Art Museum, Harvard University, Grenville L. Winthrop Bequest.

"drawing" like Corot's may look like a painting, and a painting like Van Eyck's [18], with its delicate brush work, may strongly suggest the hand of an experienced draftsman.

It is not as a matter of principle, then, that we ordinarily distinguish paintings from other graphic works, but only because oil and tempera paintings comprise an enormous and distinct genre within the arts and do have their own look functional to medium. If we distinguish oil and tempera painting from the graphic arts, it is largely as a convenience. We do so because the other media typically employ a smaller format than painting, a different and common ground material, and different tools and, frequently, reveal the artist's hand more intimately and directly. As we shall now see, *it is through the functional use of medium that each of the remaining graphic arts achieves its characteristic quality.*

Charcoal is one of the oldest graphic media and the most readily procurable. The best charcoal is produced by heating willow wood to the point of combustion within a protecting cover, but the unconsumed coals of any wood fire, if gingerly handled, can be used. The soft and brittle nature of charcoal ill adapts it to linear drawing but makes correspond-

92. Peter Paul Rubens: *Daniel*. Flemish. *c.* 1617. Black and white chalk. New York: The Pierpont Morgan Library.

93. Pablo Picasso: *Bathers*. French. 1918. Pencil. Cambridge, Mass.: The Fogg
Art Museum, Harvard University, Meta and Paul J. Sachs Collection.

ingly easy the covering of broad areas. Moreover, the darkest tones may
be made lighter in a seemingly endless succession by the simple process
of rubbing the tone down with an eraser or by diffusing the tone over
a wider area. Charcoal drawing, as noted, is functionally close to painting
because of its natural adaptability to tonal effects. The very wide range
of such effects may be noted in Corot's work [91].

Pastel, a chalky medium available in color as well as in black and
white, has an even wider range of tonal effects. Pastel is a *crayon,* a
general term applying to all dry media which are given solid form by
compression or by mixture with a stiff binder. The crayon of school days,
with its heavy admixture of wax, has the most binder; pastel, with a
very light binder of gum, has the least. Usually the term "pastel" refers to
chalk mixed with ground-up earthen pigment of different colors and com-
pressed into sticks. Whereas the wax of the child's crayon makes it adhere
quite permanently to paper, pastel has so little gummy binder that it
tends to flake off in time. To discourage this, a *fixative,* usually in the form
of a thin varnish, is sprayed on the finished drawing. Pastel could be
made with a greater mixture of gum binder, but then its flat, chalky look

94. Francisco Goya: *Two Prisoners in Chains*. Spanish. 1819. Wash drawing—brush and bister. New York: Metropolitan Museum of Art, The Dick Fund.

would be lost and its concentration of color reduced. Moreover, because of its looseness of binding, pastel can be rubbed easily on the paper, after application, to produce lighter tones; and it is smooth to apply. Its colors are very permanent, having the disadvantage only of a lack of intensity. Hence, the common term "pastel shade," with its implication of tonal softness.

All these factors make pastel a very specialized medium, useful particularly to the artist who likes to draw in color, and indeed it was this which attracted Degas to it. He himself spoke of the blending of drawing and painting in the use of pastel, but the painterly use of chalk in drawings is much older than Degas, as may be seen in the illustrated work by Rubens [92]. Here black and white chalk are used on a buff ground, with the combination of linear and tonal effect functional to the chalk media. White chalk, incidentally, is mostly gypsum (plaster), while black chalk is a crumbly, carboniferous slate.

While *pencil* and *pen* may be used to produce changes of value, these

95. Ben Shahn: *Bach*. 1954. Brush and ink. Burlington, Iowa: Mr. and Mrs. James S. Schramm Collection. (Photo courtesy Downtown Gallery)

drawing tools, because of their relatively sharp points, are ideal for the linear effect. Picasso's superb *Bathers* [93], in the Fogg Museum, is certainly among the greatest modern pencil drawings. It exploits the rhythmic force of undulating line and the variety in tone created by light or firm pressure on the drawing tool.

In contrast is Goya's *wash drawing* of *Two Prisoners* [94]. Here the tool, the brush, has a soft and pliable working end, and its medium is a flowing, translucent water color. In this drawing, Goya used *bister*, a brown pigment made by mixing the soot collected from burning wood with a little binder, such as gum arabic. He has wonderfully exploited the medium's capacity for striking contrasts of light and dark and for rich tone, producing at the same time an effect of deep pathos through the huddled isolation of the figures—in a dazzling light—against a wall and bars of enormous strength.

The artist may create an essentially linear effect with the brush by using a fine tip. Thus did Ben Shahn in his *Bach* [95], a moving evocation of the glory of that great composer's music. Shahn allowed the brush to

96. Georges Seurat: *Music Hall Artist*. French. *c.* 1887. Conté crayon. Cambridge, Mass.: The Fogg Art Museum, Harvard University, Grenville L. Winthrop Bequest.

show a feather edge, giving the line a more agitated, emotional effect than Picasso achieved with a cooler, more elegant use of the sharpened pencil. The quality of the line may contribute importantly to the psychological impact.

Next look at a drawing in *Conté* crayon, one of a number of commercial products which have a base waxier than that of pastel or straight chalk but less waxy than that of the common crayon. This produces rich, warm tones, as in the technically interesting and tonally gorgeous sketch by Georges Seurat, *Music Hall Artist* [96]. Here Seurat has used a rough paper and the flat side of his crayon to obtain a grainy, black-and-white texture—the white is reinforced—that vividly recreates the effect of shimmering night lighting. Conté and other comparable commercial crayons may be used equally well to produce sharp lines. They erase less easily than chalk or charcoal and require correspondingly greater security of application.

Charcoal, pastel, pencil, pen, wash, and the various crayons are the principal drawing tools and media, many of which may be applied in combination—most notably, the pen and wash [90]. If you look over the illustrations as a group, you will see how rich and varied they are in effect. This is so because the artist has made the most within the limitation —or, to state it positively, the excellency—of each. The drawing frankly expresses the nature of the materials used and so is functionally true to them. Seurat's *Music Hall Artist* may recreate the lighting effect of a night stage in the 1880s, but it also looks like crayon rubbed on a grainy paper. This is the texture of the drawing, the texture of its artistic medium and not the texture of the stage set or performer's costume. And it is this texture *growing out of the materials used* which gives additional visual unity and appeal to the drawing as a work of art. Again, in each of these drawings, we see the direct evidence of the hand of the artist. It is roughly comparable to the immediacy and warmth of a handwritten as against a typed letter. That which is stated may be equally clear either way, but the touch of the hand adds a warm personal note. Even so does the hand reveal the drawing as distinct from many paintings and most of all as distinct from the photograph.

Now we come to the print, the most firmly established division of the graphic arts in the mind of the art public. It is, in fact, common usage to identify graphic art solely with the print. The duplicative aspect of the print not only makes possible its vastly greater distribution than the drawing, but the artist tends not to exhibit his drawings and makes little effort to sell them. The awareness of drawing on the part of the art public, therefore, tends to center in the more widely sold and exhibited print. And it is undoubtedly true that the print can remarkably resemble the drawing.

For example, the *lithograph*, an early-nineteenth-century invention, makes possible an almost exact reproduction of crayonlike drawing [97]. One of the artist's hand tools in the process, although called a lithographic pencil, is actually a greasy crayon, and some form of fatty substance— even soap and lipstick will work—must be employed. The drawing is made directly on a smooth, flat, fine-grained stone. A bath of gum arabic and nitric acid is then brushed on the stone, and this fixes ("etches") the drawn portion, making it more impervious to water. The fixed drawing is absorbed into the pores of the stone overnight, and any nongreasy residue is wiped off with turpentine the following day. The stone is now wet down, but as this is done the water is rejected by the fixed drawing. Printer's ink is applied with a roller. Now it is the wet stone which is unaffected by the ink (since oil and water do not mix), while the greasy drawing attracts and holds the ink. Damp paper is pressed on the inked stone and the ink from the drawing is transferred to the paper with almost exactly the same tonal values as had the original drawing. With care, several hundred copies can be "pulled" from a given stone. As these are sold, the artist's overhead cost (including a commission for his dealer) and profit are spread among a large number of owners. Hence lithographs are very reasonable in cost in comparison with comparable original drawings, more reasonable, usually, than any other type of print.

The charming lithograph by Renoir [97] of two young girls reveals

97. Pierre Auguste Renoir: *Two Girls*. French. 1897. Lithograph. Private collection.

the capacity of the lithograph to reproduce effectively the look of a crayon drawing, including the crayon's wide range of light values. Lithography can be used to reproduce line drawings just as easily as those employing tone. The head by Matisse [98] reveals the artist's masterful control of linear rhythm and the positioning of shapes. Space here is as important as line. The lithograph projects this quite as effectively as

98. Henri Matisse: *Head*. French. Lithograph. Private collection.

an original drawing. In fact, lithography is essentially a duplicating process. It is possible to get special effects by directly scratching the stone and by using a grainy *tusche*—a brushed-on tone in which the grease is held in liquid suspension. But it is only the color lithograph which really looks like a new kind of drawing, a new graphic medium.

The *color lithograph* is made by successive impressions, each having parts of the drawing and each of which adds a color. Where the colors overlap, effects are produced which are uncharacteristic of any direct drawing or painting process. Hence color lithography is a separate genre; black-and-white lithography, in contrast, is more a technical means of reproducing, with amazing accuracy, an original crayon drawing.

The distinctness of the color lithograph may be suggested by Kandinsky's *Composition* of 1922 [99]. By searching carefully, you will see where printed shapes overlap. The configuration of lines and shapes here looks improvised, but was undoubtedly carefully "corrected." Kandinsky liked the idea of art being free, inspirational, spontaneous, and intuitive, but the artist in him demanded that it should express wholeness and unity. This accounts for his preliminary versions and sketches for non-objective works. He put a great deal of effort into maintaining an effort-

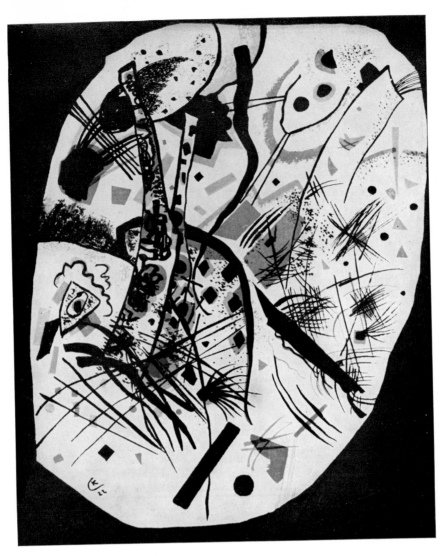

99. Wassily Kandinsky: *Composition*. Russian. 1922. Color lithograph. Columbus, O.: The Ohio State University School of Fine and Applied Arts.

less (but unified) look. If in your mind's eye you begin taking out shapes from Kandinsky's lithograph, or moving them to another position, you will see how very carefully every shape is located. Paradoxically, we have here a highly ordered spontaneity.

The *woodcut* and *wood engraving* are much older than the lithograph—they date back to medieval times—and are more distinct as art media. The woodcut is made by cutting away the part that is not to show and by inking the remainder. A damp paper is then pressed on the block and the ink is transferred to it [100]. The woodcut is unlike a drawing because of the evenness of its black tones—difficult to reproduce with a brush or crayon—and because the gouged-out or cut edges of the wood

100. Ernst Ludwig Kirchner: *The Forest*. German. 1916. Woodcut. Private collection.

reflect the use of a sharp tool and do not look like a drawn line. The woodcut is therefore functional to broad, bold contrasts of black and white, as in our forest scene. Kirchner has created a texture consistent with the gouging contour of the wood "cuts," an effective balance of light and dark, and an expressive projection of the effect of a dense, evergreen forest with its pathos of juxtaposed life and death. When its boldness of contrast is effectively exploited, as here, the woodcut can produce a very powerful impression.

The wood engraving is a counterfeit, for it still prints from a raised surface, yet approximates the fine line of the true engraving. The wood engraving is thus a tour de force, made possible by using the end grain of a very hard and close-grained wood, such as maple, and by great skill and patience in exposing ridges small enough to print as fine lines. The wood engraving does not have so characteristic a gouged texture as the modern woodcut, but it still achieves remarkable effects. In the hands of a master like Albrecht Dürer the wood block was seemingly freed from the limitations of its material and made the vehicle for a work

101. Albrecht Dürer: *The Last Supper.* German. 1510. Wood engraving. Columbus, O.: The Columbus Gallery of Fine Arts.

as finely detailed as a pen drawing [101]. *The Last Supper,* executed by Dürer in the early sixteenth century, is not only a prime example of the wood engraver's technical skill, but is a moving instance of that rich blend of humanist realism and medieval mysticism which characterized the early Renaissance in the North. Notice how effectively the bold and simple solidity of the architecture is contrasted with the agitated movement of the human beings and how marvelously the selective high lights and the crinkled folds of the drapery create an effect of emotion and vitality.

These two wood-block prints reveal a basic difference in the modern approach to the art medium. By dint of great skill and technical virtuosity the sixteenth-century carver was able to make his medium imitate another, the pen drawing. In contrast, the modern artist has not concealed but frankly revealed the nature of his medium. Kirchner's forest looks as if it had been carved. We see the clean gouge marks of the chisel, the relatively large, flat shapes which the chisel can freely and easily produce. The texture of the print is that of an imprint from cut wood.

Dürer would very probably have considered this to be too crude because his esthetic was so much closer to realism. However, "realism" is a word of many connotations. It is true that Kirchner's print does not give a realistic illusion, say, of the spruce needles, as does Dürer's of the equivalently fine human hair. But the *mass* of the boughs and the soaring closeness of the trees is very effectively suggested, so that the subjective impression of a spruce forest's stately silence is evoked. This is realism of another sort. Dürer uses a more illusionistic treatment of surface appearance, yet still expresses his own deeply felt reverence by a *different kind of arbitrariness*. It is the pose, arrangement and gesture, the vital line, and above all the effulgent light mysteriously and softly unifying the entire area and centering about the head of Christ by which Dürer achieves his own moving effect.

The Japanese have for centuries been masters of the *color woodcut* and have developed it to high technical levels. In the example illustrated [102] each change of black and white value represents a different color or tone. To produce these tones it was necessary to make separate wood blocks that would place each desired color exactly at the right spot. The correct lining-up of the blocks is called *registration* and calls for absolute precision since the error of a sixty-fourth of an inch, or less, will show. Not only must the blocks be precisely placed at the time of printing, but the section to print must, of course, have been carved so as to fit precisely into the space allowed. If you look closely along the jawline of the girl holding the tray, you will see a tiny area where the artist failed to bring the edge of the floor color snugly against the contour of the face. There are some other small "misfits," but they are amazingly few, considering that the artist required about a dozen blocks to make this one print.

The many-colored woodcut is therefore something of a technical feat, but the increase of tonal nuance thus made possible does not, of course, guarantee a better esthetic achievement. On the contrary, it has happened here, as can happen with any craft, that the delight with technical success assumes the leading rather than contributing role. There are modern Japanese woodcuts, made from a hundred or more blocks, which are marvels of precise fitting and subtle tonal gradation, but are quite lacking in the esthetic power of earlier and far simpler works. The appeal of the print as an art work still depends on form—and so on some intensifying, unifying principle of vision. In our print this lies in its balance of plain and textured areas, in the rhythmic interrelation of its figures,

102. Toyokuni II: *Serving Tea.* Japanese. 19th century. Color woodcut. Columbus, O.: The Ohio State University School of Fine and Applied Arts.

and in the fastidious delicacy of its detail, as well as in its soft color relationships. In modern Western color-print making, exact matching of edges has been de-emphasized. Ground has been allowed to appear between shapes, or the shapes to overlap as in Kandinsky's lithograph [99]; registration, while still important, does not require the extreme accuracy demanded during certain periods in Japan. The modern artist usually cuts his own blocks, whereas in earlier centuries the artist often left this to a skilled artisan whom he supplied with the original drawing on paper. The artisan made a transfer of the drawing onto the block or pasted it on and cut through it.

The lithograph is a *planographic* process, so called because it works entirely on a plane surface. The woodcut is a *relief* process, because the design is raised. The engraving and etching are of the *intaglio* process— that is, cut below the surface. To print a line that is cut below the surface of a plate, it is necessary to force ink into the channel of the line and then to press it out onto a piece of paper. This is less difficult than

103. Max Beckmann: *Merry-Go-Round*. German. Drypoint. Columbus, O.: The Ohio State University School of Fine and Applied Arts.

it may sound, technically, although there is always the problem of giving line the quality of form, which is something else again.

The *engraving* is an intaglio made by cutting directly into the plate with the *burin*, a very sharp, wedge-shaped chisel. Made on a copper plate, such an engraving is called a *drypoint*, unless the little burrs thrown up by the cutting tool—preferably having a diamond point—are polished away. In that case we would simply have a copper engraving. The drypoint line is richly dark and a little fuzzy, because the ink holds not only in the cut channel but in the excavated burrs. Very few good proofs can be "pulled" of a true drypoint, because the burred surface is quickly worn away.

Max Beckmann's *Merry-Go-Round* [103], a satire on life, is a fine example of drypoint. Along the right leg of the standing figure at the left you will see some places where the tool failed to pick up burrs, leaving a simple engraved line instead of the burred drypoint. The burred lines

104. Jean Emile Laboureur: *Autumn*. French. 1922. Engraving on copper. Private collection.

preponderate in the print as a whole, however, contributing to its richness and warmth of tone.

Compare this with a copper engraving by Laboureur, *Autumn* [104], and you will see how the absence of burr makes possible a closer spacing of lines and a cleaner, but also drier, look. The sharp line of the engraving is as suited to Laboureur's sophisticated fluff as the rich drypoint is to the emotional vehemence of Beckmann. The engraving burin does not move easily in a curving path, so that the engraver, as here, will often work mainly with straight lines.

The *etching* [132 and 105] in quality of line lies between the media just discussed, not so dry as the engraving nor so florid as the drypoint. In the etching the lines are "bitten" into the copper or zinc plate by nitric acid or other metal-attacking chemicals. Hence, the plate has to be protected against the action of the acid except where the lines are wanted. The clean plate is first entirely covered with an acid-resisting

105. Francisco Goya: *Why?*, from the Disasters of War Series. Spanish. After 1810. Etching with aquatint. Columbus, O.: The Ohio State University School of Fine and Applied Arts.

substance—such as wax or asphaltum—which has been treated with a solvent or with heat to render it fluid. The darkest lines of the future print are then scratched through the protective film with a sharp steel point. It is not necessary to cut into the metal but only to expose it. Next the plate is put into an acid bath, and the exposed lines are "bitten." The plate is removed, rinsed free of acid, and the next darker lines exposed. When the plate is placed in the bath again, the first lines get a second—and therefore deeper—bite. Hence they will hold more ink and make darker lines. The process may be carried through a number of such treatments, depending on the range of linear tone desired.

It is also possible to make the whole drawing at the outset and to "stop out" the action of the acid over *successive* portions of the plate by removing the plate from the bath long enough to apply an acid-resisting varnish where desired. The plate is then returned to the bath and the unvarnished portions are bitten deeper.

Before the plate is printed, it is cleaned of its remaining waxed surface, inked, and the ink wiped free from the top surface but left in the

106. Käthe Kollwitz: *Self-portrait*. German. 1912. Soft-ground etching. Private collection.

lines bitten by the acid. Then it is pressed under great pressure against damp paper, to produce the finished etching.

It is possible to wipe the inked plate only lightly, in order to get a certain amount of tone from the unbitten surface [132 and 104], but it is easier to get tone by means of *aquatint*, which often appears in combination with etching, as in *Why?* [105] from Goya's *Disasters of War*. You notice on Goya's print that the ground is not white but has a tone which helps to unify the picture visually and also contributes to the murky terror of the scene.

The aquatint process consists of dusting finely powdered resin on the bare plate and then heating the plate until the resin adheres firmly to it. The resin is acid-resisting, so that when the plate is bitten, countless fine pits are produced which will hold ink and give a finely textured tone to the print. In recent times acid resists have been developed which can be brushed on and actually produce a painted look.

Before leaving Goya's etching, note its very masterly quality. The arrangement—that is, the composition—is perfectly balanced: the two men at the sides who turn inward "close" the composition and create a balanced vista for the two in the center. An undulating line from the leg of the man at left up the arms of the man at right runs across the picture and unifies it laterally. Position of swords, tilt of the bodies, even the line of the twig above the doomed man—all contribute to a wonderful unity of rhythm, counterrhythm, and appropriate emphasis. But the most remarkable thing of all and the sign of Goya's artistic maturity and genius is the fact that this detailed organization appears completely natural and uncontrived. It actually helps to make more vivid and convincing the casualness and therefore the moral hopelessness of the brutality, also reflected verbally in Goya's title. Beauty of form, elimination of nonessentials, psychological and dramatic realism, a timeless and terrible human theme are wrought together, as if without effort, into a tragic-beautiful vignette of man.

Experiments have been conducted with a very soft acid resist made of wax and grease. A paper is placed on the resist and the drawing is made through it onto the plate, without tearing the paper. This method gives a lithographic and more textured look to the print's surface and is called *soft-ground etching*. The *Self-portrait* [106] of Käthe Kollwitz is a splendid example. The artist has increased the effectiveness of the design by scraping and burnishing that portion of the plate marked by the white hair, which is visually balanced with the darkness at right, so that psychologically the head seems surrounded with murky shadow (the past?) and shining age. Lines engraved directly on the plate intensify some of the shadow in this highly subjective portrait.

One of the most versatile modern experimenters with print media was Georges Rouault. He showed great ingenuity in combining various techniques and did more, perhaps, than any other artist to stimulate new tendencies in the intaglio process. One of his most spectacular achievements was a rich, wash-drawing effect using aquatint [107]. Our illustration is of a study made in 1930. Note the look of brush work and the extraordinary richness of the blacks, greater than that possible to the lithograph. Rouault first made a brush drawing of the figure, photographed it, and had a halftone photoengraving made of it. He then worked on the photoengraving plate as on a regular etching plate, heightening the high lights by burnishing and building up the richness of the darks with added aquatint and varnish stops which give a painterly look. The result is a phenomenally extended range of values and richness of tone. Compare this intaglio work with Renoir's *Two Girls* [97].

Rouault, a master colorist, also experimented extensively with the *color aquatint*. His *Clown* [108] is an example of the technique which involves the careful registration of successive plates. The fine-grained texture of color aquatint diffuses the light and is rich and luminous to the eye.

We come finally, and briefly, to the *stencil* process, called the *serigraph* or *silk screen*. In this process, a silk cloth is first stretched tightly across an open frame. That part of the design which the artist wishes to

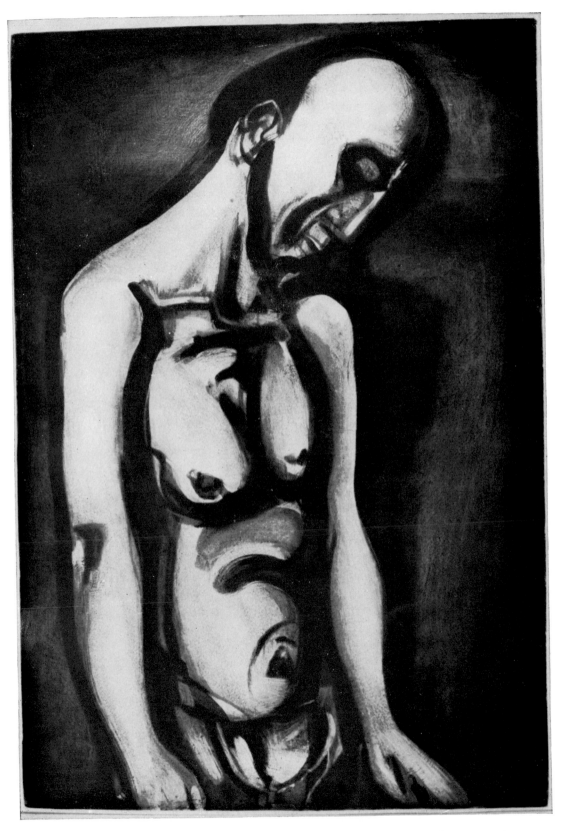

107. Georges Rouault: *Figure Study*. French. 1930. Aquatint on photoengraving plate. Columbus, O.: The Ohio State University School of Fine and Applied Arts.

108. Georges Rouault: *Clown*.
French. 1935. Color aquatint.
Private collection.

show is left untouched on the silk, and all the rest is "stopped-out," using
shellac, glue, lacquer-filler, or other liquid hardeners for which there are
solvents. A popular method is to paint the desired portion of the design
on the screen with a tusche which is allowed to dry. A glue resist is then
flushed across the whole screen, and after drying, the screen is treated
with a grease solvent which attacks the tusche but not the glue. This obvi-
ates having to outline the design.

The desired color, which may have an oil or a water base, is mixed to
the consistency of thick cream. The frame is then placed on top of the
print paper, and color is brushed on the silk and squeezed (squeegeed)
through the silk onto the paper. The resist prevents its going through the
treated points. The silk mesh creates a characteristic grainy effect which
is, however, relatively inconspicuous. Additional colors can be applied by
preparing another screen and again stopping out all but the desired portion. Hence there is a problem of registration in serigraphy, too, just as in
the colored woodcut or lithograph. The serigraph is much easier to work
with, however. Its materials are physically lighter; its design is brushed

109. Sylvia Wald: *The Wave*. 1952. Serigraph. Private collection.

on and can easily be removed with a solvent; and it can be used with a variety of kinds of color.

Its chief technical limitation is that it is not easily adaptable to rendering smooth transitions of value, as in a chiaroscuro drawing, but the scope it does have is so broad that the resourceful printmaker can make it a vehicle for personal expression and a wide variety of effects. Sylvia Wald's serigraph *The Wave* [109] shows how effectively the medium can be used to project bold free forms, and how adaptable it is to rendering painterly contours and interesting textures.

It has been said that the serigraph is not a print at all because it is not made with a press. This may technically be true, but it looks like and has characteristics in common with other print media. It will probably continue to be grouped with the print, and in any case, it is certainly one of the graphic arts.

Discussion of the *mezzotint* (made by selectively burnishing down or scraping away a surface which has a rich over-all burr) and some refinements of the other processes have been omitted, but the techniques covered are those principally in use.

I hope my reader will be stimulated anew to an interest in the graphic media. They are vastly more reasonable in cost than most paintings or sculpture and are of a scale to grace the average home. But these are only practical considerations. On the basis of outright quality, the graphic work holds its own. It may include, as we have seen, a very wide range of techniques. It has the great advantage of an intimate relation to the hand of the artist and a correspondingly personal effect. Part of the beauty of the drawing or print develops out of a technical problem well solved. While the graphic media are not so restricted as the "school figures" in figure skating, in both we may enjoy the triumph of the polished performance—when it occurs—because of its sheer perfection within technical boundaries.

In looking at architecture we saw how the nature of the materials used and many other factors combined to establish functional restraints on the nature of the product, *but also functional opportunities* for it. We may also realize, now, that functional problems exist equally for the modest pen drawing and all other graphic media. Some artists have sought to meet these problems by stretching the functional possibilities of their media; others have worked comfortably within their limitations. It is clear that the artist is obliged to adapt himself in some manner to the peculiarities and the potential of his tools and materials. The nature of art is inescapably bound up with its techniques of expression, its freedoms and restraints. Even the inspired hand needs discipline and the respect for method. The graphic works are an absorbing side of the arts because they show how the spirit can soar and find expression even within modest means. Indeed, they show that, for some, graphic works can provide art's most intimate and subtle fulfillment.

11-The Medium
in Painting
and Sculpture

Many callings and activities have rewards peculiar to the techniques involved in solving their problems. These rewards, often, may be felt by the participants to outweigh arduous and onerous difficulties in the solving process. The politician, for example, may encounter frustration, altercation, and boring obligation in his work, but, if he is a seasoned professional, he still loves politics and the political life. He develops a feeling for political compromise, timing, and persuasion, and in the end he is able to enjoy for their own sakes the finesse and subtlety of a well-executed political maneuver. In short, the experience has become creative, based on training, practice, specialized technique, and an individual contribution. Similarly, the satisfaction of a figure skater in executing a complicated sequence may be very close to that of a mathematician solving a complex problem or of a poet finishing a poem, even though the resources required of each are quite different. In working persistently at his calling, each has become an initiate through skillful control of the limitations and positive characteristics of the medium. Through the satisfaction of mastering them, the elements involved become more and more interesting for themselves, easier to handle, and a source of self-realization.

To be sure, there is a basic difference between such occupations as politics and that of soldering contacts in a TV assembly line, or between the practice of art and the operation of a cash register. All require special

154

110. G. B. Tiepolo: Allegorical ceiling painting, Berti Palace. Italian. 18th century. Nervesa, Italy. (C. Maya photo)

techniques and skills but in only two does the practice of those techniques and skills allow for any self-expression. The medium is of interest for itself only where it can be *manipulated* in a personal way which yet takes into account the medium's peculiarities. Whereas politics and art— to select contrasting activities—may be a means to self-discovery and personal growth, the operation of a cash register does not hold this promise. It lacks creative possibilities—except for the thief or for its designer. A great dilemma and tragedy of our time is that industrialism, the mechanism which has provided economic security—or at least abundance—for so many, by its nature fetters the self-expression of the millions who do its routine operations. Yet in educational thinking, relatively little consideration is given to encouraging avocations, such as the practice of art, which would at least provide a spare-time focus for creative self-expression.

Now the medium in painting and in sculpture, no less than in the other arts and more than in most activities, offers what may be termed

111. Giotto: *Flight into Egypt*, detail from Arena Chapel. Italian. 1305. Fresco. Padua, Italy. (Anderson photo)

creative limitations. The artist must paint on a flat surface, but it may vary in size and shape, both of which create interesting special problems. His oil paint must be malleable, but within this limitation may be mixed to apply thickly or thinly. His tools are mainly the brush and palette knife, yet they may be used with a variety of emphasis. And these variants may be vehicles for the expression of particular temperament and of particular epochs.

The people of the seventeenth and early eighteenth centuries, for example, with their intense curiosity about the nature of space—epito-mized in the researches of Kepler and Newton and in the cosmology of Milton—in art developed to a peak of expression the great ceiling mural [110]. Here the entire surface became a single composition denying the presence of the wall. It presented an illusion of space reaching from be-fore the wall to infinity beyond it. To produce these grand compositions, seen best from a distance, a virtuoso technique was needed and also a medium—oil pigment—flexible enough to serve it as a vehicle. But before considering some specific characteristics of oil painting as a medium, let us look more broadly at the nature of paint and at some of its types.

The coloring matter in pigment is finely-ground earthen or mineral materials or chemical compounds which need a binder to hold them permanently in place against the wall, panel, or canvas. One of the earliest binders was the lime or plaster on the wall itself; the painting was applied while the wall surface was still wet. Hence the Italian term *fresco*, meaning fresh. Because of the rapidity with which the fresco dried, it had to be painted quickly from carefully prepared working drawings. These drawings were first enlarged in outline on the wall. Over the preliminary sketch was laid a thin layer of plaster through which the sketch could still be seen, and the final painting was executed on the wet surface of this outer layer. The relative transparency of the medium made corrections difficult so that the artist dared not take chances with spontaneous effects. Fresco was thus best adapted to monumental compositions having broad, simple masses. In the hands of a master like Giotto, it was raised to a very high level of plastic expression [111]. The great murals of the medieval period and early Renaissance were mostly frescoes. In fresco, the coloring is absorbed into the wall surface—in fact, the painting and wall surface become one—so that it is extremely permanent, unless the wall surface gets damp or sweats.

Related to the fresco is *tempera*, which was also used in mural painting and which employed egg yolk (sometimes both yolk and white) as a binder. Tempera was used primarily on wood, following the preparation of a well-seasoned panel with several coats of *gesso*, a mix of glue and plaster. Egg tempera is rather flat in color, but this was offset—as may be seen in the Tuscan *Madonna and Child* of Figure 147—by the luminous tones resulting from the translucency of the medium against its white gesso ground and also, in many early works, by the surrounding presence of gold leaf.

Today tempera is commercially available in tubes, where it has a chemical binder in place of the egg yolk. The poster paint used commercially and in art classes is related to it, although these modern "temperas" might better be referred to as opaque water colors. If competently applied to a well-prepared surface, true tempera will not crack or flake off. A considerable degree of surface luster can be obtained by waxing and burnishing the surface of the finished painting, or by varnishing. Andrew Wyeth's *Northern Point* [170] is a modern tempera painting which shows the medium's power to project an exhilarating brilliance of light and, in the darks, to achieve a certain hardness of contrast not possible to the more transparent water color.

Water color makes use of a water-soluble binder, usually gum arabic, and of coloring materials—both chemical and vegetable—which remain in the water in very fine suspensions when mixed. They are applied by the artist to an absorbent material like paper, sometimes, for crisper, less soft effects, especially treated to resist absorption. Because the particles are relatively diffuse, the whiteness of the paper continues to show and imparts a characteristic lightness of ground. The transparency of water color also allows attractive overlays of color, when one color is brushed over the other. The color washes easily onto the paper, permitting very

112. John Marin: *Breakers, Maine Coast*. 1917. Water color. Columbus, O.:
The Columbus Gallery of Fine Arts, Ferdinand Howald Collection.

free effects. This is evident in John Marin's *Breakers, Maine Coast* [112].
Yet the same transparency and fluidity which make this work luminous
and vital make water color a medium requiring great skill. The transparency almost prevents corrections by means of overpainting and hence
requires experienced knowledge of the application and appearance of
overlaying colors. Marin's picture of surging water—one of the most "advanced" paintings made in this country up to that time (1917)—shows
his acquaintance with oriental shapes as he combines them with local
references in an essentially abstract arrangement.

Because of its difficulties as a medium, transparent water color has
been supplemented increasingly by various modern temperas and opaque
water colors, of which the most important is *gouache*. Here the binder is
lead or zinc white, which imparts a characteristic softness of tone to the
colors.

Less in use today but of very ancient provenance is *encaustic*, pigment
with a binder of hot wax. The moisture-resistant waxy surface produces
a soft, glowing effect in the colors, but the difficulty of handling a heated

medium has kept encaustic from having more than sporadic revivals.

The foregoing indicates the primary importance of the binder in a color's use and effect as a medium. The binder controls the transparency of the color, its consistency, its reflective brilliance, and the surface to which it is best applied. Not surprisingly, the word *medium* still refers, in technical usage, to the binder alone, although it also has the more general meaning followed in this book. Thus the words *oil medium,* depending upon the specific usage, may refer to the finished pigment in the artist's tube, to the properties of oil paint, or only to the binder itself (usually linseed oil) in which the coloring material has been thoroughly ground.

The oil medium—using the term now, in its broad sense—displaced all other paints in popularity soon after its discovery in the fifteenth century. Its extraordinary versatility was soon apparent. It could be applied thickly, an *impasto,* or—reduced with turpentine—very thinly. It could be applied opaquely or—thinned with varnish—could produce a *glaze,* or translucent overlay. With the addition of a little linseed oil, it could be made to dry more slowly, permitting the working up of a canvas or panel in a "wet" state. Again, agents could be added to speed up the drying, in which case changes could be made by painting over the dried, underlying sketch. Finally, oil increased the refractive index of the pigment to light, making possible rich and glowing effects which almost rivaled stained glass in brilliance. Although the oil medium could not duplicate all the effects of other paint media—the high transparency of water color, for example—its wide range of effects, ease of application, and richness of color have established it as the leading material for the painter.

The spatial and material illusion in the detail of Tiepolo's Berti Palace fresco [110] is so brilliantly executed that it would be almost impossible to believe that the architectural framework shown is only painted were it not for the clouds and figures in front of it. Here is an example of the adaptability of the oil medium to illusionism. True fresco would have been ill-adapted to and almost impossible to use for such effects, and tempera would have lacked the necessary brilliance of tone.

Tiepolo painted with a rather broad brush, an aid to rapid coverage of the huge areas of his ceilings and to the achievement of a broad effect that would project well. Other artists developed their use of the medium in other ways. At times they have enjoyed the scumbly appearance of pigment, for example, and Rembrandt, as we have already seen, deliberately allowed the paint to show in a texture which was only partially illusionistic [19]. The artists of our century have been particularly prone to emphasize the texture of the medium. In Abramofsky's *Three Faces* [113], the artist has changed the texture within the area of the canvas, applying it in a scumbly way here and a smooth way there, using a palette knife. This richly varies the appearance of the surface and contributes to the painting's subjective effect of serious vehemence.

An outstanding modern exemplar of the enjoyment and emphasis of medium for its own sake is the work of Jackson Pollock. His *No. 5, 1950*

113. I. Abramofsky: *Three Faces*. 1945. Private collection.

[III] shows the complete elimination of subject, unless we accept the medium itself, given form, as the subject. Pollock painted this work mainly by dripping the paint on the canvas from a broad brush. Paint—as such—assumes major emphasis. It can be argued that by totally avoiding presentation, the artist actually achieves it here. He *presents* color, texture, paint. Realizing this, some artists have called art of this kind *concrete art*, and with good reason, although many of the public thought the designation a cynical hoax. Textures in a painting like Van Eyck's *Madonna and Child* [18], marvelously convincing though they may be, are still illusionistic—related to the appearance of something that existed outside the painting. The texture in Pollock's painting is literally texture. Touching the hair on Van Eyck's canvas would be a disillusioning experience, while touching the paint on Pollock's would confirm exactly what we had seen, and no more. Here we may reach the artist not through any physical illusion he created but via the immediate evidence of his physical contact with the canvas. Thus the form he creates and the content—of which more in another chapter—are projected with a certain superdirectness, uninvolved with an intermediary subject and having the theoretical potential, at least, of heightened expression.

III. Jackson Pollock: *No. 5, 1950*. New York: The Museum of Modern Art, Gift of Mr. and Mrs. Walter Bareiss.

In sculpture we find the same tendency for medium to receive increasing emphasis for its own sake. At first thought, it might seem that the very nature of sculpture would preclude its being involved in the kinds of illusionism we have seen in Van Eyck and Tiepolo. But this would be to underrate the ingenuity of the artist. One way the sculptor surmounted the limitations of his material was to paint it. This was done occasionally in almost every period (for a late Gothic example, see Figure 145) and was common in the time that Tiepolo was creating his vast spatial illusions. The sculptor was a part of the same cultural ferment as the painter and he participated by creating groups of realistic figures in space. They might be in the form of saints around an altar or, if angels or putti, might often be suspended in the air, with the illusion of defying gravity [114]. In the same period the sculptor was also able to stretch the capabilities of his material, making plaster composition look like marble, as here, carving marble to look like lace, or giving bronze the look of pliant textile.

In the early part of our century such practices were condemned as being "untrue to the material," but lately the sculpture of the Baroque has been enjoying a collectors' revival, and the argument, no doubt as logical as the earlier condemnation, has been advanced that anything the material can be made to do is, *ipso facto,* true to the material. Despite repeated excursions into tricks and illusions, however, over the centuries the sculptor has learned the way his material works most readily and has developed a liking for the material as such.

Baked clay, stone, wood, and bronze are the sculptor's chief media, although ivory, gold, silver, and lead have also been used extensively. Recently, welded steel, iron, and built-up plaster have found favor. Let us look briefly at some of their characteristics.

While *baked clay* may be associated with pottery and the utilitarian products of the ceramist, we are here concerned with *ceramic sculpture,* a branch of ceramics more exclusively concerned with artistic purposes. Such sculpture has often been called *terra cotta,* but technically this term refers only to a particular clay that is brownish-red when fired. Terra cotta was especially popular during the Italian Renaissance because it was easily procured, resisted warping or cracking, and could be fired safely in large sizes. The modern ceramic sculptor has made use of many other clays and mixtures of clay. While the sculpture may be left in its original fired, or *biscuit,* state, it is usually put in the kiln a second time after applying solutions whose chemical or suspended ingredients bake into a hard, surface *glaze.* A wide range of colors may be obtained in glazes, and they vary in sheen from dull, or matte, to a high gloss.

Ceramic sculpture, although subject to chipping or breakage if carelessly handled, is remarkably resistant to deterioration and is one of the most durable of all the artist's media. Because it begins as malleable clay, ceramic sculpture can be produced in a mold and therefore duplicated any number of times. Many of the greatest works in this medium are unique pieces, however, for it is not only its duplicative potential but also other positive qualities that have made it survive. Among these are its

114. Altar putti. German. 1738. Plaster composition. Rottenbuch, Germany.

115. Luca della Robbia: *Madonna and Child* (*The San Donato Madonna*). Italian. 15th century. Glazed terra cotta. Toledo, O.: The Toledo Museum of Art, Edward Drummond Libbey Collection.

ease of maintenance—it can be washed without harm—cheapness, and permanence of color and finish. Esthetically it has the ready impact of shiny surface and bright, clear color, which, unfortunately, can be tawdry and garish in effect. But handled with reserve, as in the *San Donato Madonna* [115], by Luca della Robbia, the medium points up the subtle nuances in surface treatment of the clay model and has an exhilarating clarity combined with softness of light. The only contrast of color here is in the background and in the eyes. This work is an example of relatively *high relief*. It stands out from its ground yet is attached to it. Without an attached panel, it would be *free-standing*, or *in the round*. If the design does not project beyond its ground but is cut back at its contours, as on the columns in Figure 116, it is *incised relief*.

Stone exists in an enormous variety of color, texture, and hardness. Power-driven chisels have greatly accelerated the sculptor's work with it, particularly the roughing out, but it is still a hard and resistant medium and a physical challenge. Once a piece is chipped away, moreover, it cannot be put back; the worker in stone has to be secure with his chisel. Rendering tractable this heavy and hard material and subjecting it, at last, to the vision of the artist is a creative joy which the finished work may reveal even to the spectator. Weiner's *Figure* [15], as we have previously noted, openly accepts the rough and hard look of the stone as a part of its effect in contrast to the smooth sweep of the contours. Henry Moore's *Figure* [13] depends not so much on the static beauty of a shaped mass as on the flowing interaction of mass and space. The softly rounded curves and undulations of the figure are made more convincing, visually, by the smooth texture of the stone.

We need not draw the negative conclusion from the above examples that were we to have illusionism in texture it would necessarily destroy a feeling for the material. Although the ancient portrait of Augustus [129] suggests the texture of skin and hair with almost uncanny realism, the sculptor still maintains the look of marble throughout. He does so by exaggerating, ever so slightly, the smoothness of the skin and by allowing the hair and wreath a "stony" simplification. It takes a master to bridge this dualistic trap, for there is a certain inherent conflict in seeing realistically and with an eye to form. Another superb example of the combination of formal and realistic elements is seen in the ancient Egyptian statue of Ramses II [116], still standing in the temple at Luxor. Here the polished texture of the surface unifies the whole and combines with the simplification in handling of mass to give a realistic effect of majesty and physical power.

The modern sculptor and painter often have avoided the conflict of realism and form by de-emphasizing realism. Why is it that so many of us find it difficult to accept this shift of emphasis? Perhaps in the past the realistic or illusionistic aspect of art has attracted more than its share of attention, so that the quality of form, the underlying abstraction and visual intensification in works like the portraits of Augustus and of Ramses II, has gone largely unnoticed. Yet it is this very formal quality, the unifying vision of the sculptor working with a resistant material, which gives these works their distinction and lifts them above the level of life mask.

Wood, generally, is much easier to work than stone. Extremely hard woods—such as teak—are usually avoided by the sculptor; those with a beautiful color or grain, such as rosewood, walnut, and mahogany, are favored. On the European continent, linden has been popular. It has a close grain that yields easily to carving, and it is resistant to splitting.

In the Breisach Altar [17] we saw how love of the material and its rich yielding to plastic effects under the chisel caused the artist to exceed the bounds of realism. Cashwan's *Harp* [117] suggests only wood. The texture is that of the chiseled material, indicated by the sharp edges and contin-

116. *Ramses II.* Egyptian. *c.* 1250 B.C. Stone. Luxor, Egypt.

uously gouged surfaces along the right side. The modern artist simply gives more *exclusive* attention to designing his material.

Bronze is highly susceptible to rich surface effects because it begins with—and is finally a duplication in metal of—a clay model. Within limits, anything that can be modeled in clay can be cast in bronze, usually done by the *lost wax process.* In this, a negative plaster cast is made of the original—that is, a cast with inside surfaces conforming to the outside of the model. After the cast is taken off the model, in previously planned pieces, it is reassembled and coated inside with hot wax. The wax is built up to the thickness desired for the bronze. The mold is again removed, leaving a wax model of the original. As wax works easily, the artist may then make any desired final adjustments in his work before it is cast. Now the hollow wax model is coated inside and out with a heat-resistant, semiliquid mixture of silica and plaster which hardens around the model. The whole thing is now slowly baked in an oven. The wax melts and is "lost" through tubes previously placed in the mold as drains. When the wax has all run out, the now hollow mold is packed around with foundry earth to resist

117. Samuel Cashwan: *Harp.* 1946. Mahogany. Private collection.

the high heat of molten metal, and the bronze is poured into it. After cooling and removal from the earth, the mold is chipped away. Any appendages—such as those caused by the wax drainage outlets—are carefully cut off; the bronze is then buffed down to the proper texture for the surface. And there you have a bronze casting, a very expensive process requiring technical knowledge, experience, and skill. Bronze not only is extremely resistant to deterioration, but develops a beautiful green incrustation, or *patina*, through the years. Its reflective surface when smooth or polished is very effective in creating flashing contrasts of light and dark. You will see this at once in Rodin's bronze representing St. John the Baptist [127].

Contemporary artists have emphasized even more the reflective, metallic look of polished bronze. Max Bill's *Three-Part Unity* [118] may be compared with Cashwan's *Harp* which it rather resembles as a design, yet the change from wood to metal alone results in a quite different effect. Bill has exploited to the full the potential of his material for brilliance of surface and for displaying hardness and strength. While a wood shape could conceivably be carved as thin, its fragility in this form might leave us psychologically uncomfortable through the feeling that it would crack. Cashwan's heavier forms are much more woodlike and have been treated as such. Bill's work in its way is equivalently metallic. The nature of the material has governed its treatment in both cases; the sculptor has exploited those effects inherent in his medium which have interested him.

The give-and-take between the artist and his material is well exemplified in Ibram Lassaw's *The Constellation of Perseus* [119], a welded

118. Max Bill: *Tripartite Unity*. Swiss. 1947. Bronze. Private collection.

wire construction. The heated welding stick has a tendency to flow into globs or little lumps, and Lassaw has used this functional tendency to build a rich variety of textures in his design. The flow of space through this strong, yet delicate, frame keeps space its most unifying aspect. This the sculptor may wish to identify as part of the vastness of the universe, defined by the mysterious interconnection of its countless suns—here symbolized by the complexly interrelated cage. However, we need not engage in such speculative interpretation to see that this work is indeed intimately the outgrowth of its material—metal rods—and of its technique of construction—welding—and that it took the creative imagination of an artist to combine these in a unified visual expression.

Indeed, we may well return to the artist at this point, and to the projective nature of art. The particular properties of a material still have to be recognized by the artist to be projected. If the sculptor of Ramses II [116] had disliked stone and, say, inordinately admired textiles, he could have tricked up his stony surface to deny itself and suggest only cloth. The material may make one effect easier of achievement than another, of course, but is the easier effect, therefore, more *fundamental* to the material? Philosophically, the answer to what is basically a philosophical problem is no. All we can conclude is that through the ages and wherever he

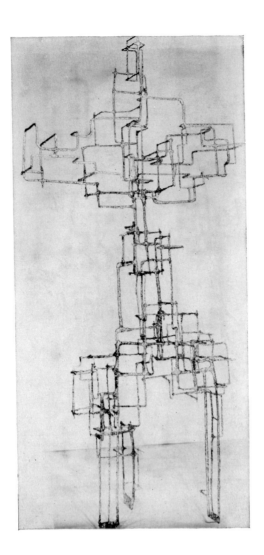

119. Ibram Lassaw: *The Constellation of Perseus.* 1951. Welded wire. Rio de Janeiro: Modern Museum.

has wrought materials into form, the artist has developed the properties which *he* felt to be peculiar to those materials. As he worked he grew to love materials and to try to turn the properties he found in them ever to better advantage. Even if one man exploited a material in a way that seemed "unnatural" to another man, or to a later age, he still was developing a consciousness of material *as such.* We have seen how this consciousness, whether applied to painting, sculpture, the complex field of architecture, or a simple medium like the woodcut, has deeply influenced creative endeavor, making of art an interplay of the artist's creative power with his conception of materials as vehicles for expressing his feelings and insights.

Levels of Approach to Art

12-Introduction

Looking at the *Madonna and Saints* [120] by Hans Memling, we recognize that in its most objective aspect it is the illusionistic *presentation* of a scene. Two men, two children, and two women are grouped around a woman and child in a columned porch. Details of costume, individual appearance, gesture, position, and setting are all part of this external subject. These are the facts we can observe without any knowledge of the *representation* involved, of what the scene stands for or means.

Most of us know immediately, however, that this group represents individuals within the Christian story. They are identified for us by certain *conscious* or *apparent symbols.* St. Catherine was martyred on a knife-ringed wheel and also by the sword. It is unusual to find both these instruments of her martyrdom in a painting—the wheel usually suffices—but these are symbols of this particular saint's martyrdom. The Christ Child is identified not only by His association with the woman who has the leading position in the group—obviously his mother, Mary—but also by His placing a ring on St. Catherine's finger. This is an allusion to her mystic marriage to Christ. On the right is St. Barbara, doer of charitable deeds, identified by her missal, or book of prayers for the mass, and by the tower associated with her martyrdom. The tower is also the façade of the church in Sts. John Hospital, Bruges, Belgium, for which the painting was destined. At the back on the left stands St. John the Baptist, who lived in the desert and is identified by the lamb and the slender staff in the shape of a cross. The other man is St. John the Evangelist, writer of the gospel, identified by the poison chalice, which he neutralizes and transforms by the blessing of right. The children would ordinarily be angels. The omission of their wings could be a sophisticated reflection of the realism of the time. However, the presence of two small angels, holding the crown above the throne, indicates that the other two are mortal. One child is playing music on a portable organ; the other is holding a book, probably the Bible, for the Madonna to read.

120. Hans Memling: *Madonna, Christ Child, and Saints*. Flemish. 1479. Bruges, Belgium: Museum of Sts. John Hospital.

Such elements of identification in an art work are technically known as the *iconographic* elements. As indicated, they are presented through identifiable objects which are symbols—apparent and intended—of action associated with specific individuals.

We notice that the group is located in a sumptuous setting. The open porch is supported on monolithic columns of imported marble, there being no such marble in Flanders. A handsome Oriental rug is at the Madonna's feet and a gorgeous damask decorates the back of her throne, which has a canopied top. The floor is of inlaid marble. The ladies' gowns are of the

finest materials. The Madonna wears a robe of beautiful rose silk over a velvet undergarment of dark green. St. Catherine also has a bodice with velvet sleeves and her gown has a magnificent damask skirt. The border of the Madonna's gown at neck and sleeve is richly jeweled, and both she and St. Catherine wear coronets. St. John-Baptist's undergarment is edged with fur, and he and his counterpart wear robes of the finest material. The bare leg of St. John, an allusion to his life of rigorous self-denial in the desert, appears through such clothes as an incongruous element, rather than as characteristic. In fact, the Bible at no point associates these people with such evidences of wealth. The Bible not only points to the humble circumstances of Mary, for example, but gives them dignity and justification through the precepts and life of Her son. Why, then, did the artist not select a setting more appropriate (so we would think) to the recorded circumstances of his principal subjects?

The answer to this lies in the area called *unconscious symbolism*. It is meaning which goes beyond identifiable and intended representation. It indicates the significance, *not realized by the artist*, of what he has done as a matter of course or for some other reason. Whether Memling considered the clothes and setting appropriate we cannot know, although his other paintings give us no reason to suspect he did not. We can be reasonably sure that the patrons who commissioned the painting and the church dignitaries who accepted it—it was for years the chief altarpiece in the Sts. John Hospital Church in Bruges—and doubtless most of the congregation, saw nothing incongruous in it. Why?

In the first place the patrons of art of the day, both lay and ecclesiastical, were either wealthy church orders, the nobility, or wealthy members of the middle class. Most of these were accustomed to sumptuous surroundings, avowed and displayed them as a matter of right, and might well have felt uncomfortable to see their Lady in a lowly setting. The painting thus becomes an unconscious symbol of their values, values which they might have held quite as a matter of course.

Unconscious symbolism plays its part in other respects. Objectively we see that the artist has created an illusion of real space and has peopled it with flesh-and-blood people like those around him. The two women saints are particularly individual and realistic, and the Madonna, too, appears to have been a specific model, possibly someone whom the artist wished to honor. The Christ Child is depicted as an ordinary infant and the large "angels," as previously noted, are not immortalized with wings, but appear as children.

Such are the apparent factors. What do they signify? We will throw light on this first by noting what they do not signify. We do not have here a mystical concept or one based on the denial of the flesh and of the world. Even the marriage of St. Catherine, a highly symbolic and basically spiritual conception (to our view today) is represented with the most matter-of-fact realism. Neither the Christ Child nor St. Catherine even looks at the other, which gives a curious, perfunctory look to the incident. No, here is

no avowal of the primacy of Spirit and of the approach to it through a life of self-denial and meditation. Rather it is by good works that we can imagine these people seeking their reward; by good works, moreover, in the world around them, in the charitable pursuit of daily tasks. In the placement of the Madonna in the center and in the general refinement of the treatment we find a reverential quality, but it is on an essentially humanistic basis.

There is no intent here to approve or disapprove the way of life made implicit by this painting. That is a matter of personal values, and besides, it was a way which existed nearly five hundred years ago under conditions very different from those of today. A conception of the nature of that life, to be sure, or of the group of people it represents, may throw a revealing light on our own. But that is another problem. Here our concern is with the apparent symbol, the intended content of the artist and his patrons, and how it *may be seen in a larger symbolic way*, turning out to be, in this case, the hidden symbolism of a humanistic Christianity.

The objective facts of Memling's painting, together with their intended symbolism, are its *apparent reality*, the story it tells, the details it reveals. We have seen that in the *way* the subject is presented lies an unconscious symbolism that reveals much about the values of those involved with it.

How reliable are the interpretations reached by us in such a case or in another which we might analyze? The answer is that, for the most part, they must remain hypotheses. Depending upon the evidence we accumulate regarding a specific work of art, we may feel more or less secure in our conclusion. But the fact remains that these interpretations are projections by us. Inevitably, our own limitations will limit the breadth of our perception or cause errors of judgment. While this should remain a sobering realization, its value is not in inhibiting interpretation but in promoting an openness of viewpoint. Meanwhile we proceed on the basis of that hypothesis which reason, reflection, study, and experience convince us makes the best sense—for us.

There are, then, a number of levels of approach to the art work, the enumeration of which may serve to summarize for us the point we have reached in our investigation of art. The art work may be approached, then thus:

1. As illusionistic presentation of physical phenomena, of visual facts about setting, nature, people.
2. As interpretation of the subject, achieved by emphasis or distortion —that is, by symbolic referents, conscious and unconscious.
3. As self-expression—discernible partly through handling of content, partly through symbolism of form.
4. As form, esthetic organization for its own sake.

It is quite possible to regard a work from any one of these levels and to ignore the others. The unsophisticated viewer is not likely to get beyond the first. The purist, particularly today, tends to confine himself to the last. My own bias, as the reader has doubtless divined, is that the broader the

framework of reference, the broader the grasp of a phenomenon. But it is a bias in favor of a multiple level of approach with this qualification, that the artist's intent should be given first consideration. And there can be little doubt that the artist's own concern is usually with esthetic unity and quality. That is what makes him an artist and differentiates him from one who only describes or reports. Nevertheless, the ramifications of art are rich and varied, more so than we can even touch upon in this book, and there is no single approach that answers for all the others.

13-Nude and Portrait-Influence of Subject

It happens infrequently; yet most of us eventually find ourselves revisiting the zoo, usually under the pretext of making company for a child. When we pass the tigers' cage, we are likely to stop in admiration, especially if the great cats are pacing back and forth in the fruitless and pathetic boredom of their confinement. It is easy to be fascinated by their velvet-cloaked power. But it is not alone this physical, vaguely frightening presence of menacing strength which stops us there. It is also their sleek lines, the trim grace and smooth texture of their bodies, the rhythm of their gait. With different subjective overtones we could admire these in a gazelle and in many other animals.

Neither the alligator nor the yak, however, has such *visual* appeal, although the one may have a terror-fascination and the other at least evoke the image of remote cultures. They are quite as functionally designed as the others, yet we speak of the tiger and gazelle, not of the alligator and yak, as "beautiful." Why is this?

It is another example of the projective, "human" nature of our seeing. We subconsciously relate even animals to ourselves. We have nothing apparently in common with the alligator, whereas the gazelle has smoothness of build and grace of movement, attributes which we admire in human beings. The shagginess of the yak, in contrast, makes him seem "unkempt." His proportions are angular in comparison to the smoother and more supple body of the tiger, which is correspondingly closer to our own. Even the tiger's gliding step is akin to that which a human dancer may create and whose rhythm we accordingly admire, whereas we cannot imitate the step of the yak or alligator, except in comedy. Their equally functional gait seems undistinguished. To our human eyes, again, the gambols

176

of a hippopotamus would appear preposterous but those of a lamb charming, only because our own actions are quite unrelated to the huge pachyderm. Our visual reaction to animals, in short, springs more from an anthropomorphic bias than we may have realized.

There can be little doubt, moreover, that the human element in our approach to the physical body has sexual undertones. This is the reason the human body itself is more attractive to us than that of any animal. A shark or hummingbird is just as beautiful from the criterion of the relation of form to function and from their "design" having a unique appearance of consistency and wholeness. Indeed, in the abstract, the human female figure, with its broad hips, narrow shoulders and protruding breasts, is less dynamic than the less complex but visually consistent and streamlined form of the shark. The male human, with his smoothly broadening build, reaching a climax at the shoulders, also has a more unified "design." The preponderance of female nudes in Western art is a reflection of the preponderance of male artists, rather than of any visual superiority of the female body, and is a manifestation of sex interest.

The choice in art of the unclothed human figure, however, though it may have sexual or erotic roots, is also the response to an inherent esthetic challenge. The harmonious proportion of the human figure: the springing of the body in easy balance from feet to head, the subtle union of part with part, the dynamic play of curves in the change of contour—from ancient times these have supplied the artist with ready-made visual relationships of a unifying sort. In the mere copying of the human figure the artist has confronted the visual problem of relating mass to mass and of creating rhythmic effects. The nude has been an unending esthetic resource and stimulus, and it is no wonder that it has contributed to the artist's development in all ages where its representation was not culturally taboo.

Artists and also art-minded observers like ourselves have both a perfectly natural erotic interest in the human body and an interest in the body's unusual esthetic potential. A great deal of confusion about the nude in art would be dissipated if it were frankly seen in this dual light. At the same time it is undoubtedly true that the relative weighting of erotic and esthetic interest may vary widely. The observer's own predisposition, naturally, is a guiding influence. "To him with a carnal eye shall it appear carnal," to paraphrase the well known maxim. Nevertheless, as we shall see, the artist still plays the intitial and, if we allow him, the controlling role.

The *Venus* by Brescianino [121], a competent Italian artist of the early sixteenth century, in certain respects appears more realistic than that by Lucas Cranach, a sixteenth-century German [122]. The Italian painting, in the main, is convincing in proportion and detail. Cranach's *Venus*, in contrast, shows many distortions. The whole body is attenuated, drawn out—an effect which is emphasized by making the chest and shoulders unusually narrow. This attenuation has a double function. It lengthens, abstracts, and emphasizes the body's sinuous contour, thereby

121 (*left*). Brescianino: *Venus*. Italian. 16th century. Rome: Borghese Gallery. (Alinari photo). 122 (*right*). Lucas Cranach the Elder: *Venus*. German. 1532. Frankfort am Main, Germany: Städelches Institut.

allowing the artist to give its rhythm a more expressive visual flow. It also serves to emphasize the subject's sex, exaggerating the thighs and the femininity of the narrow chest and shoulders. Although the figure seems to be facing us almost squarely, the artist has emphasized the contour of one breast and placed the navel to one side so that the roundness of the abdomen can be included in the contour.

Attenuation as a device tends to create the effect of refinement (in contrast to grossness or stolidity, for which compression or broadening of the subject is used). The elegant refinement in Cranach's painting is heightened not only by attenuation but by the artificial position of the arms and hands, which abstractly carries on the effect of rhythmically undulating contours seen in the treatment of the body. The gossamer veil, as transparent as glass, conceals nothing of the body, although it goes through the motion of doing so. It also adds another rhythmic element,

especially striking against the dark background. Necklaces and contour of face and hair reveal other curving rhythms, all subtly varied.

Cranach's nude provided him the opportunity for a masterly play of visual rhythms which he has combined with a sophisticated emphasis of the erotic nature of his subject. The erotic element is heightened even more by having the subject look toward us—thus increasing the effect of immediate "presence"—and by giving the subject's face a highly individualized look. This is no abstract study of ideal womanhood but a heightened portrayal, if not of a specific person, then at least of a seductive and knowing type.

Brescianino's *Venus* has been conceived in quite a different way. In most places the contour of his figure is made fuzzy by a shadow and does not have that incisive clarity which adds continuity and linear design to Cranach's painting. Brescianino is far more concerned with volumes. Where the light plays flatly and evenly across Cranach's nude, it *models* the body of the other figure. It also models the space back of it—if one speak thus of the creation of a void—giving the figure a freestanding, tridimensional veracity. Such form or visual unity as the work possesses is achieved by the simplification of its volumes and their surface texture together with the clean and simple articulation of these volumes.

A distinction is often drawn in art literature between the naked and the nude figure. The latter is shown to have the refining abstraction of form, where the former is merely undressed. The distinction is worth attention, but it should be added that the art work—in this case, the nude—does not thereby gain any automatic superiority of *content*. The naked figure, actually, is neutral in content or, if not that, is inherently chaste. Any other reaction is projected upon it. And this is precisely what the introduction of the element of form permits. It permits the artist to make of the unclothed figure a vehicle for a broad range of symbolic overtones reflecting himself and his culture.

Compare the two Venuses once more. We have seen that Brescianino's is more illusionistically three-dimensional and "real"-looking and has less distortion of accepted anatomical norms. In brief, it is nearer to nakedness. But it is also more idealized, detached, and, yes, more chaste, than the far more abstract and erotic work by Cranach.

Law suits have been held in which the admissibility of the unclothed figure was at issue. The defense of the art work has usually been based on the premise that the presence of art quality removed the figure from the moral opprobrium that would attach to it if it were truly naked. "It is above criticism because of being an art work." Yet this overlooks both the essential neutrality of nakedness and the variability of content in art. *There is nothing inherently superior or above reproach, morally and ethically, about an art work.* A work can have art quality and also stand for the most depraved ethic. To establish a polarity of nakedness and art is to dodge the true issue. The polarity only sets up a would-be bypass of the deeply ingrained folkways which still see something shameful in the human body.

In Cranach's work we have seen the union of a strongly esthetic and erotic expression; in Brescianino's, a lesser intensity in both respects. An infinitude of varying balances of these elements is found in art, including many instances where the decorative or formal concern is paramount and where the sensual becomes at most the sensuous. Indeed, use of the nude as a decorative subject dates back to ancient times and has been so employed in many other periods, notably in the Baroque and Rococo of the seventeenth and eighteenth centuries.

By *decoration* we mean *a design or visual organization which contributes through repetition to the attractiveness of an ensemble.* The decoration must have an interest on its own account, but not too much. It is always subordinate to a larger frame of reference. It is an embellishment and therefore must not be too intensely wrought or achieve too serious a status. In its subjective function, decoration appropriately serves our lighter moods, although its effect may be dignified, too. In the Baroque and Rococo periods it often contributed to an atmosphere of joy and elation, and the nude, with its wonderful possibilities for gesture and movement and with its human association, was an ideal decorative vehicle. It may have been with a feeling of joy that the eighteenth-century church decorators, particularly in southern Germany, took up their task. And it is with this psychological insight that we approach their complex designs.

Let us look again at the putti from Rottenbuch, a church in southern Germany which is almost oppressively rich in decoration but is very charming in detail [114]. We see the corner of the altar, above which the nude putti are so cleverly supported that they seem to be truly free in space. The effect of movement is enhanced by the glancing light which animates their bodies and breaks up the architectural regularity of the altar section where they fly. Notice how the highlight on the right corner of the altar interrupts the look of continuity of its mass, creating a painterly effect. The continuity of mass is further interrupted by having the lower putto's leg come down over the altar ledge. This is an art of *movement* in space, of freedom and joy, and it is this repeating movement everywhere which is decorative.

In the background beyond the upper putto may be seen a part of the ceiling decoration in relief stucco. Notice how the charming gesture of this putto's arm and the swirl of his drapery find a sympathetic, if unintended, reflection in the ceiling decoration, just as the extended arms of his playmate have a rhythmic reflection in the sweep of the marble architectural element between the two figures. From almost any angle some interesting new relationship of the putti to one another and to their setting is discovered. And note: these cherubic aerialists are not necessary to their location for reasons of content—for their contribution to a Christian schema. *Their true function is esthetic,* and their nude bodies, having movement both of limb and of flashing highlight, are excellent decorative additions to the general effect of the interior.

To see, here, the integration of figures and setting (field) requires a certain imaginative effort on our parts, because we are dealing with architecture, sculpture, painting, and relief decoration, each of which may also be of independent interest. Moreover, at the actual site, we see them in depth and from changing points of view. All this makes more exciting, but also more difficult, the integrative process. The union of various elements into a decorative ensemble is clearer in our example of Baroque mural painting [110], where a single artist's hand, or at least his design, provides an additional unifying element, as does the paint medium itself. Here the figure, whether nude, clothed, or seminude, is combined with the painted architecture in a magnificent decorative ensemble that characteristically suggests both the pathos and the grandness of gesture of the period. The decorative and ecstatic exuberance of an ensemble combining these many elements will be recalled by looking once again at an interior such as that of the Church in der Wies [30].

Flickering light and rhythmic contour are the esthetic subjects again in Boucher's *Venus Consoling Love* [123], where Venus, though the center of attention, is still only part of a decorative ensemble.

In the modern era of art—since about 1885, in France—the nude has increasingly been treated as a point of departure for esthetic experiment. This is well exemplified by Pablo Picasso, who has rendered a developing series of nudes, based on a single theme. In 1946, a year in which he expressed a strong renewal of interest in woman as a theme, he made eighteen lithographs of the same subject, a pair of nude women. As with his famous series of the bull, these began quite realistically and became increasingly abstract. The two reproduced here [124 and 125] show the kind of change that took place. The earlier version [124] is based on a balance of light and dark and on contrasts of texture, rhythmic contours and balanced shapes. However, the figure at the right—indeed, the whole right side—is treated more realistically than the figure and ground at the left. The later version [125] pushes the whole design to a more abstract level. Even the drapery is made flatter and more nearly a straight texture. This is a particularly instructive comparison because it clearly shows the shift toward a "purer," more formal expression in which the beauty lies only in the nicety of the arrangement of essentially visual elements, in the economy of means, and simplicity of execution.

When you know the other designs of the subjects, you see the whimsy in the transformation. It is a kind of music of the crayon, in which the flowing lines form the theme and the spaces the supporting harmony. If we saw only the later version, labeled *Two Women,* we might think the artist was having fun at our expense, whereas, knowing the prototype of the work, we can see that the title is quite right and indeed emphasizes the amusing metamorphosis the two women have undergone. This fanciful bit of experimental fun is perfectly understandable if seen in the context of an imaginative variation on a theme. It also demonstrates how far the treatment of the nude can turn towards abstraction and how far away from a concern with either erotic or ideal womanhood.

123. François Boucher: *Venus Consoling Love*. French. 18th century. Washington: National Gallery of Art, Chester Dale Collection.

A delightful variant of the nude-as-esthetic-vehicle is Mario Carreño's *Two Dancers* [126]. Here the technique, scratchboard, is worth noting. A white ground, usually a mixture of plaster with a little glue and water, is brushed on and allowed to dry. A colored wash is next applied. (In the *Two Dancers* this was given varying concentrations of color to produce a textured look.) Then the figures are literally scratched out, using a sharp point, which removes the wash and exposes the white ground. Carreño has produced the paradoxical and amusing effect of making his figures seem both massive and light—even translucent—at the same time. This rhythmically conceived work shows further that lightness of effect and vitality do not require sylphlike proportions.

124 (*above*). Pablo Picasso: *Two Women*. French. 1946. Lithograph, State 10. Mrs. Meric Callery Collection. 125 (*below*). Pablo Picasso: *Two Women*. State 17. Mrs. Meric Callery Collection.

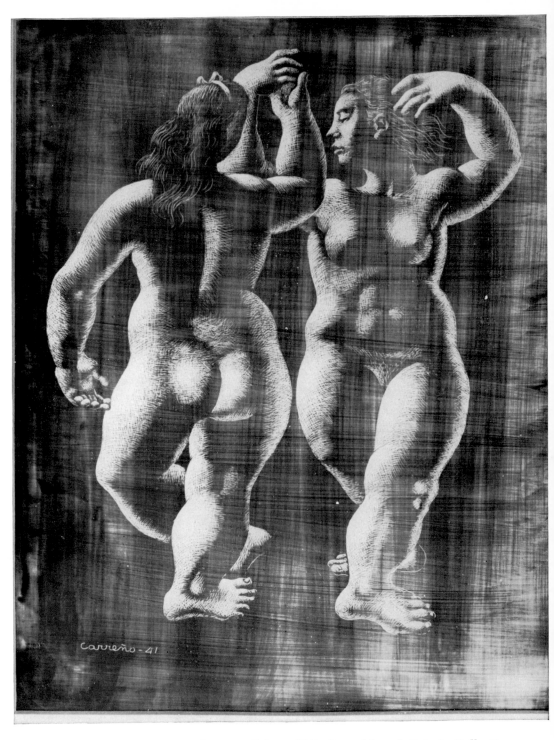

126. Mario Carreño: *Two Dancers*. Cuban. 1941. Scratchboard. Private Collection.

For an example in another medium, sculpture, see again Henry Moore's *Figure* [13]. Here there are neither masculine nor feminine facial distinctions, and the distinction of sex is entirely subordinate to the work's dignified and massive formal rhythms.

The adaptability of the nude to abstract treatment makes it suitable not only for experiments in pure form but for the expression of many attitudes and states of awareness. These may be appropriate both to an underlying cultural norm and to individual expression within it. We have already seen examples of how the nude served the spirit of gaiety, release, and expansiveness that was one facet of the eighteenth-century mood [110, 114, 123]. The Greek *Youth* and Parthenon *Theseus* [141 and 14] come from an ancient culture which honored and in a sense worshiped the human body. The two works reveal different stages in that culture's development: a gradual increase in the discovery of the individual and in the complexity of his nature.

In contrast to the two Greek works, Henry Moore's *Figure* [13] reveals no concern with ideal human proportion or with the body as a potential of action and accomplishment. The *Theseus* is 2400 years old and has been subject to centuries of indifferent care and to the erosion of the elements. Yet it is Moore's work, rather, which looks weathered, like a massive piece of driftwood or like a great stone that has been subject to the timeless washing of the sea. Moore's figure does not imply a culture, or at any rate an individual, having an uncomplicated ideal or youthful zest. The weight of centuries seems to hold it down, making the Greek works, in comparison, look young and confident. Yet Moore's figure, despite its melancholy association with the immense warping and eroding assault of time, rises with dignity and strength. Please check this against your own subjective reaction to it. Moore's work, which expresses a part of our culture, seems to be in part weary and disillusioned, yet in part calm, grave, and having a certain nobility. It is the product of a late age. Esthetically, of course, as we have noted, it represents the rhythmic interaction of space and plastic volume.

The nude can also be the vehicle for expressing a more agitated and emotional state, as in Rodin's *St. John the Baptist* [127]. Compare this with the sculptures just discussed and note how much tenser and more emotionally charged is Rodin's work, an effect created by its nervous surface and tight musculature. The Greek *Youth* [141] resembles it in pose, but the mood is completely different. Notice that the areas from the *Youth's* hips to the knees and from the elbow to the wrist are quite smooth and volumetrically conceived. The same areas of the *St. John*—and other comparable areas—are constantly varied by surface changes, producing an agitated, or at least a vibrant, effect in contrast to the smooth and poised articulation of the Greek work. Again, the bronze material is wonderfully functional in showing off the tense body of Rodin's work, for the polished metal catches the light as from countless mirrors and emphasizes, indeed exaggerates, the rippling surface. The resulting strong highlights are like dazzling brush strokes (a kinship with the then-contemporary Im-

127. Auguste Rodin: *St. John the Baptist.* French. 1878. Bronze. London: Tate Gallery.

pressionism is suggested). They disturb the volumetric consistency of the work. The stone of the Greek work, in contrast, has a less reflective surface, permitting the light to fall with a more even and form-defining tone. It is a purely sculptural conception, and even if we think of it as having been colored, it has no suggestion of the painterly look of the nineteenth-century work. Thus do the two cultures, though "seeing" differently, still find through the flexibility of art a means to self-revealing expression.

As for the Gothic world view, with its denial of the flesh and its insistence upon the primacy of spirit as embodied in Christian dogma, we rightly would not expect the nude to be its consistent vehicle. When unclothed figures do appear on Romanesque and Gothic church façades, as in the treatment of Adam and Eve or of the Day of Judgment, we find no emphasis on the human body as a thing of beauty or as a means for symbolizing an ideal. At best these nudes have architectonic simplicity, that harmonious fusion of decoration with structure which was a glory of medieval art.

But whatever its neglect in the medieval period and at other times, we have seen how the nude may be the basis, in a more appropriate psychological climate, for the expression of both individual and cultural differences.

Although attempts have been made by some social anthropologists and psychologists to equate physical body "types" with personality, most people are relatively unconcerned about the meaning, if any, in disparity of human proportion. It is a matter of indifference to most of us whether a friend has an oval or round face, a tall and thin or a short, plump body, tapering or short fingers. That is, we maintain a fairly sharp separation between physical and psychological dimensions. This frees the artist, in turn, to make use of the human body for esthetic experimentation without doing violence to our sense of the personal integrity of an individual.

This will be seen more clearly in contrast as we turn from the nude to the portrait and so to the representation of the human face, for here we are immediately involved in a sensitive problem of the subject's "rights." Although the individual's clothing, his personal activity, and setting have at times been considered a valid part of his portrait, it is still the face which distinguishes him most as an individual. And to alter the appearance of the face *for esthetic reasons* is therefore to do violence to the subject's individuality. This is the great dilemma of portraiture.

To be sure, intensely collective societies have placed little emphasis on personal individuation. This was the case in the medieval period, when the highest precept of behavior emphasized not the self, but self-denial. Other cultures, like the Islamic, have considered it a usurpation of Divine power, and therefore a sacrilege, to create realistic human images. But in the Orient, in ancient Greece and Rome, after the Renaissance, and at various other times, the portrait has been broadly explored. During these periods the artist, in his drive for esthetic unity, eventually found a conflict, or at least a problem, created by the individuality of his subject.

The portrait of *William Moreel* [128] by Hans Memling was painted during that brief period in the Renaissance when man seemed to establish a delicate balance, at least in art, between the ideal and the real. It gives the impression of being candid, but in a sympathetic way. Individual characteristics such as the unusually prominent nose no doubt were faithfully rendered, but no effort was made to suggest the personality and the inner man. We have here an extremely realistic portrait which nevertheless idealizes, but it is an idealization by omission rather than commission.

A more positive idealization appears by comparison in the Roman sculptured head of Augustus [129]. A very rich and detailed modeling of the surface gives this work a more realistic look, even, than that of *William Moreel*, yet it appears no more related to the inner man. All the nuances of modeling remain surface manifestations and fail to suggest the little

128. Hans Memling: *William Moreel, Burgomaster of Bruges.* Flemish. 1480. Brussels: Royal Museum.

distinctions which must have given power, character, and individuality to the face of as great a leader as Augustus. *Augustus* is the artist's idealized conception of a Roman emperor, even though it probably looked a good deal like a specific incumbent. Realism, in other words, may be only of the surface and not of the soul, or again, through the artist's vision, the ideal may be made to look real and convincing.

In a deep sense, all portraits are self-portraits of the artist. This becomes most apparent in periods such as the Baroque when admiration for

129. *Augustus Caesar*. Roman. 2nd century A.D. Marble. Munich, Germany: Prince
Karl Palace, Glyptothek Collection.

130. Rembrandt van Rijn: *Self-portrait*. Dutch. 1659. Washington: National Gallery, Mellon Collection.

the individual was combined with intense self-awareness. Rembrandt, for example, was acutely responsive to his own feelings and was also moved by a deep compassion for others. This is evident in a comparison of his *Self-Portrait* in the National Gallery and his *Portrait of a Rabbi* [130 and 131]. Note that in both portraits the light does not alone shine upon the face but also seems to emanate from it. It is this use of light which most powerfully creates the inner effect of Rembrandt's works. How is the effect produced? You may already have noticed that the light on the subjects' clothing is either nonexistent or very suppressed. It would be impossible to produce a natural light strong enough to reveal the face as here

131. Rembrandt van Rijn: *Rabbi*. Dutch. 1657. London: National Gallery.

without also illuminating the surrounding surfaces. Rembrandt has simply created a new light which cannot be explained as coming from an external source, but which realistically reveals the features. We ultimately discover that it has the effect of a light from within as well as from without, and that it searches out those surface nuances which reveal mature years and a reflective insight.

132. Pablo Picasso: *The Frugal Repast*. French. 1904. Etching. New York: The Museum of Modern Art, Gift of Mrs. John D. Rockefeller, Jr.

One does not speak of the *appearance* of such a face so much as of its *look*, for it is above all the eyes which are charged with understanding and which reveal suffering without bitterness. It is almost embarrassingly self-revealing. We also see how Rembrandt in his portrayal of the Rabbi, who, being a Jew, was a pariah to many, expressed his kinship and sense of brotherhood with him. This was not achieved in any sense by giving the subject an actual likeness to the artist, but by investing the portrait with the same symbolic form, the same tragic sense of life as appear in the *Self-Portrait*. In this sense, Rembrandt, more than any other artist of his time, allowed his portraits to become self-portraits—particularly in his later years.

133. Pablo Picasso: *Figure*. French. 1938. Pen and chalk.

134. Charles Despiau: *Paulette*. French. 1907. Bronze. Private collection. (Bernès-Marouteau photo)

With variations, we find the tendency to self-portraiture-in-others a frequent recurrence. In terms of their content, there is no difference in principle between the approach to Rembrandt's *Rabbi* and Picasso's etched double portrait of 1904, *Frugal Repast* [132]. That is, in each the presence of the artist dominates and supersedes, but does not eliminate the individuality of the subjects. The realism of the *Frugal Repast* serves to point up Picasso's self-identification and sympathy with those who suffer from deprivation. The attenuation of the man's arms and fingers, the distortion of proportion which shrinks the man's forearm and lengthens that of the woman, the angularity of the poses, and the exaggerated emaciation and boniness of the subjects, particularly of the man, all go beyond realism and serve to express Picasso's own intensity of feeling. The reality of the scene becomes Picasso's feeling of sympathy, which overwhelms the subject and somewhat strains our credulity concerning it.

But the dominance of the artist and the retreat of the subject is much greater in the witty and biting *Figure* of 1938 [133]. The subject appears to have had long hair and to have worn thick glasses and a wide-spreading hat. But if these distinctions are true at all, they still refer only to the woman's accessories. The facial distinctions which truly mark the individual are entirely absent. Thus the work becomes not so much the caricature of a particular person, although this may be an element, but, what is more important, of women generally. Clearly a great change has taken place in the artist's outlook, from one of sympathetic self-identification to one of

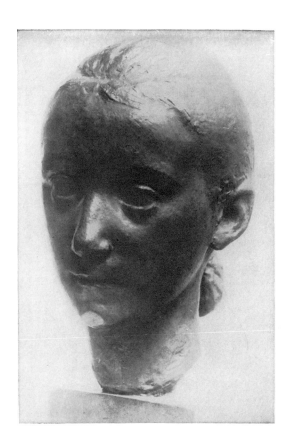

135. Charles Despiau: *Country Girl*. French. 1904. Bronze. Private collection. (Bernès-Marouteau photo)

greater distance, independence, and even of hostility. For if there is an element of spoofing here, the violence in the extent of the facial distortion suggests a scarcely concealed bitterness. Picasso's portraits of women have ranged over a tremendous emotional gamut.

In between the detachment of Memling and the emotional self-expression of Rembrandt and Picasso lies a third approach, which we may call that of *objective insight*. It is a clinical insight, rather than a subjective one, as with Rembrandt. Let us, for example, compare Despiau's *Paulette* of 1907 with the famous head of the ancient Egyptian queen, *Nefertiti* [134 and 136]. Whether the Egyptian sculptor deliberately elongated his subject's neck to heighten her aristocratic appearance or refined her features for the same reason, we cannot be certain. Evidence from other representations of her point to the Berlin head's being a good "likeness." However, the point is that we see only the externals of this handsome queen. Despiau has given the contour of Paulette's face a similar knifelike continuity and with a similar precision has defined the features, particularly the mouth and eyes, but with this difference—that they combine strongly to evoke individuality and a particular personality. Despite their realism and distinctness, Nefertiti's features, by comparison, appear generalized. We can tell little about her, whereas we can imagine Paulette as a woman who is sophisticated and perhaps witty, but also calculating and even ruthless. Paulette's portrait, furthermore, has a convincing look which makes her attributes seem really to belong to her.

136. *Queen Nefertiti.* Egyptian. *c.* 1400 B.C. Painted limestone. West Germany: National Collection.

Despiau's penetrating ability to perceive the inner person is demonstrated again in the *Country Girl* [135], whose open-eyed shyness and innocence are in striking contrast to the steely, if feminine, sophistication of Paulette.

Neither of Despiau's portraits has the artist-dominated look of Picasso's nor the externality of *Nefertiti.* Therefore, we have here a relationship between artist and subject in which the artist is using his creative sensitivity as a vehicle for expressing his *understanding* of others rather than for a description of others, for the statement of an ideal, or for a self-statement using the subject as a means. The Egyptian sculptor of *Nefertiti* was a sensitive artist and highly competent. It is not a difference of ability which separates his results from Despiau's but a difference of understanding of the problem of portraiture—differences deeply rooted in the sculptors' respective cultures. Where such differences result in a self-conscious art, the artist's statement of himself, if he be a genius, may have significance for his time and also for the future. But, especially in the area of portraiture, there is much to be said for the less spectacular but mature and psychologically modern approach of Despiau.

Finally, and in diametrical contrast to the works discussed above, we have the portrait as *esthetic experimentation,* in which state it virtually ceases to be a portrait in the sense of a likeness, either external or in spirit. Naum Gabo's *Head of a Woman* [137], a constructivist work, was made with pieces of cellulose acetate. The subject, of course, may have had broad cheek bones, a narrow chin, a long nose, and small mouth—all of

137. Naum Gabo: *Head of a Woman.* 1917. Celluloid and metal. New York: The
Museum of Modern Art.

which characteristics are evident in the work illustrated. But even if the subject had these facial characteristics, here they have been made too abstract to carry much power of evoking a human individual. This is essentially an *experiment in form* in which the clarity of the shapes, the consistency of their texture, the imaginativeness and economy of their assemblage, and the use of natural light and shade as a means of differentiating the planes all give to the study an intriguing organization. The nature of the subject may have been lost in the process, but in her place we do have a personal expression of creative clarity and originality.

The difference between this work and Picasso's of 1938 [133] is that Gabo's appears less concerned with emotional overtones involving the subject; Gabo is more nearly detached from his environment and engaged in independent and "pure" self-expression.

The story of the portrait, then, is the story of the pathos of man's individualism. Man as an individual realizes his separateness from others and the loneliness of that separation. Yet in proportion as he achieves a community of insight and feeling, he must sacrifice that very freedom, distinction, and identity, which is the glory of an individualized life. So the result is generally a compromise in which the individual walks a tight rope separating his personal identity from that of his fellows. He desires to assert himself and to develop more richly his uniqueness as a person; yet he constantly desires oneness with others. In no other phase of art is this conflict so clearly revealed as in the portrait.

The nude, on the other hand, has had as its variable factor no such potential conflict between the artist and the "rights," or individual integrity, of the subject. Here the variable has rather been one of attitude towards the human body. In the end both subjects have served as vehicles for the re-expression of a world or cultural view, as well as for drawing out the formal resources and personalities of the artist.

In considering how art may involve problems which are strongly affected by subject, the nude and portrait have been selected as examples because they are of general interest. The landscape and the still life could equally well have been chosen and are as distinct in character. While bearing in mind that the art work may have its uniqueness of effect resulting from the subject, let us remember that the subject may be of only oblique influence in the rich totality of the art experience.

14-Art and Self-Revelation

So far our discussion has touched but lightly on the question of the artist's revelation of himself in his art. Which aspects of the self go into creative effort? It is tempting to think that the "total man" is represented there, more intricately concealed than are the complex stereophonic sounds of a symphony in the microgrooves of a phonograph record. It must be recognized, however, that not all aspects of the personality are apparent at the same time. One's moods change and one's reactions vary in accordance with the impact on the self of a changing environment. While it is entirely possible for a poet, composer, or artist to create under the spell of a particular mood or cluster of feelings, more often art is only broadly related to the artist's personality.

Art is a controlled—and also partly uncontrolled—sublimation of the emotions and drives, the psychiatrist would say, and we need not go the whole way of Freud or his followers to recognize that any made-to-order symbol-producer like the esthetic impulse would inevitably relate to the inner man. What makes it acceptable is its over-all esthetic control. Thus when Beethoven introduces violent and sudden changes into his music, as, for example, in parts of the *Appassionata Sonata*, we accept it as "exciting," but when he introduces violent changes into his social behavior, as when in a pique he threw a bowl of soup into a waiter's face, we are less impressed. The form of art is a kindly veil. To put it another way, the pent-up energy and tension implicit in the incident of Beethoven and the waiter become a positive force in his music. Negative behavior may be the misdirection of a positive potential.

Art goes deeper than any one-to-one correspondence with behavior patterns. It is a synthesis and therefore overshadows individual traits, al-

199

though occasionally some aspect of the artist's personality may be so strong that it comes through as a dominant element.

Under the favorable stimulus of free creation, moreover, the artist is able to express his idealistic or romantic yearnings, or any of a number of other drives which he might have no opportunity for expressing in his social environment. An example of this is Caravaggio, who was a roisterer and even a murderer, but whose paintings reveal a deep human compassion. The creative climate of his art made possible a constructive release of forces which, in a less favorable environment, were directed in an antisocial way. Salvator Rosa was a brigand; Benvenuto Cellini was a mountain of conceit; Michelangelo had so difficult a personality that no assistant could work with him without discord; Pontormo was so excessively withdrawn figuratively that he literally withdrew to an attic accessible only by rope ladder. Yet all of these men were excellent artists whose personal eccentricities, if concealed somewhere in the form-symbolism of their art, were not prominently in evidence.

Which was the "true" Caravaggio, the brawling tough who fled Rome to escape arrest, or the compassionate human being who saw normalcy in Mary Magdalen and Everyman in the Christian story? No doubt both were true—different outpourings of the same nature under a different challenge—but it is clear which solution comes closest to fulfillment for the artist: it is the art work, for here the artist has a freedom of action very seldom found in the environment of the world.

But we are better able to discern how the artist felt about his *subject* than what kind of person he was. Attempts to discern the personality of the artist from within the form of his art vary from psychoanalytical probings to subjective hunches. The most fruitful area of speculation, here, is in what we may call the expressive *tone* of a work of art. But first let us discuss several works with the aim of arriving more specifically at insight into the personality of the artist, in order to show how very subjective such a search becomes.

In a way this is pressed upon the modern follower of art, because the trend in Western art, on the whole, has been toward more and more intrusion of the personality and so of the symbolism of the artist. Presentational elements, objective phenomena, story: these have been relegated to decreasingly important roles. Art has tended to become self-expression minus other elements instead of self-expression plus, as it was before.

Alexander Calder's *Mobile* [138] not only has no story, but its shapes do not refer to anything in the objective world. To be sure, Calder has closely observed nature, and in the movement and shapes of such natural phenomena as leaves, branches, waves, clouds, and wings has found inspiration for his own swinging forms. Yet these forms do not *imitate* those in nature. Starting in some cases from natural observation, Calder still develops his shapes so that they are personal to him. Where the wheel in Memling's painting [120] is both a realistically presented illusion of a wheel with knives and a symbol of a particular saint, the shapes in Calder's work are neither objective nor apparently symbolic. Calder's shapes repre-

138. Alexander Calder and mobile. (Herbert Gehr photo, courtesy LIFE Magazine)

sent him, almost exclusively. This is the measure of the great swing—so significant for us all—from group to individual expression since that early Renaissance time, from a common faith to an individual philosophy.

When you look thoughtfully at Calder's shapes, you see that they have certain very distinct characteristics. While they are varied, they are also the same. The unity is apparent: similarity of thickness and color, curving rather than straight edges, a preponderance of convex curves, basically parabolic or triangular forms. Their individual areas, too, with contrasting exceptions, strike a mean in size.

In our illustration, Mr. Calder is holding one side of the mobile down below its normal position, but even with the mobile irregularly placed we can see that the shapes have a consistency in their spacing. When released, the mobile will take its place as a three-dimensional thing, visually organizing a segment of space while moving through it. The holes through some of the shapes merely reveal the interchangeability of solid and void.

Space pushes through the shapes, as around them, so that the free interchange is psychologically expedited. The originality of the work is its frank incorporation of change as an essential element of its effect.

If we grant that the work is expressive of Calder, it may suggest to us the following: The shapes are wonderfully distinct and clear. They are not jagged, fussy, complex, but smooth, flowing, distinct. At the same time they are varied in a delightful way and integrated into a visually cohesive whole. The character of these shapes and their arrangement suggest to me a free, affirmative spirit, orderly and also fun-loving, adaptable yet independent, not complex yet subtle.

These observations are thrown into relief when we compare Calder's mobile with a wire sculpture by Richard Lippold, *Full Moon* [139]. The actual work extends beyond the limits of the photograph but not much, so that we see it substantially in its entirety. In the central portion are a number of boxlike shapes, refined in their appearance through their finely-drawn borders. These hollow shapes—placed one inside the other (or one outside the other, depending on how we begin)—start from a small cube at the center. From the center of this cube also radiates a series of pyramids with interconnecting bases, or apexes. The sculpture, like Calder's, is based upon the penetrability of solid and void, the fluidity of matter and space.

Esthetically the work is not so self-contained as Calder's, but this may be in keeping with the artist's own intent; the shooting out into space of the work's extremities could merely imply more units unseen and endlessly proliferating. There is a fascinating interplay of shapes and lines here, and the balance among elements, the extremities again excepted, is quite astonishing.

What, then, is the hidden symbolism, the subjective quality evoked by this work? What imprint of Mr. Lippold's personality do we find in his selection and organization of forms? There is a clear emphasis on the logical relationship, the natural flow of one element into another. Although at first glance the work appears intricate, a little study shows it to be basically simple and logical. It is made of delicate wires, and it looks gossamer in comparison with the sturdier shapes of the mobile. All this suggests a more intellectual and a more introspective personality. Its subjective effect is refined, delicate, logical. It might be argued that it is also pretentious, but to me it is rather the opposite—modest, because the logic of it is allowed to develop from the nature of the forms, without any hint of arbitrariness or caprice. While this modesty strengthens and renders consistent the work, it also limits it. The work does not carry the sharp hand of the arbitrary; neither does it have the playful touch of the unexpected. It clearly shows a different feeling for rightness of form from Calder's and does so, we may assume, because it springs from the wellspring of a different personality.

Lippold's work is called *Full Moon*, but this does not mean that it is supposed to remind us of the appearance of the moon, that it is supposed to be an abstraction of the moon's appearance. The sculpture radiates out

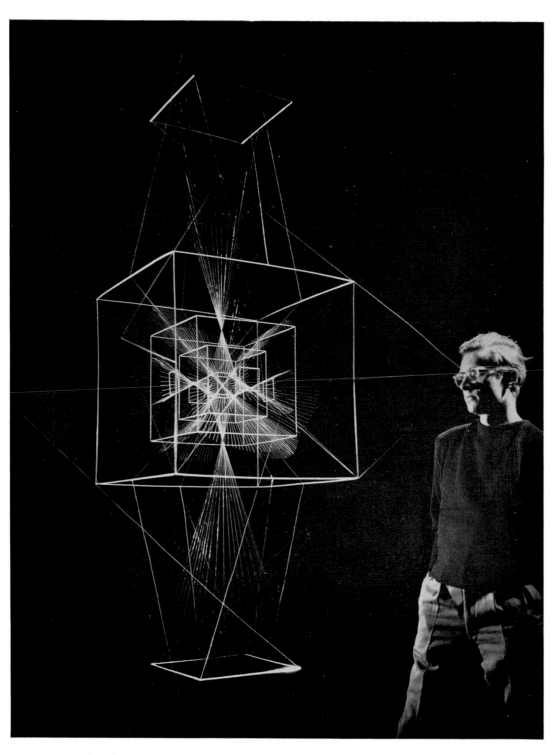

139. Richard Lippold and wire sculpture, *Full Moon*. 1950. New York: The Museum of Modern Art. (Walter Sanders photo, courtesy LIFE Magazine)

from a central core and in a very free, subjective sense can be related to the spreading out of the moonlight in all directions into the darkness. The fact that Lippold has given us a title referring to something objective in nature raises the whole question of when to use the terms "abstract" and "nonobjective" or "nonfigurative." Etymologically the word "abstract" implies a summarizing reference of one thing to another. The term "nonobjective," of much more recent usage, means the absence of reference to any objective phenomena. These might seem to provide the needed distinctions between art works which make continuing reference to something in the objective world and those which have no such origin and make no such references.

But we have only to look at Calder and Lippold works to see the difficulties of drawing any such clear distinction. Does Calder's mobile make any reference to the exterior world? Does Lippold's? They both do and don't. They may be sufficiently remote from objective connections to merit the term nonobjective, but the number of works is small which can claim outright independence of any objective connection in any way.

The fact is that we have not yet developed a good term for describing a state which is *nearly* nonobjective and therefore still an abstraction of something, though remotely so. "Abstract art" is a reasonably good term for the "nearly nonobjective," although in the literature on art one frequently sees the word "abstract" used in the full nonobjective sense. "Pure abstraction" is another equivalent of nonobjective, as is "nonfigurative." "Abstract expressionism" refers to a particular kind of nonobjective art which is more impulsive, emotive, and charged with feeling. This semantic digression indicates how imprecise the art vocabulary still is. The alert reader must watch for differences of meaning from author to author.

Returning to the problem of art as revelation of the artist, let us look, now, at Alberto Giacometti's *Pointing Man* [140], selected for its contrast with the two sculptures discussed above. Whereas both Calder's and Lippold's works depend mainly upon their *form*, their visual organization, for their effect, Giacometti's work provides a greater proportional emphasis upon *content*. In visual comparison with the other two works this one seems lacking in variety, either rhythmically or in the balance of its parts. It has consistency of texture and also of shape, for it is attenuated, delicate, but it is no match in esthetic interest for many contemporary works which are more richly organized. What is fascinating, haunting, about this figure is the conception of man it evokes.

Here is no secure and robust person like the ancient Greek *Youth* [141], perfectly poised between rest and movement, apparently satisfied with the physical world he sees and standing in it self-confidently. Here, in contrast, is a frail man whose body has wasted away. He reaches out to the world. The gesture (and please interpret it differently, if you like) is a combination of defiance and suffering. There is a pathos, even a tragic quality, in this ungainly stick of a creature, and a curious nobility. By comparison, Calder's and Lippold's works suddenly seem to be removed from

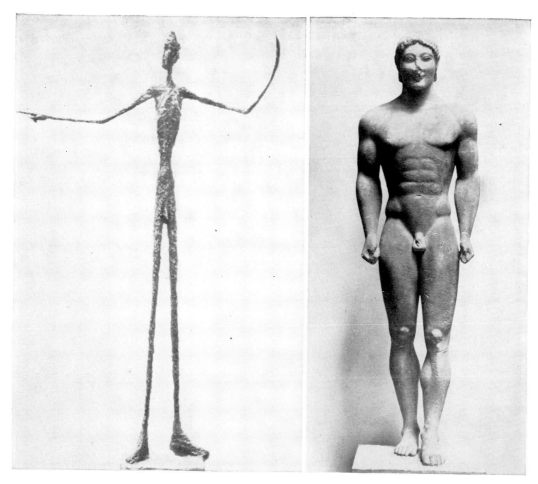

140. Alberto Giacometti: *Pointing Man*. Italian. 1947. Bronze. London: Tate Gallery. 141. *Greek Youth*. 6th century B.C. Stone. Munich, Germany: Prince Karl Palace, Glyptothek Collection.

the stream of modern mankind's struggle. The *Pointing Man*, in contrast, appears to be at the heart of it.

While it is, of course, unfair to the others to appear to criticize them for what they are not, notice how much more vivid these subjective factors become through comparisons.

Because of the fluid character of its medium and its relatively low cost, painting is well adapted to experiments in nonobjectivity. Let us look again at the work by the late Jackson Pollock [III]. Before he died, Pollock was re-experimenting with brushed-on pigment and appeared to be moving in a somewhat new direction, but *No. 5* is typical of his work over a long period. That is, he let the pigment drip onto the canvas, which was laid flat on the floor. For accents, he could use the brush directly on the canvas. Here, he first covered the canvas irregularly with a light green. This ground, in turn, he almost completely covered with black, again loosely and energetically applied. Over this he dripped or brushed—in stabbing or sweeping motions—accents of white, yellow, blue, with a few touches of violet and orange. Note that in spite of the imprecise control inevitable to such a technique, the artist has achieved a general balance of values (light and dark) and of shape placement while still maintaining the effect of energetic movement. In building his painting, Pollock might add more of a color from time to time to this or that area. He would do the same thing with the other hues, weaving, now here, now there, in a different direction, deliberately preventing any tendency toward a consistent movement. His aim was a *final* consistency.

Now, the question is, do we have merely an over-all pattern here, a kind of freehand wallpaper or terrazzo floor design? Can we imagine this work extending indefinitely in all directions, as if what we see were merely a section, chosen at random, from a huge decorative surface? Some of this artist's works may affect us that way—but not this one. Notice, for example, that none of the demanding white and yellow shapes is allowed to touch the border. Most of the important black shapes of the ground avoid intersecting the borders and tend to turn parallel to them. The painting does achieve a dynamic balance within its particular plane.

As to the meaning of this particular choice and organization of shapes, the painting suggests the following: Whereas even Calder and Lippold chose shapes which find their prototype in nature or—as in the cube—the intellectual mind of man, here we have no prior or external source. Here the shapes are partly spontaneous and partly derived from the artist's sense of the developing esthetic needs of the canvas as he worked on it. The difference between these shapes and Lippold's or Calder's, again, is that Pollock's shapes have no conception governing their form other than their conformity to a visual ensemble, as against shapes which have references outside their ensemble. The Pollock painting is thus as self-sufficient and independent as it is possible for an art work to become. Its only dependence is on Pollock and its symbolism is entirely related to him. This is in striking contrast to Memling's *Madonna and Saints*, which has many elements with referents other than to the artist. Pollock's exclusion of all elements referring to nature or the world of man and his emphasis on movement and contrast may represent a volatile, emotional disposition. If not actually anti-intellectual, which it may be, it certainly indicates a strong reliance on impulse. The most affirmative aspect of this work is its openness, its hopeful employment of controlled spontaneity. It has a *complete freedom from the cliché and stereotype.* Calder finds roots in a serene contact with nature, Lippold in the discipline of mind and spirit. Pollock found it in an atmosphere of spontaneity and freedom. This will be taken up at a later point, as a recurring aspect of art today in this country.

Artists sometimes create works which, in their content, reflect the mood of the moment. But in their most serious efforts it is amazing to see how consistently the same impact of the artist's personality comes through. It is this expressive element in art, an impact of content engendered by form, which enables us to achieve a heightened or intensified awareness of and rapport with the artist through his creation.

Let us look again at the Greek *Youth* and Giacometti's *Man Pointing* [140 and 141]. The underlying effect of the sculpture of the *Youth* is that of enormous yet self-contained physical vitality. This is the essence of that part of the content which is related to *form*, and to feel it is to come close to the artist himself.

Giacometti's figure produces almost the opposite effect, that of the frailty of the body and the fortitude of the spirit in a tragic and knowing relationship with the world. Again, awareness of this effect puts us in contact with the feeling presence of the artist.

In some instances, effects such as we have seen in this chapter have been consciously attained and in others unconsciously. The sculptor of the Greek *Youth* achieved his effect of vitality, very possibly, without being aware of it as such. If this be so, the vitality in the *Youth* would be at the level of unconscious symbol, where Giacometti's effect, which is certainly more knowing, achieves the status of conscious symbol. It may be helpful to reflect again that meaning in art may be projected either way.

The content actually related to the artist may easily and through misunderstanding become identified with the subject. Thus, we see the *Youth* as a vital man, where actually he is vital only because the artist was vital or because the artist was capable of the conception, for the *Youth* is a type, an ideal, rather than the portrait of an individual. The artist invests the subject with himself, even in trying to be objective. In nonobjective art, he invests his choice of rhythms, shapes, hues, and textures and his organization of them with himself. The form he develops, in order to satisfy him, must conform to his own expressive needs. And if it satisfies him, it almost certainly makes possible the evocation by someone else of this satisfaction. Through this empathic involvement we understand or intuit the signs and symbols of the artist's nature and world and so that nature and world itself.

Even where the artist develops a traditional religious or mythological theme, he may yet treat it in a self-assertive way. In fact, he cannot help doing so. What has obscured this is only the very much more apparent self-assertion in some works than in others. In Memling's altarpiece [120], the artist was modestly intent on giving convincing visual presence and identity and appropriate setting and demeanor to his figures. While he undoubtedly took pride in his craftsmanship, he could hardly have thought of the painting as revealing more of him than of his subject. It is as a byproduct of his main intent that we discover in the meticulousness of the work, in its placidity and calm assurance, and also in its externality, a personal statement and the revelation of an individual.

Jacques Lipchitz' magnificent bronze representing *Prometheus Strangling the Vulture* [142] may not reveal any more about the artist, in the end, than Memling's painting, but the self-expressive element is relatively more prominent. That is, where Memling's work gives at least the illusion of objectivity, Lipchitz' is frankly a personal expression. Prometheus, defender, part creator, and symbol of dynamic man, and the vulture, symbol of the relentless, destructive forces he confronts, are seen in a death strug-

142. Jacques Lipchitz: *Prometheus Strangling the Vulture.* 1943–1952. Bronze. Minneapolis, Minn.: Walker Art Center.

gle in which Prometheus (man) is the victor. This is a parable of Lipchitz' hope, esthetically expressed in a work of monumental simplification of form. The rippling contours and sturdy masses give the effect simultaneously of earthiness and lightness, suggesting a personality of ardor, vitality, and richness.

The interrelation of artist and subject is varyingly complex, and where a first—and therefore tentative—insight may readily be reached in one case, it may be far more difficult in another. Consider, for example, Picasso's *Girl before a Mirror* [II]. The artist has made no public statement about the meaning of this work and it may be no more than a lively organization of color shapes, yet it seems to have more to it than that. Notice that the reflection in the mirror appears to be a face somewhat different from that outside. The inside figure has a strange eye that may be blind, yet releases an orange tear. If the reflection symbolizes the inner self which the outer self seeks to find, then is it an inner self of blindness and remorse? The groping of the self that this suggests may be further indicated by the mirrored figure's seeming to reach back to the one outside and by the multiple aspects of personality suggested through the dual views of face and body. Although one aspect of the outer face is turned towards the mirror, and although the arm reaches towards it, both eyes look out and away from the mirror, as if the outer figure longed to find itself, yet feared or was unable to do so. Other ambivalences are the simultaneous nude and clothed states of both figures and the subjective contrasts of color—for example, the sunny yellow of the forward-looking portion of the outside face and the eerie violet and orange of the side view and of the face in the mirror.

Whereas the subjects chosen by Lipchitz and Memling are well known and provide the means for a comparative revelation of these artists' interpretations, the girl—or Venus—before the mirror is a much more illusive theme, and Picasso's abstract handling of the subject pushes the meaning even farther into the realm of speculation. We conclude only that this work *may* symbolize the ambiguities in relation between the inner and outer nature of man. And what of the painting's more direct relation to Picasso? The bold shapes and color of his painting and its intricate formal design suggest to me an exceptionally assured, complex, and passionate personality. This stands in contrast to the much more tentative expression of Giacometti [140] and the refinement of Lippold [139], to cite two other comparisons.

In view of the uncertainties of these interpretations, it is reasonable to inquire if such speculation is worth while at all. The answer lies in the level of understanding to which the art lover aspires. The person who suspects no symbolism in Picasso's painting or who is not intrigued with the relation of art to the individual or to states of feeling or consciousness, may safely avoid the risks involved. Others are not so easily satisfied and are impelled by inner necessity to seek deeper meanings. The uncertainties of the answers mean only that they must not be taken dogmatically but as working hypotheses upon which a richer and, gradually, more secure awareness of art may be developed.

As we have seen, symbol relates both to the artist's conscious reaction to his subject and to the revelation of himself inherent in the nature of his form. His conscious reaction may be essentially descriptive, like Memling's respecting his *Madonna and Saints,* or it may be emotional, like Bellows' respecting the fight scene. The awareness of the symbolic character and the grasp of the expressiveness of an art work may require an effort on our part and normally will. The reason is simple: we may be stretching out to a way of life sharply different from the one we know. Small wonder that our adaptive resources are sometimes stretched. Yet one of art's rewards is the intimate perception it gives us of ways of life and of human nature contrasting with our own. Art is partly a conscious, partly an unconscious self-revelation, not only of the artist, but of and for the spectator as well. The subject, too, may have its own evocative potential. Spectator, artist, and subject are all interlocked in a mutually influencing way. The understanding of art is a dynamic of these interactions. While not neglecting the manysidedness of art created by these factors, we need to find a central element in it around which our understanding may orient and develop. And it is this problem to which we now turn.

15-Expressiveness

Personality has been defined as the total effect on behavior of the individual's habit patterns. If a man has developed the habit of politeness, it becomes "natural" to him and an aspect of his personality. He may also have developed the habit of being unscrupulous. The unscrupulousness, of course, he would try to conceal, but it would be bound to color his personality in various ways. For example, he might unconsciously be impelled to compensate for his antisocial machinations by being extremely sociable. This would have the double potential of further disarming his victims while giving him a certain illusion of treating his fellow men like a brother. Thus the outer manifestation of politeness or sociableness, while it might be the direct reflection of a genuine considerateness and harmonious gregariousness, might in part be a hidden reflection of something else.

Although outer behavior may not always be acceptable at its face value, it nevertheless has a certain validity of its own. Whatever the motives or compulsions behind it, for example, politeness is a generally admired trait. The fact that someone is polite, clever, and sociable unfortunately does not necessitate his being anything else, yet the favorable disposition assured by such traits has often led to unjustified suppositions as to other traits.

We must grant, however, that in the formation of the personality a particular cluster of traits may combine to give a *dominant external "tone" or expressive quality*. This may not reveal and, indeed, may even conceal other important elements, yet by its very persistence still carry with it a valid and summarizing effect. Thus the personality, if it is the expression of an intricate combination of *all* the habits of the individual, is not just a summation of them but a new emergence in which the original influences may be sublimated and lost to view. That which emerges is partly voluntary and partly involuntary.

The individual knows what interests him, and he has varying degrees of awareness of his assets and shortcomings. But he can see himself only partially through the perspective of other viewpoints. His outer behavior, accordingly, evokes in part that which he wishes, is conscious of, or understands, and in part that which others varyingly perceive. If he is ahead of his time, as creative people have often been, the perception of him on the part of others may prove to be less valid than his own understanding of himself. In fact, the perception by others—like that respecting Van Gogh, Rembrandt, John Donne, Franz Schubert, and many more—may in time undergo a virtually complete reversal, although there are always a few who recognize genius in its day.

The differences of perception, then, between the individual and his critics do not possess any *inherent* superiority or rightness, one way or the other. But they do emphasize the inevitability or our seeing others in a different light from that in which they see themselves. This sense of strangeness in others, of seeing them according to *our* lights, may reveal the impossibility of perfect communication and understanding; but it should not obscure the possibility of a very considerable degree of understanding, which may in part be achieved through a sympathetic experience of some characteristic expression of the other person. Since the nature of the artist's approach to his art work is peculiarly his, by perceiving its nature, we establish the basis for a shared experience. And in the degree that compatibility enables us to share the experience, we enjoy a vivid rapport with the artist. This is a hidden cause of the gripping power of art—that what moves us is not only an experience of our own but a *shared experience* with the artist.

This shared experience is made possible by contacting and understanding a certain pervasive effect of the art work—its *expressiveness*. It is that about the art work which is intensifying, unifying. It is that which the artist, knowingly or unknowingly, has given most passionately to his creation—and it may be of the mind as much as of the feelings. It may be revealed through a primary interest in form or a primary interest in content or through a combination of them. It may evoke a very simple or a very complex mood or awareness. In brief, it springs from the artist himself, not in his every aspect of personality, but in some characteristic perceptions or feelings which the expressiveness of his art enables us to reach. Moreover, this expressiveness is likely to be more than perfunctory, in contrast to many aspects of behavior which are outer gestures only. The art activity is conventional only to the degree that the artist is himself conventional or is forced to be conventional by agreement with a patron. Where he works for himself, the artist may pour his own most ardent, deep, and personal effort into his creation. And he may often do so even if he is working for a patron, since the form, not the subject, may provide his expressive release. Or again, he may feel quite as sympathetic toward the subject as does the patron.

For an example, look at the *Grieving Madonna* by Tilman Riemenschneider [143], a work which shows the artist's expressive feeling for both form and content. The Madonna is erect but a little unsteady in bearing, her right shoulder down and her head tipped in counterbalance. It is

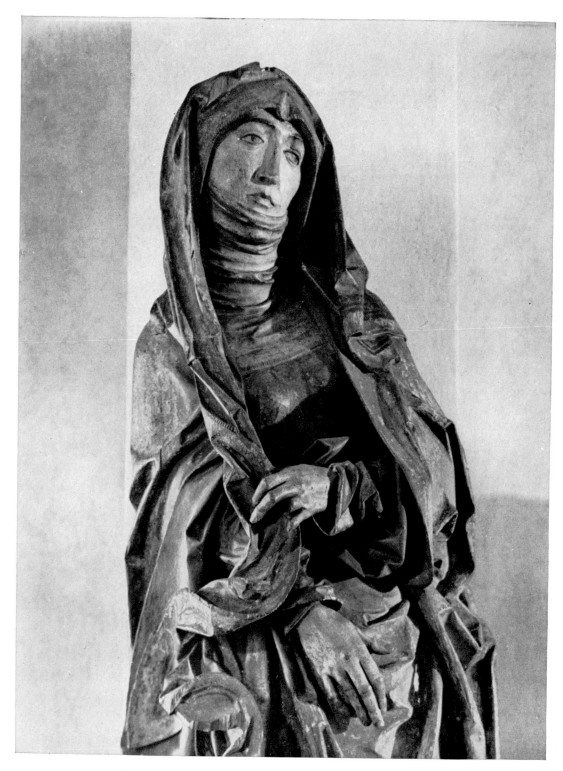

143. Tilman Riemenschneider: *Grieving Madonna*, detail. German. 16th century.
Linden wood. Würzburg, Germany: Mainfränkisches Museum.

144. *Madonna*, detail. German. 13th century. Stone. Bamberg, Germany: Cathedral.

as though her grief had affected her physically. Her hands are open, one absently touching the cloak, one listlessly hanging. The real subject of this sculpture, however, is not her physical state, important though this may be, but her inner experience. The inner effect is heightened by the eyes, which do not focus on anything, are lost in thought. The broad, plain face is wonderfully dignified. Grief is shown by a very slight down-turning of the mouth and by the treatment of the planes of the face. The features do not come forward in an outgoing, psychologically lively way but appear almost to be struck flat. Heightening the effect further is the hood of the cloak, with its trembling and delicate fall. The indentation in the hood above the nose marks the visual axis of the head and has the effect of an agonizing cleft in the brow. The neckpiece is rather heavily modeled, which accents the smoothness of the face and, in its horizontality, serves as a contrast to the fall of the hood.

We see the evidence almost everywhere of the wood carver's tool, lovingly working the material and giving the sculpture a splendid esthetic vitality. The rhythmic treatment of the falling border of the cloak is especially effective. Its reversal of direction near the lower hand, illogical in terms of realism, is visually meaningful in varying the character of the rhythm; the effect is repeated on the other side by tucking in the robe. It also provides a temporary halting or horizontal feeling to the design by paralleling the sharp turn of the falling cloak with the lower hand and a bulge of drapery to the right. Thus, the strong shape of the hand is not left isolated but is given a positional emphasis by the drapery. In addition to the main rhythms of the drapery, there are many counterfolds which enrich the surface in a vital way. Indeed, the formal expressiveness here lies

145. *Madonna and Child*, detail. German. 15th century. Painted wood. Colmar, France: Unterlinden Museum.

in this rhythmic and incisive carving of the wood, both in the large compositional sense and in the richness of the surface texture—another example of the influence of medium.

The expressiveness of the *Grieving Madonna*, then, derives from a marvelous union of a vital visual effect with the creation of a mood of mourning recollection and thoughtful melancholy.

If we compare this sculpture with another Madonna, from Bamberg Cathedral in Germany, done over 200 years earlier [144], the contrast is almost shocking! In place of the Riemenschneider Madonna's reticence we have an almost aggressive energy. A hearty barmaid could have posed for this study. The expressive effect here is dynamically physical and external, in contrast to the introspectiveness of the other. The effect of the Bamberg *Madonna* is heightened by the preponderance of bold, deep, folds, which may be contrasted to the far greater variety and refinement of surface treatment in the other's drapery. Incidentally, the Bamberg *Madonna* shows that realism did not have to wait for the Renaissance.

An in-between approach is marked by the lovely Colmar *Madonna* of the fifteenth century [145]. Its expressiveness suggests neither deep introspection, unalloyed externality, nor exclusive formal emphasis. With exquisitely delicate modeling the sculptor has rendered the softness of flesh and played it visually against the opulent rhythms of the cascading hair and the rich and rhythmic folding of the drapery. The esthetic interest here competes for our acclaim and is not so closely integrated with the subject matter as in Reimenschneider's *Madonna*. Nevertheless, the Colmar *Madonna* is more than a "figure study." Its expressive effect in content is that of gravity and maturity in the Madonna and of vital, almost saucy babyhood in the Child. This effect is combined with an independent interest in the visual beauty of contrasting textures and rhythms.

We thus may have a certain dichotomy between the form and content. Indeed, it often happens in art. In the Colmar *Madonna*, the artist definitely had a conception about the woman and child he was representing, but the conception was one which could be expressed by a simple realism. At the same time the artist was independently interested in the artistic problem of carving a draped female figure holding a baby. This excited him quite as much as—and probably more than—the coincidental circumstance that the couple were to represent Mary and Jesus. We have here a double expressiveness in which form and content are not entirely interrelated or of the same level.

We have already seen, in the case of the Breisach Altar [17], that the artist may be more interested in his medium than in his subject matter. The same is frequently found in music—for example, in *Così fan tutte*, where Mozart wrote some of his most moving music for a farce that is itself of little interest. Again, many of Shakespeare's plots are trivial. It is the greatness of Shakespeare and of Mozart that they could invest an unpromising subject with lasting appeal; in these instances, therefore, it is not the subject which appeals, nor the artist's concern with it, which may be slight, but the expressiveness of the form in which it is cast.

It often happens in life, as in art, that the individual is obliged to deal with a task or subject which is not of deep interest to him. It is no wonder that in such circumstances he may try to achieve satisfaction and self-realization through discovery of a *personal way* of approaching the problem. When this happens in art, as it frequently does, we find a separation between form and subject-content.

If the subject is something in the world or is connected with social or cultural tradition, it has properties, visual or in content, which belong to it and are separate from the artist. The artist's use of form, in contrast, belongs to the artist and is intimate to him. In his treatment of content he may merely be bowing to social, religious, or political conventions toward which he has no deeply-felt alliance. But he does have alliance to art. In treating an outer subject, the artist is reaching out to something about which others may already have fixed views or attitudes, and to a certain extent he is therefore inevitably involved in a give-and-take with the conventions and culture of his time. But insofar as he can exercise artistic freedom—that is, freedom of form—he is responsible only to himself.

Conflicts and inharmonies between the artist and his society will therefore find expression in the nature of his approach to the accepted symbols of the time. One senses that for Riemenschneider the concept of the mourning Madonna was a significant and absorbing challenge and a means of expressing his own devotion. The sculptor of the Bamberg *Madonna*, however, was willing to create the symbol of Mary, but he was unable, or unwilling, to invest it with any deep or perceptive feeling.

This split between the artist as a creative individual and as an interpreter of commissioned or traditional subject matter is one of the aspects of art which most easily causes confusion until it is exposed. The same split may occur when the artist picks a subject that has but a mild interest for him or which excites him largely or only by its stimulus to his creative imagination. Realization of this simple phenomenon can forever put to rest any doubts as to the validity of "distortion" or of any departure from appearances. If the artist is not interested in appearances—or, for that matter, in meaning—he can not do a heartfelt or convincing job of presenting either. The artist can not make a profound interpretation of the Madonna if the Madonna arouses in him no profound insights or deep empathic involvement. Yet he may be able to make a great painting or sculpture using the figure of a woman as his initial stimulus, and he may even call such a figure the Madonna; or he may be commissioned to depict a Madonna and give it the necessary attributes to reveal what it is intended to be. Yet for him, all the time, it may be intended only as an expressive esthetic form.

In the Colmar *Madonna* [145] we have a compromise in which the artist by no means rejects his subject—treating it, as he does, with humanistic dignity—but in which greater passion is lavished on the designing and carving of the figures. He achieves a certain expressive intensity both ways. In grasping the contribution of an art work, *we have to be able to discount the element of subject—or to give it importance—as readily as does the artist.* This does not preclude our adopting yet another view or facet of view—indeed, that is inevitable. But the artist's approach, in so far as we can divine it, should be our own preliminary to creative personal interpretation.

Let us look at two works in painting which treat with striking contrast the same theme we have been regarding in sculpture: Dürer's *Virgin and Child*, painted early in the sixteenth century, and the thirteenth-century Tuscan painting of the same subject [146 and 147]. In the Tuscan painting note the suave almost imperious gesture of the Christ Child's right arm and hand and the tilt of His head. Note the exceptionally large and knowing yet mysterious eyes of the Madonna and the attenuated refine-

146. Albrecht Dürer: *Madonna and Child* (*Madonna of the Iris*). German. 16th century. London: National Gallery, formerly Cook Collection.

ment of her fingers. Note the elegance of the way she holds the Child and the richness of her veil. Note the emphasis of the crowns. Here the Madonna is no ordinary individual but rather is given to the impressive fulfillment of a role, that of queenly mother to her royal son. The underlying effect or tone, here, is *aristocratic, sophisticated, elegant, regal, mysterious*. The subjective impact of these words, I hope, is evocative of the expressive effect of the painting.

Yet the work is also expressive in form, and the same qualifying terms, "elegant" and "refined," apply to the rhythms of the drapery, to the textures of the veil, to the rendering of the features, and to the rich color of

147. *Madonna and Child.* Tuscan (Italian). 13th century. Tempera on
panel. Florence: Academy. (Alinari photo)

the robes against the gold ground. Form and content here are simultaneously expressive and interlocking.

Dürer's *Madonna* is entirely accessible. She has become a lovely young woman such as one might know. She holds her baby warmly and tenderly and nurses Him. The baby is completely dependent on her and is in no way indicated as unusual or extraordinary. The two are no longer awesomely isolated from the world, as in the other painting, but are intimately associated with its nature, the bounteous grape vine—an allusion to the Eucharist—and its surrounding construction of man. The underlying tone of the painting, then, its expressiveness in content, lies in *human warmth and graciousness, in a love of life and the world.*

In form Dürer's work leaves something to be desired. The Madonna's robe is rendered with expressive vitality and the grape leaves with a certain heightened realism; the Child, and the head and shoulders of the Madonna, are centered in the over-all field; the darkness at the lower right is balanced by the highlight at the upper left. The curving drapery, the masonry to which it leads, the vineyard's poles and the tree—all help to enclose the composition. Despite these aspects of form, there is a visual conflict among closely observed elements in this painting. They compete for our attention and therefore deny us the easy unifying look of the Tuscan artist's work. Dürer's is composed of *beautiful parts* in a balanced arrangement which lacks an over-all intensive and unifying impact. The painting's most compelling expressiveness is in its reverent humanism and in the zest and vitality of its lavish realism.

More often than not, and it is unfortunate that this should be so, it is not easy to put one's finger of clarification quickly and securely on an art work's expressiveness. The reason is that the brew of art can combine a complex of background factors—as well as the artist's insights—into a single expression which no word or even group of words can exactly characterize. Moreover, the artist has sometimes approached his task with mixed, even contradictory, feelings, which have prevented a clear or unified expression. Finally, the artist has sometimes lacked the cohesiveness and vigor of personality to make a forceful personal statement.

Yet even a person with an anemic or neutral personality can learn a trade and achieve technical skill, especially through apprenticeship. Many of the workshop paintings of the Renaissance, and, indeed, many modern works, fail to impress us because the artist had technical skill but lacked the personal fire to give an *expressive* unity to his work. The result may have a certain competence, but be dry and even vaguely repellent.

However, it is not the neutral, the empty, or the confused that we seek in art, but the positive, the unifying, the enriching. Therefore it is valuable to be able to recognize even the absence of expressiveness, which allows us the more easily to pass on to another work of art.

Understanding the nature of expressiveness helps to clarify the relationship between the personality of the artist and his treatment of a subject. Why is it that for Riemenschneider the Madonna was a sensitive, mature woman, whereas for the Bamberg *Madonna's* sculptor she was almost

148 (*left*). *Senator* (?). Roman. 1st century B.C. Stone. Munich, Germany: Prince Karl Palace, Glyptothek Collection. 149 (*right*). *David* (?), detail. French. 12th century. Stone. Chartres, France: Cathedral. (Etienne Houvet photo)

a hoyden? Clearly, these men have projected *themselves* into their conception of the Madonna. If these works were typical of each, it would not be difficult to believe that Riemenschneider was the more complex and introspective and the other a hearty man of the world. While the expressive tone gives us a conception of the Madonna in each case, *it is really the artist we are contacting subjectively and only apparently his theme or subject.* This is not to say that we may learn nothing objectively true about an artist's subject, but this would happen only in so far as he was capable and desirous of an objective statement.

In short, we must be very cautious in assuming that we are learning much about the artist's subject. Oddly enough we are closer to the artist himself and to the culture of his era, even though he may have sat before the subject and endeavored to copy it for us. We gain objective data about the subject only in the art works of those eras in which objective observation was a facet of the cultural expression—and in the history of man such eras have been surprisingly few.

We may suppose that objectivity was possible in the culture producing the Roman portrait head [148]. Such a work, although giving the impression of verisimilitude, suffers from the defects inherent in art as imitation. We are given a good idea of the probable external appearance of the man, but externality is made an end in itself and so leaves us at a loss to "perceive" inner individuality. We surmise only that such a conception must

150. *St. John the Baptist*, detail. French. Early 13th century. Stone. Chartres, France: Cathedral. (Etienne Houvet photo)

have belonged to an intensely practical and "realistic" age or artist. This hard-bitten realism is the sculpture's expressiveness. It is given intensity by the emphasis on, and no doubt the exaggeration of, the head's many surface planes and wrinkles.

The head from Chartres Cathedral thought to represent *David* [149] is as subjective in its implications as the other is objective. The sculptor had only to create a young man wearing a crown, but in so doing he provided a characterization of faith and idealism in the twelfth century. No furrowed brow is here, no sign of the wear and tear of life implicit in the other work. This is a conception, not a report. It radiates serenity, openness, earnestness, confidence. Its unspoiled and uncomplicated idealism is as striking as the lack of illusions in the face of the Roman. Here are the pathos of faith untouched by doubt and of doubt untouched by faith.

In the modern army there is a dictum: "Don't do as I do; do as I say!" Implicit here is a cleavage between aims and reality, but it still follows that both aspects of the dichotomy are a part of the reality of military life. We know that life in the medieval period fell far below the exalted level suggested by the *David*, yet the *David's* expressiveness provides us direct rapport with an aspect of the twelfth-century aspiration which marked it as one of the most exalted epochs in the history of man; and we achieve this through contact with one who may have been considered, in his time, no more than a simple artisan.

But just as the expressive tone of the personality fails to capture the full richness of the individual, so no art work can fully symbolize its creator or epoch; it can only illuminate aspects experienced by the individual. Through the magnificent *St. John* [150], also at Chartres, we touch a different and later side of the culture from that just projected. In place of the confidence suggested by the David, we have here a profound pathos, a deep, perceptive sadness. In form, the simplified, incisive treatment of the features and the planes of the face, the softly mingling rhythms of the texture of the beard and the intertwining rhythms of the hair shirt provide a marvelously tender complement to the facial expression, making this one of the most moving achievements in Western art.

It is true that the subject, St. John the Baptist, having lived a life of meditation, self-denial, and even of self-punishment in the desert, might reasonably be "interpreted" in this way by the sculptor. Yet we have only to look once again at the very different St. John in Memling's painting [120] to see how much more the treatment is related to insights of the artist and his time than to any fixed or inevitable interpretation. The *St. John* and *David* at Chartres evoke in a wonderfully expressive way contrasting aspects of the medieval outlook.

The look of sadness and of pathos in the *St. John* at Chartres is patent; and yet, however acceptable, this interpretation is still subjective and uncertain. The lack of objective precision and proof in interpretations of expressive meanings in art makes it desirable to think of them as insightful hypotheses, as revealing speculation, at the most as probability, rather than as fact. May the reader keep this in mind in reading the interpretations here! Yet the expressiveness of art not only opens the way to a deeper understanding of meaning in art generally, but points to its subtlety and power to evoke the finest distinctions.

For example, the underlying tone of Quentin Metsys' *Portrait of The Virgin* [151], like that of the Chartres *David,* appears to be that of an open, unquestioning faith, but there are important nuances of difference. The *Virgin* is more individualized than the *David* and the emphasis on her eyes in the painting, like that on the delicacy of the contour of her face and veil and on the effect of radiance created by the lighting, makes the subjective effect that of a delicate *inner* experience of the subject (and so of the artist and ourselves). The *David* is less self-conscious.

A sharply differing concept of faith is suggested through the underlying tone of the *Christ* of the Cathedral at Worms [152]. It suggests a faith sustained by authority rather than by the voluntary experience implied by the other works. Christ is here shown as a ruler, a commander, looking at the spectator with driving penetration and making clear with the written word His assertion: "I am the way, the truth and the life." The largeness of the sculptured shapes of the face, the textural, linear simplicity of the drapery—a manuscript derivative—and the bold frontality of the figure combine esthetically to evoke this reaction—and much more powerfully than by a "realistic" approach.

As for the quality of pathos, which we have also been discussing, it too finds through art extended subtleties of revelation. The *Jewish Rabbi*

151. Quentin Metsys: *Portrait of the Virgin in Prayer.* Flemish. Early 16th century. Antwerp, Belgium: Royal Museum.

152. *Christ*. German. Late 12th century. Stone. Worms, Germany: Cathedral.

[131] is an example of a more personalized pathos than the Chartres *St. John*. The *House by the Railroad* [153] by Edward Hopper reveals through its blank sky, stark lighting, physical isolation, and outdated architecture the pathos of bygone cultural patterns whose outer shell is still vividly real but whose substance is gone. The projective nature of the expressiveness of this painting is made clear by the circumstance that Hopper painted it in his studio. The convincing effect of reality is there because of Hopper's sharp recollection of the visual character of Victorian mansions, but he has added his subjective reaction to them. The house has become a vehicle for expressing an outlook on past and present, embodied in a personal mood.

The few examples above suggest the remarkable responsiveness of art to the expression of nuances of feeling or insight and that this often comes through to our subjective perception as an underlying, pervasive tone or

153. Edward Hopper: *House by the Railroad*. 1925. New York: The Museum of Modern Art.

effect, made expressive by the artist's treatment of the subject and his handling of form.

Our perception is frequently a compound of the influence of feelings or emotions and of reason. The expressiveness of an art work may reflect either or both modes of awareness. The underlying tone of Van Eyck's *Madonna and Child* [18] is that of objectivity, orderliness, and calm. It is essentially reserved and unemotional. Compare it with Rembrandt's *David* [19]. Immediately we realize that Rembrandt's work is far more subjective and personal, having an inner significance, and that the perception of it depends on contacting the nature of this inner quality, whatever it may be. Whether the effect is one of depth of feeling or of sparking intellectual understanding, it is *pervasively present,* an underlying, dominant tone.

In Cézanne's lithograph *Bathers and Mt. Ste. Victoire* [154], the subject matter has no importance, and the work's impact comes from the inner excitement of solving a problem in form. Here Cézanne shows the peculiar relationship of figure to ground which he also carried out more complexly in color. You will notice that the "interior" of most of the shapes is simply the paper or ground on which the print is made. Considered from one point of view, we may look right through the bathers, right through the mountain, and right through the trees and clouds to a common plane and tone. Moreover there is a tonality to the shading itself which is re-

154. Paul Cézanne: *Bathers and Mt. Ste. Victoire*. French. *c.* 1898. Lithograph. Private collection.

lated to *designing the plane* rather than to creating the effect of atmosphere or distance.

The general tonality of the trees in the middle distance is the same as that along the lower edge of the picture. The lighter tones in the mountain are the same as the clouds and, more importantly, are the same in many places about the foreground, especially in the area of the reclining figure. Notice also that the lines of the lithographic pencil show as distinctly in the upper part as in the lower and that the white spaces show parallels in size between top and bottom. That is, Cézanne does not allow the sky to be blankly white nor the foreground to be uniformly shaded but creates a kind of evenness of balance between light and dark in both areas. The one very dark area in the lower right corner is balanced by the large, very light area in the upper left corner. The picture's distribution of dark is along the lower border, at the sides, and across the middle, but there is no unrelieved darkness, and everywhere the light ground keeps coming through. The eye—that is, our visual perception—does not move along continuous contours but, through a dynamic grasp of the interlocking elements, sees the whole plane as at once stable and moving. Finally, we see that the avoidance of perspective (there are few in-leading lines although they are important) and of atmospheric illusion does not destroy the effect of depth. Change of size and overlapping of near upon far, plus the rhythmic progression of light shapes or "spaces" from foreground to background, convincingly suggest spatial extension.

Further, as if to bring us ever back to the plane, Cézanne links many contours of near and far. For example, the contour of the tree at the right continues around into the cloud; that of the standing figure in the distance at left continues into the contour of the mountain; the curve of the head of the man at the right continues along the distant horizon; the arms, head, and shoulders of the largest figure parallel elements in the background.

Thus we are able to see this work either flatly or in depth, so that while seeing it in depth, *it remains organized in its plane.* Moreover, it is not a static balance of shapes but a dynamic equilibrium which is dependent for its effect upon the "eye" picking up a succession of relationships.

It is not necessary for the formal problem to be complex to have primary appeal, as we may note from Matisse's lithograph [98]. In both this work and Cézanne's the artists were absorbed in their formal task. *The joy, challenge, and interest in an essentially artistic problem was the driving force.* While Matisse may have been attracted by his subject, and while Cézanne undoubtedly enjoyed the view of Mt. Ste. Victoire, which he often painted from nature, the basic interest in either case was not so much subject as the artistic problem. Hence *the expressiveness is largely formal,* and we should grasp it as such.

Some works may have a subject which was significant to the artist but which is of much more casual interest to others of his time or to a later age. The thirteenth-century Romanesque capital from Autun [155] represents the angel awakening the Three Kings to advise them to fol-

155. *Warning of the Three Kings*, fragment from capital. French. 12th century. Stone. Autun, France: Museum.

low the Star home and not to succumb to the blandishments of King Herod. As represented, the angel has just touched the hand of one king, whose eyes have opened, while his royal bedmates remain peacefully in dreamland. With the other hand the angel points to the Star. The sense of drama here in the choice of a specific moment and the directness of its rendering give vividness to the scene. We can appreciate the rhythmic sweep of the robe, the variety of texture, the simplicity and directness of the carving. Yet the expressiveness of this work for our later age lies in its charming ingenuousness. The work becomes expressive to us according to *our* lights. We cannot be sure how the Romanesque believer would have felt about it, although we can admire the sculptor's skill as artist and appreciate his succinct powers as a storyteller.

This sort of cultural barrier is even more evident in the case of truly primitive monuments such as the stone head carved by a prehistoric Indian of the Columbia River region [156]. We are unable to make any contact at all with the probable "meaning" of this face, yet we can see that the sculptor had a bold, simple, even powerful grasp of form. The sweeping eyebrows visually link together the two sides of the head, and the large shapes of the eyes are consistent with the massiveness of the head as a whole and contribute to its effect of power.

156 (*left*). Stone mortar, by a prehistoric Indian of the Columbia River region. Portland, Ore.: Art Museum. 157 (*right*). Head, from the Dipylon, Athens. Greek. *c.* 620 B.C. Stone. Athens: National Museum.

Or again the archaic Greek head illustrated [157] is so remote from us in content that we cannot even be sure of its sex. (Actually it represents a man, perhaps an athlete who won an event at the Olympic games.) In comparing this head with the Indian, we see the greater refinement of the "primitive" Greek. The expressiveness here for us is all formal, created by the remarkable clarity and simplicity of the carving, its sensitive feeling for the material and secure balance of parts.

Thus, much art that may have been highly important in content and meaning to its creators is expressive to us only as form. The impossibility or great difficulty of reconstructing the original meanings has led to what the original artist might well consider an overemphasis of his artistic achievement; that is the privilege of a later age.

Child art offers another case in point. The *Child in Tall Grass* [158] by nine-year-old Angela was made with pieces of colored paper cut out and pasted in place. The "grass" was a shredded strip, allowed to stand out from the surface in front of the subject to indicate that the "girl is coming this way." In front is a large flower and in back are snow-covered hills with green trees artfully suggested by small triangles, decoratively applied. While in adult terms the flower at the right may seem too large, in general the picture is well organized and reveals a clear sense of form. In fact, it is more expressive in form than many adult works. But

158. Angela (age 9): *Child in Tall Grass.* Colored paper.

it is also childlike in content and we see that the level of the content behind the form does affect our final appraisal. However delightful and heartwarming child art may be, it can never equal the effectiveness of a mature work that is also expressive. The form of child art lacks a correspondence in significant content. Its expressiveness lacks depth.

If the subject in many instances, as in the Indian and Greek heads, has become inscrutable, in many others it may have an expressiveness of its own, even before the artist begins to treat it. A starving man holding out his hand for food or money is such an expressive subject. The sight of him—the gesture, the stoop of his body, the boniness of his hands, the look in his face—heightens or intensifies our feelings, whether in sympathy, pity, outrage, or revulsion does not matter. Expressiveness of content, in short, may be *inherent in subject*, although even when it is, the artist may and in fact usually does control the nature of the expressive effect, imparting to the treatment the means of evoking his own reaction.

Finally, in the case of *nonobjective art*, it is clear that the expressiveness must derive wholly from the form since there is no subject—except as we apply the term to the work's shapes, color, and organization. Let us examine contrasting works by Franz Kline and Mark Tobey, contemporary Americans [159 and 160]. Although the paintings by Kline that appear in the illustration are not finished, they already have organization and give an excellent idea of what his painting is like. It would be hard to find a greater contrast in nonobjective art than that between the introspective and brooding minutiae of Tobey and the bold and brash

159. Franz Kline and paintings. (Fritz Goro photo, courtesy LIFE Magazine)

160. Mark Tobey: *Meditative Series, No. 9.* 1954. Tempera. Darthea Speyer Collection.

power of Kline's big shapes. The first is as withdrawn as the other is assertive. This comparison may suggest to you the enormous range of subjective expression possible in the contemporary forms.

In Kline's works the ratio in size of dark shape to ground is sensitively felt, in spite of the seeming spontaneity of their application. Compare them with the Mondrian [8]. Kline may be regarded as a "descendant" of Mondrian via Oriental calligraphy, without his being too derivative to achieve a personal and independent statement. The difference is one of temperament, and Kline's canvases have an emotional quality in contrast to the fastidious, intellectually poised, aloof treatment of forms by Mondrian. In comparison, Kline's seem bluff and open, ingenuous, yet powerful. Compare them also with Kandinsky's [7]. The vastly greater sophistication and complexity of Kandinsky's expressiveness is transparent. Kline's forms are like a bold, simple, heartfelt cry or shout that ends with itself.

The brooding effect of Tobey's painting is created partly by the insistent use of small, irregular, rectilinear shapes. Psychologically this creates an effect of patient persistence, of the power tirelessly to explore a single theme. The little shapes, never quite the same, are unified overall in endless variations. Here is not one figurative navel to contemplate, but hundreds making the effect of one. And the brooding oneness is achieved not only by the repetition of the tiny rectilinear theme, but by pervasive warm tones ranging from red-orange to mustard-gold to pinky-violet, each appearing in a variety of values. Even in black and white they produce a rich tonal effect. A generally higher value in the lower central part of the picture helps to close the visual design and to create both a focus of attention and a certain subjective effect of emerging light. It is this centered light area and the darker tones to the right and left which give the painting its organization in the broader sense. A subjective reaction to this work might be that it represents a near-complete introspection or turning within, a rejection of the practical world for pebbles on the beach, "pebbles" which the power of contemplation invests with a warmth and strange serenity. This work also suggests a vastly more subtle, calculating, and complex personality than that of Franz Kline, whose paintings, by comparison, appear direct, open, impulsive.

What has been said of the canvases of Kline and Tobey may be reinforced by comparison of both with a drawing by Pieter Brueghel the Elder [161]. It is an interesting experience to confront this sixteenth-century work with the modern. A drawing rather than a painting has been chosen for comparison, because the traditional drawing comes closer to the intimacy and personal expressiveness so characteristic of nonobjective works. Where Tobey's patience seems turned entirely within, Brueghel's equally minute and careful attention is directed to a drawing which establishes an inner concord with nature. It is a nature in which man, at the lower left, plays a tiny yet seemingly harmonious part. This is not a threatening, but a soaring, majestic landscape. The distant strip of lake with its mirror calm invites us into the heart of the scene. Brueghel's delicate realism is also skillfully decorative, and for all the naturalistic detail in this landscape, the light that shines on it is of the imagination, an inner light. Brueghel's conception is both his own and of the world. Compare Kline's massive and impulsive shapes with Brueghel's delicate meditation and ponder this moving revelation of the difference of two worlds.

Metaphor and simile have been useful in discussing the works-without-subject because they provide the most fruitful way to penetrate to the underlying tone. Unquestionably expressive in form, the subjectless works carry a powerful effect of the presence and nature of the artist which we can reach only subjectively. Yet in each case our reaction is related to the *kind* of forms and the *kind* of organization employed by the artist. And assuming that the interpretation of these works is correct, does it not help to break through the barrier between us, the art work, and the artist?

To conclude, we cannot assume that insight into the expressive in art

234 EXPRESSIVENESS

161. Pieter Brueghel the Elder: *Landscape* (*Waltersburg*). Flemish. *c.* 1554. Pen and ink. Brunswick, Me.: Bowdoin College Museum of Fine Arts.

is a means of access to the "whole man." But as indicated earlier, there is no single human expression which can imply every trait of character or every aspect of the personality, even though each played its near or distant part in the outcome. Nevertheless, because the art work, into which the artist pours his most intensive effort, certainly means much to him, we may suppose that the resulting expressive effect will bear at least a serious and even a profound relationship to his nature. Despite its inevitable hiatuses and subjective uncertainties, expressiveness in art opens a way to reaching beyond the art work to the artist and his time. And the point is that we need not lose contact with the artistic achievement in the process but can come back to it with an enjoyment compounded of a larger understanding.

Whether expressiveness is of content, form, or both, it invests the work with its pervasive presence. In perceiving its nature we go far toward solving the enigma of art, for through it we discover that art is no more and no less puzzling than the nature of man. Art through its expressive power becomes the measure of man, becomes a catalyst through which we reach not only aspects of the individual personality, in the form of feelings and insights, but of the environment and culture. Through art's expressiveness the art work ceases to be isolated and is discovered to be the intermediary between ourselves and a sensitive man or woman.

Part Three

Toward a Personal Judgment of Art

16-The Question of Taste

All customs undergo a formative period when they are clearly matters of taste. A thoroughly established custom—like the wearing of skirts by women—while representing a preference, is so deeply rooted in human folkways as to be relatively unconscious. We therefore do not usually think of it as a taste, because it admits of so little deviation. Indeed, it is the *deviation* that is the revealer of taste—when to wear blue jeans or shorts, for example—and even this may become so firmly established in local custom as to permit little individual choice. *Taste implies a preference among alternatives having esthetic implications.* The factor of taste is therefore central to the arts and to allied fields, such as manners.

Many people hang coats in their cars during the summer or when traveling, a practical expedient which gets the coat out of the way yet leaves it readily accessible and free of wrinkling folds. Many other people abjure this useful practice because the hanging coat recalls the closet, a place associated with a private or closed-off part of the home. This illustrates how a taste may be influenced by factors beyond the instance in which the taste is exercised, and how the esthetic aspect may affect one person and not another.

In the same way, preferences in art can reflect all manner of elements which may be unknown or only incidental to the artist. Life gives its meaning to art and not vice versa, although the art work may serve to call attention to previously unrealized aspects of life. This accounts for the wide range of possible approaches to art, a phenomenon irritating to many artists but actually an asset, revealing art's roots in the breadth of human perception.

It is possible, for example, to regard art with the Freudian psychologists as an expression of *wish fulfillment,* as a link with the subconscious. Freud's study of Leonardo is an example of this approach, in which considerations of form are neglected for analysis of the symbolism of Leonardo's art, linking it with abnormalities of the artist's childhood. Actually, the intuitive and "freely" selective nature of art does open it easily to influence from the subconscious. That is, hunch and impulse play a role in the guidance of the artist.

Another approach associates art with the *creative act or process,* which is seen as more significant than the finished product. The "essence" of art, then, according to this theory, is the *experience* of producing it.

The idea of art as process is linked with that of art as *play.* This view does not exclude serious intent but carries with it, as in any game, the idea of adaptability to a changing situation and of fun or pleasure in the doing. The art work does not exist full-blown in the artist's imagination but is an emerging thing which may require a certain give-and-take between the artist and his objective. That is, an attitude of expectant openness leads to unforeseen results, to self-realization, or at least to creative realization. It also leads, sometimes, to a better result than expected, yet one which is still a personal achievement. This approach, in combination with that emphasizing "process" generally, is seen as the key to success in other fields of human activity and is the exalting of the creative endeavor above all else.

A related concept sees art as *pleasure,* derived, however, from contemplating the finished product. It is recognized that the sensation of pleasure in art may be linked with something—as with tragedy in drama—which is not altogether pleasurable. Most of us are hedonists enough to find much appeal in this theory. Once the esthetic faculty is sharpened, art does indeed provide a great deal of sheer delight, but one trouble with the theory is that the term "pleasure" is so broad that what is a pleasure to one may be boring or even distasteful to another. The theory must be applied projectively—that is, according to the particular meaning of "pleasure" employed.

An extension of the pleasure theory is to regard art as a stimulus to the emotions more broadly, to see it as *emotion, esthetically expressed.*

The theory of art as *form* does not preclude the pleasure and emotion concepts but regards them as by-products of a more central element—experiencing the work's unifying organization. To make the distinction sharper: only that pleasure or emotion coming from the experience of form is significant, because—so the theory goes—art is form and form alone. Moreover, this form is found only in the art work and is its meaning, end, and justification.

A related approach to the form theory sees art as *formal styles.* Here the emphasis is somewhat less on the isolated esthetic experience of the work and more on an *understanding* of the work as part of an ever-changing approach to form, both within the activity of a given artist and from other points of view. Thus formal style reveals national characteristics, as Italian versus French; period characteristics, as Renaissance versus baroque; local characteristics, as Roman versus Venetian, or Northern European versus Southern; and stylistic types, as Impressionism versus Post-Impressionism. Many an art historian is partial to this viewpoint.

A corollary to the above sees art as a *cultural manifestation.* According to this view, form and content relate not only to the artist, but through him to the outlook and cultural nature of his time. The differences in form of a Medieval and Renaissance work can be traced to the differing worlds of the two periods. The chief value of art, then, would be as a cultural mirror of its time.

Or again, art has been seen as *lyrical intuition* and as *unified symbol.*

Books, and in some cases many books, have been written according to each of the above approaches. And with such a bewildering array of possibilities—only the most prominent are mentioned here—it is not surprising that partisanships for a particular view, rather than a synthesis of various views, tend to develop. This is accounted for partly by the sheer complexity of trying to coalesce and keep before the mind a variety of approaches, some rather antagonistic to each other.

And yet, the fair-minded reader may well have developed the suspicion, even from these thumbnail sketches, that *each* of these approaches has some validity. And indeed, form and content, as we have investigated them, may be the basis for a broadening approach to the meaning of art.

Still, we have not accounted for the multiplicity of these concepts nor for the partisanships, earnest and even violent, which may accompany them. Let us return to the element of taste, defined as preference among alternatives having esthetic implications. Could it be that these various approaches to art are matters of taste, rather than of right and wrong? Seen thus, the puzzling disparities of viewpoint on art are recognized at root as projections of differing personalities. *The individual's approach to art, in the last analysis, becomes a form of his own self-expression.* And why not? The artist himself is certainly engaging in self-expression, if he is satisfied with his work or if he enjoyed working on it. Why should there not be different approaches to art for the connoisseur, critic, historian, lawyer, engineer, businessman, or housewife? No two of them could be expected to bring the same type of interest, let alone the identical approach, to as subjective a creation as art.

The value of a "process-oriented" viewpoint, then, is partly that it dignifies the creative act and is therefore bound to appeal to the artist. In contrast, the person who has both an esthetic eye and a flare for synthesis of ideas is almost sure to be fascinated by the evolution of artistic forms and their cultural grounding. The philosophically disposed person will look with interest at all approaches and seek or develop that which seems in harmony with his particular philosophical outlook. And so on.

If each of us has a more natural affinity by temperament for one approach to art than another, it follows that we also have an affinity for a certain "level" of art. It has not been sufficiently recognized that the contemporary taste for chrome plate and even the juke box, is positive and not the result of a mere lack of exposure to something else. While education can and no doubt should play a part in calling the attention of young and old to a broader range of esthetic expression, it should be remembered that taste in art is more than a general sensitivity to form. It is sensitivity to the kinds of form appropriate to the individual's outlook and personality.

The ruins of antiquity were just as available in the twelfth century as in the fifteenth, and there were esthetically sensitive people at both times. The twelfth-century people remained much more aloof to the classical remains because *they lacked the underlying affinity of outlook needed to make the classical forms seem vital*, not because they were unexposed to the forms or lacked the esthetic capacity for their appreciation. The mature esthetic understanding must surely include a broader readiness than that of esthetic training alone. The art work represents a way of life and the person who lived or lives it, and so does the taste for art and for one art form above another. It is also entirely possible for the circumstances of an individual's life not to have proffered him the motive to develop his esthetic faculty, so that it has largely lain fallow.

We may designate three broad levels of taste in art—the popular taste, the cultivated taste, and the uncultivated taste.

In the sweep of history, popular art is known as folk art. It has roots in the dance, in song, and in the crafts, with occasional ventures into painting and sculpture. It is characterized by a vivid sense of form which may be quite simple or quite intricate though not intellectually complex. In music, its content ranges from the melancholy ballad to the gay harvest song, and although fundamental in the sense of touching feelings which are common to mankind, folk art is emotionally uncomplicated. Small wonder that in a sophisticated age like ours, with its many insecurities and tensions, people with cultivated taste are turning back to the simple but strongly felt emotions and the appealingly clear and simple forms of folk art. It is a very interesting sign of our times that two important folk art museums should recently have opened in this country. For folk art as such is directly functional only to those for whom it was intended, and to put it in a museum is immediately to recognize the immense gap in the ways of life of its creators and those who collect it. The number of collectors must be small indeed who can wear a folk costume unself-consciously, or even sing a ballad without feeling its remoteness. Yet the simplicity and emotional directness of these folk expressions have a powerful appeal.

It is one of the phenomena of our country today that we have no traditional folk art to speak of. Not that there is no craft work or that there are not "primitive" artists—like John Kane and Horace Pippin— but folk art is certainly not the vital expression of the contemporary small American town that it still is of the small town in India, or that it was in our frontier days of the limner and the traveling cabinetmaker.

What do we have instead as popular art? Jazz music and dancing come the closest today to a folk expression that is widely participated in, although there are some other popular arts which we shall take up later. But in jazz, for example, Louis Armstrong has approximately the qualities in his music that one expects of folk music: basic simplicity of structure, vital energy, and a felt but uncomplicated emotion. Louis's records are already and properly collector's items, along with those of his great predecessors, like Bix Beiderbecke and Jelly Roll Morton. Furthermore, he brings to his performance, and it shows in his playing, the appeal of a hearty, open, and warm personality.

But along with the brightness, directness, and fire of Louis Armstrong we have the treacle of Wayne King and the sheer rhythmic noise of many others. If jazz is our folk music, it reaches heights both of sentimentality and of frenetic, explosive energy hitherto unscaled by the folk artist.

In *form* jazz is a remarkable enough achievement, but it is what it reveals to us about our age that is disturbing. If we compare it with the folk music of the past, we may find nothing comparable in creative zeal; on the other hand the earlier forms express a poise, a melancholy realism, or a heartfelt joy that is alarmingly absent from the nervous tempos or the sentimental banalities of most of today's jazz. With this the chrome-plated automobile, the dazzling neon lights of our city streets, the hop of the jitterbug, the violence of our pulp stories of crime and sex play their various complementary roles.

The vast, sprawling, energetic field of popular taste is accompanied by the equally heterogeneous range of the cultivated taste. The borderlines between the two groups are indistinct or, better, blend together. The best of the popular jazz, for example, is very widely appreciated outside popular levels.

But the instant we reach Beethoven, Shakespeare, and Rembrandt, or even Gershwin, Shaw, and Renoir, we are in the area of cultivated taste, which counts among its following, today, a large and growing group. These people are concerned with the kind of art, by and large, that we have been discussing in these pages, and the reason these art forms represent cultivated taste is exactly that they require a certain effort to be appreciated. Whereas the developer of a cultivated taste is aroused by a challenge in cultural matters, the follower of popular taste takes things as they come.

Some psychologists attribute a conscious desire for art to insecurity and the drive for status—to the snob appeal of culture. This may be a motivating factor, but it cannot be productive of a genuine love of the arts. And in the eighteenth century we have the example of many noblemen who enjoyed both social and economic security but who also became excellent amateur artists or musicians. No, I believe the explanation for the cultivated taste lies in a superior capacity to integrate, fostered in a life situation making for a degree of detachment, and the ability to perceive more easily the uniqueness and character of other people and other expressions. It requires, paradoxically, *detachment, accompanied by perceptive warmth.*

These are the qualities, I contend, that we must develop, if we are to make such art works as we have investigated here a meaningful part of our experience in life. If the temperament is ready, then the awakening is a continuous process of growth.

We must also account for the fact that not all people of imagination and creativity are interested in the arts, which brings us to the third level of taste, the uncultivated. Andrew Carnegie, a man of enormous creative gifts, although respecting the arts, provides an example of such a taste. So does John D. Rockefeller, Sr. So today do numberless politicians, lawyers, businessmen, and scientists. People of uncultivated taste generally have little awareness of the element of form and so feel that their intelligence is being insulted by nonimitative art, particularly the nonobjective. It is they who have openly attacked contemporary art and who have placed the creative artist, in whatever epoch, on the defensive. These able people include among them large numbers of potential enthusiasts for the arts. Unlike the lover of popular art, who within his limits is an ardent fan, these people have very little positive identification with art of any level; yet if once reached by the simple realization that art is a form of personal unification and therefore must be more than imitative, an esthetic chain reaction might be set in motion which could turn many foes of art into growing friends.

Taste, then, does not relate so much to the art object as to the way of life and the experience of the individual; the approach to the art object is its sympathetic projection. This is why equally sensitive people may prefer different art forms and also why explanation of art may fall on "deaf"—that is, unready—ears.

17-Utility and Abstraction in the Contemporary Art Scene

If the proverbial man from Mars were to guide his flying saucer over United States towns and cities in search of public evidences of art, he would have only about fifty chances among thousands of finding even a modest art museum. Yet at hand everywhere would be countless examples of commercial art and of product design. In Europe, to be sure, many parks are decorated with sculpture, and many churches as well as museums are treasure places of art. But all this comes largely from an earlier time. Europe today is not unlike America in its pervasive manifestation of the arts of industry.

If this is a modern trend, it also has ancient roots. Art in its origins was almost certainly linked with utility, either in the embellishment of tools and utensils or in the creation of images having magic powers. Very gradually, the art element achieved independence of utility, particularly in the fine arts—painting, sculpture and architecture—as distinct from the applied arts—pottery, weaving, and other craft or "commercial" art work. But even the fine arts retained a utilitarian overtone—for example, in the instructional aspect of religious art or the glorifying aspect of religious and aristocratic art. Society remained homogeneous enough for art to repre-

245

sent the common values of large groups and even of society generally. Art for art's sake, an essentially modern doctrine, is characteristic of a more diverse society in which the nonesthetic, but culturally cohesive, aspects of the fine arts have little importance.

The causes of this change are complex, but among those affecting art most directly were the decline of the church and aristocracy as great patrons and the rise of the middle class in a cultural climate devoted to science and industry. The artist received considerable patronage from this new class but with few exceptions was no longer serving a grand social or religious design. The success of the machine in producing the goods of the world was accompanied by the growth of a new urban society having materialism as its tacit, if not avowed, philosophy. Whereas in the Baroque the material evidences of success had to be hand-produced, in the nineteenth century they became increasingly machine-produced. And today, instead of viewing his art collection or making music with a group of friends, the successful man can turn for satisfaction to color television or stereo sound, a change which can be spoken for or against, but which represents, in any case, a deep shift in values. Whereas in the day of Henry VIII it required a master craftsman to carve and emplace a fine stairway railing and newel post, today a stairway may have no individual decoration at all and be admired for its engineering or functional simplicity. Moreover, the designer of the modern version, the fabricator of its materials, and the builder who puts it in place may never see one another. In his own labor, modern man often reflects the impersonal routine of the machine and assembly line.

Art museums everywhere continue to exhibit works of the fine artist, but his audience is extremely small and his apparent influence even smaller. Among the modern fine arts only architecture, after an up-hill battle, has held its breadth of appeal. Where yesterday it was the fine artist, today it is the commercial artist or industrial designer who embellishes and designs the most sought-after luxuries. And these luxuries are likely to have a mechanical, electrical, or scientific genius at their source, rather than an artist or hand craftsman.

Substantial differences are evident in the training of the industrial designer (machine-made products), the interior designer (architectural interiors), and the commercial artist (advertising and popular illustration). But in the broad sense they are all members of the commercial art profession, since they work with machine-made or reproduced products, for clients who have to pass on what they do and who may request and obtain design alterations. In contrast, the fine artist works for himself and deals with the public, on the whole, on a take-it-or-leave-it basis. Commercial art, moreover, is frequently a group enterprise the final product of which may reveal the genius of a particular designer but to which a supporting team has nevertheless contributed importantly. The fine artist has no such involvement with organization. One of the groups he may join, Artists Equity, exists in part to protect this independence.

We must frankly recognize that the commercial art profession in all

162. Charles Eames: Molded chairs.

its broad ramifications is the dominant art profession today and produces, in the public sense of the term, the dominant art of our time. This is so in the quantity of art produced, in the number of the public directly affected, and in influence on public taste. Commercial art has become a pervasive aspect of our culture. It reflects both the astonishing degree to which mechanization has superseded the crafts and, the effort to give the products of the machine and their presentation to the public a visual as well as a utilitarian-economic appeal. It is a direct outgrowth of our competitive economy. In this connection, a representative symbol of our culture—and perhaps the most so—would be the automobile. It manifests the triumph of industrial organization, the economic advance of the masses, and the astonishing vitality and creative energy of our society. It mirrors also its restlessness, impersonality, materialism, and frequent taste for the garish. But if the automobile suffers from occasional excesses of chrome plate or grossness of proportion, it still reveals a significant advance in over-all design from the time prior to the industrial designer. And towards this an awareness of pure forms, as seen in the sculpture of Gabo and Calder, was a needed preliminary.

The fine artist, in fact, has had more influence on commercial art than has generally been recognized. His emphasis on texture and color for their own sakes, on simplicity and clarity of shape, on the nature of the material worked with, on visual relatedness—in short, the approaches to form he pioneered—have profoundly affected commercial art. Furthermore, an increasing number of commercial artists and designers have had training in the fine arts or architecture and are really fine artists working in the commercial field. They have a refined sense of form and a creative awareness of the original opportunities growing out of design for mass produc-

163. Wire chair and aluminum-Plexiglas table.

tion. However, such men may still be regarded as prophets in the wilderness in a profession which has produced the jukebox, the neon sign, the roadside billboard, the worst of Grand Rapids furniture, and chrome decoration. For reassurance we ought to look very briefly at a few examples of better works.

There is the basic chair designed by Charles Eames for Herman Miller and Company [162]. The Fiberglas seat, stamped out with a press, is virtually indestructible and will not burn, scratch, lose its finish, or wear out. The smart black steel legs, functional to the enormous strength of this material, are slenderer than those of any traditional chair. Indeed, the whole design reveals creative adaptation of new materials to methods of manufacture. Instead of producing a traditional chair with machine methods the designer approached the whole problem in the light of new techniques and materials, including the difficult problem of bonding the metal leg to the seat without piercing the plastic.

The possibilities for variations on such a basic modern design may be suggested by the all-wire garden chair illustrated [163]. Influenced by Eames, it nevertheless shows imaginative variations—is properly more jaunty. The slight suggestion of a wingback and the dipping line of the front edge of the seat give this chair a lilt. The strong continuous wire edge has a delightful rhythm and the curving mesh of the seat and back have an almost gossamer effect against the background. In contrast the narrower, central back of Eames's arm chair and its high arms give it a graver look. Instead of emphasizing a linear rhythm, it reflects the beauty of subtly curving plastic form. Eames's side chair is a smartly curving simple shape with a comfortable seat and a back having a little spring in it.

248 UTILITY AND ABSTRACTION

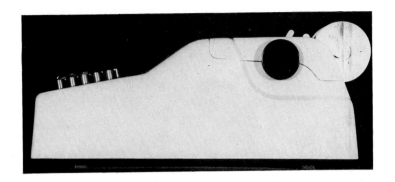

164. Marcello Nizzoli: Olivetti printing calculator.

The out-of-doors table [163] is another example of anonymous modern design showing creative use of modern materials—in this case, an alloy of magnesium and aluminum. With its strong, virtually unbreakable Plexiglas top, it weighs only fifteen pounds and is immune to damage from the elements. Here is an extension of the idea of tubular furniture, first developed in Germany by Marcel Breuer. Notice again how this garden furniture is essentially free in space. One looks through it as well as to it. It takes its place graciously outdoors.

Sound creative design has been applied to all manner of household aids, from the can opener to the vacuum cleaner. In packaging, dazzling ingenuity has been expended to flatter the customer's taste. Machines are made so attractive to the eye that one becomes convinced—sometimes against one's better judgment—that they would be a pleasure to operate. Such is the case, for example, with the Olivetti Printing Calculator [164], designed by Marcello Nizzoli. First came functional considerations—the convenient sloping of the keyboard, readability of the tape, compactness of design, and so on. Then the trim housing was fitted around the ensemble. Note how right angles and sharp edges are avoided, promoting a relaxed approach. Sharp edges are psychologically "cutting," and a rigid rectilinear shape is unyielding. Note, too, how the good-sized winding knob is recessed. Its color contrast makes it readily accessible to the peripheral vision. Finally, the over-all color is optimistically light, promoting the conviction that one's fingers will find the right keys and produce favorable balances. Olivetti's small portable typewriter, the well-known Lettera 22, is another outstanding product of modern industrial design. Very neat in appearance, it is so compact it can be fitted into a brief case.

Leaf-raking is a chore that is pleasant or onerous according to one's disposition at the time, but whatever the raker's emotional predisposition, the job is made visually and physically easier by the Kenco Products Company adjustable garden rake [165]. Made of aluminum, this rake is strong yet light to handle. The wide fanning out of the blades assures a good spread and the blades fold together and slide up the handle for safe storage. Visually speaking, the general shape and the contrast of sturdy rod with trim, slender blades is very successful. Here is a modest abstract sculpture, as well as a tool.

For an example of packaging let us look at Chanel No. 5 for the Purse

[166]. Perfume companies long ago learned how to make a quarter-ounce bottle appear to hold approximately an ounce, but only recently have they displayed a similar resourcefulness in packaging. The exterior box is a straight forward white rectangle with contours edged in black. The size of letter and choice of letter face are planned to carry easily at a distance so that the customer may be reminded of this particular aromatic thrill, in case it should have slipped the mind. We proceed in well-ordered stages down to the bottle. The inner package is a discreet black and gold and, with its rounded ends, has a slightly more informal note. The ensemble makes a fitting and sophisticatedly plain container for its precious cargo.

These are but random samples in several fields of commercial design. Adapted to the functional and psychological requirements of the particular item, they are also valid visual expressions which make a worthy esthetic contribution. But however much the commercial arts may retain prominence in our culture and continue to improve in quality, the independent fine arts will still have a contributing role. The tie of commercial design to machined product and its strong grounding in the practical make all the more important the individual experimentation of the fine artist. For it is he who is free from considerations of the client's or consumer's taste and from restraint imposed by cost of manufacture.

And it cannot be denied that the fine artist today is experimenting with pure form as never before. There are at work excellent artists whose achievement is still based partly on presentational concerns, but the majority of the leading artists all over the Western world are working either very abstractly or nonobjectively. This is a phenomenon that needs further explanation, particularly in view of the smallness or opposition of their audience, the obliqueness of their influence, and the spread of commercial forms.

The opposition of some to both abstract and nonobjective art has been based on the feeling that they are "dehumanizing." But this is to overlook the very personal—and so human—character of all activity requiring integrative effort. No one charges music with being "dehumanized," yet it is certainly nonobjective. And are not the stereotypes of art, for all their folksy subject matter, actually far removed from the deeper human concerns of our time?

The charge has been made that abstract and nonobjective art have been put over by a few zealots and powerful self-interests, the Museum of Modern Art in New York and the art dealers being cited as the chief perpetrators. It is true that some of the panegyrics on these arts, whether written or in the form of exhibitions, have been extreme, but we must remember that they have had to overcome and still have to overcome not only ridicule and contempt but the more deadly opposition of indifference. The opposition to the abstract arts is deep-seated and widespread; this, more than anything else, accounts for the almost overpowering zeal of some of its supporters.

If a satisfactory explanation is to be found for the nature and persistence of abstract and nonobjective art, it will have to be found in a deeper

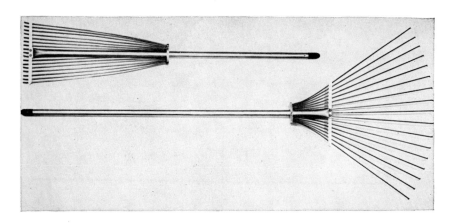

165. Aluminum rakes.

probing of the nature of art in our time. It has been said that abstract and nonobjective art are a reflection of the new scientific view of the nature of matter. Certainly it is true that the *surface appearance* of things and their point-to-point, static relation in space are no longer an adequate abstraction or statement about the fundamental nature of the physical world. Recent discoveries are pushing the concepts of matter beyond that of a succession of ever-symmetrical subdivisions. It is found that the *element of chance* plays a larger role than had previously been recognized in the interaction of electronic forces, and that the submicroscopic world is not necessarily one explicable in terms of neat geometrical solids or symmetrical relationships [167]. The general resemblance of the illustrated electron microscope photograph to some nonobjective paintings, like the work by James Brooks [168], is striking, just as the perspective and volumetrically conceived mass of the Renaissance artist coincided in a general way with the then-current scientific viewpoint.

The integrative capacity of the successful artist is its own indication of his high intelligence, and this is frequently combined with sensitivity and an inquiring outlook. Without understanding the theoretical basis for current scientific theories, the alert artist picks up enough of their conclusions to be influenced by them. We know, for example, that Picasso spent hours in friendly association with a young mathematician, that x-rays were discovered near the turn of the present century, Einstein's theory of relativity in 1905, and that cubism, with its transparent planes and simultaneous opposition of viewpoints, is consistent with the then-developing picture of the physical world. Such artistic parallels to scientific thought do not *require* a rationale of the artist. An x-ray photograph might have been quite enough to continue the chain of visual experimentation leading to cubism. Or again, an artist's view of an electron microscope photograph, without any understanding on his part of its scientific import, could yet start a whole chain of creative visual ideas.

In this general way nonobjective art does reflect new scientific attitudes, even though its purpose as far as the artist is concerned is the crea-

166. Chanel No. 5 packaging.

tion of form. Its frequent emphasis on probabilities and on spontaneity and movement is all a part of the same ferment and is likewise a reflection of the state of flux and the transitional character of our times.

Among earlier factors making for a change in the artist's status and a new emphasis of form was the invention of the photograph in the 1820's and its wide usage in the 1840's and after. The photograph effectively broke the artist's monopoly as an imitator or recorder of the visual appearance of the world. It did not entirely supplant him in this respect, but it was undoubtedly one of the factors causing a re-appraisal of the nature of art by the more advanced artists. In this century, development of the motion picture has only accentuated the challenge and helped further to free the artist for activity which is more comparable to that of the poet or composer—a purer emphasis of form.

And to the above factors must be added, today, the tensions and pressures resulting from life in a world in deadly international conflict and in which the anomalies between science and orthodox religion are painfully evident. The artist is in a world emphasizing applied science and materialism, while tending to belittle pure research, with its closer affinity to the fine arts. His is a world dominated in daily life by an industrial psychology which involves millions of people employed in the operation of machines which offer no leeway for personal expression, a world in which other millions of white-collar workers and executives are governed or inhibited by the overriding demands of the group or corporation. And—

167 (*above*). Aluminum magnified 24,000 times. (Albert Prebus electron micrograph) 168 (*below*). James Brooks: *Cauthunda*. 1958. Collection the artist.

169. Jack Levine: *Feast of Pure Reason.* 1937. U.S.W.P.A. Art Project, on extended loan to The Museum of Modern Art, N. Y.

especially hard for the artist—his is a world in which a substantial number of his country's leaders and large sections of the people ignore or even look down on art. These and many other factors of our culture are creating an environment of tension and insecurity for many, but especially for the creative and sensitive artist and for the individualist. Whereas prior to the nineteenth century the artist had been sought after and respected, he then came to be regarded as an odd fellow and misfit. And to this situation in the twentieth century have been added all the other factors mentioned above and more, making for an insecure and tense life. Is it any wonder that many contemporary artists, in these circumstances, have turned within themselves to seek peace and adjustment?

It may be argued that more people are looking at art and listening to music than ever before, that art works command higher prices, that the artist is finding economic security in the academic community, that status has been given the practice of art by prominent political figures who paint, and so on. These and other like considerations do reveal a trend toward greater support of the arts, but it would be missing the deep, symbolic character of art to suppose that all the artist needs is economic security. To be sure, he has to be able to earn a living. He may succeed in supporting himself, however, and still be sensitive to the underlying character of his time.

But there is a reason for nonobjective art residing in the nature of art itself. While there have been periods when the artist became esthetically side-tracked by problems of realism, the overwhelming bulk of the art of man is governed by some principle of abstraction, by a feeling for visual form. As the artist's exterior world supplies subject matter which seems to him less and less significant, the formal element of art—in which he is fundamentally involved, anyway—becomes that much more important. A total interest in form, therefore, becomes in part a matter of momentum, a tendency which accelerates, given the background conditions indicated. And given these conditions, nonobjective art also offers the means to a continual personal expression of mood or feeling unlinked to external subject. If there is little that contributes hopeful or positive values in the external world, the world of inner resources is all that is left, and nonobjective art, like music, serves this world. Hence there develops an art which mirrors the intimate feelings and moods of many artists in a tense and inhospitable culture.

Finally, ours is an age in which the great advances in communication have enormously multiplied the facets of life and of the world to which the inquiring and intelligent individual is exposed. In these circumstances, abstract and nonobjective art offer the way to expressing complex mixtures of feelings and insights for which no external subject provides a ready focus, as did the Virgin Mary for the thirteenth century.

The fine arts, in short, reflect the enormously complex nature of our culture and are a search for equilibrium in that culture. It is this which accounts for the puzzling disparity of styles today, for no style can adequately express our many-faceted age. Where Giotto summed up the spirit of the beginning Renaissance with a single, consistent, religio-humanistic expression, an equal genius of our own time, Picasso, has had to resort to a dozen ways of working; and many lesser artists have found it necessary to alter their styles drastically.

Is there, then, any underlying force which is finding frequent expression in today's multiplicity of art? I think there is, and that it is protest. To be sure, the kind of specific, deeply felt and bitter social protest that characterized the 1930's [169] is now seldom seen. Moreover, some artists have continued to find security in the world about, as has Andrew Wyeth in his *Northern Point* [170]. Here is a lyrical outlook whose hyper-realism seeks integrity in the commonplace, attaching dignity to that which exists before the eye and mutely in nature. In Wyeth's painting there is an almost ecstatic reverence for the bright light of a summer day, a deep joy in the lofty vista from a position near the unpretentious roof, with its hand-hewn shingles and its craftlike, old-fashioned lightning arrestor.

170. Andrew Wyeth: *Northern Point*. 1950. Tempera. Hartford, Conn.: The Wadsworth Atheneum.

Wyeth brings an intensity to his work which makes his realism lyrically expressive and successful.

Yet, even here, in spite of the realism, there is a kind of nostalgia, an echo of the simpler and more conservative life of another day. The effect of the vista across the flat roof and steel railing of an International Style house would be quite different. Very few artists of our time have been able to create for themselves a security of this Emersonian or, perhaps better, Whitmanesque variety.

The view of the past and present by another realist, Edward Hopper, affords a sharp contrast. On the surface, his paintings may seem to be quite objective reports; they are more than that. In his *Hotel Room* [171], the woman is shown naked, but in a way to heighten the realism of the situation. The body seems to represent, rather than her sex, the bleakness and lack of adornment in so much of modern life, an effect heightened by the barren room and its glaring light. Works like this and the *House by the Railroad* [153] are not protests in the positive usage of the word but constitute a quiet statement of the irony and pathos of life in a world which—for this artist—substitutes clear light for romantic illusions.

171. Edward Hopper: *Hotel Room*. 1931. New York: The Museum of Modern Art.

In spite of these and other very competent continuations of realism, the tendency of the fine arts in our time—for the many reasons already indicated—has certainly been towards increased abstraction and a more exclusive emphasis of form. And here the element of protest is also frequent. Willem De Kooning's *Woman* [172] has none of the presentational elements found in the work of Wyeth or Hopper. It presents no illusion of real space, three-dimensional form, or of normal proportion. Rather, it is a symbolic image, of experiences and feelings of the artist which were too strong and deep to represent realistically. Distortion became a necessity because of the expressive poverty of externals. The artist painted a whole series of this subject, each one more violent than the preceding. There is nothing gracious, sentimental, or flattering about them. On the contrary, they appear to be savage attacks in which the artist is emotionally reacting to a complex experience and, perhaps, is destroying a mem-

172. Willem De Kooning: *Woman, I.* 1952. New York: The Museum of Modern Art.

ory. The color, to be sure, happens to be handsome and is applied with bravura, but what of the almost ostentatious vulgarity of this work? Can we accept it as good art? This is a problem in judgment with which we will deal in the next chapter; for the present, let us note that whatever its ultimate merit, and whatever its essentially personal sources, DeKooning's work does constitute, in its broad suggestion of personality, a protest. It is openly violent, openly nonconformist. The mere fact of its being exhibited projected it into the area of rebellion against that which is routine, suppressed, safe, because it is forcefully evident that De Kooning is not that kind of man. His work becomes a protest against conformity in general, even though it may have had no such intent.

The same is true of the work of Franz Kline [159]. As we have already observed, there is a kind of savage power to those great strokes; they are like a magnified cry which—to continue the musical simile—is all fortissimo. Kline's works, in general, are fortissimo. This painting is not polite, genteel, "other-directed," or conformist; it is aggressive self-assertive, individual; it is an insistent personal statement, without yielding grace, and, to the extent that this is an age of conformity, it is rebellion.

Jackson Pollock [III] does the same thing in a different way. He flouts the notion that all is tidy and secure. Yet with the untidiness of dripping paint, he creates a unity of his own at last. This is a more modest statement than Kline's, more subtle. Kline comes through because of sheer clarity and freedom from the extraneous—strong and unified, but creating an over-simplification. Pollock accepts the accidental, the uncontrollable, and imparts to it a measure of stability. This is why his protest is more of our age, if it is also counter to it.

In contrast to these distraught, aggressive, or withdrawn artistic solutions to stresses of our time is that which does not complain, shout, nor yield, but creates an orderly world of its own, accepting only such fragments of the world about—or none at all—as the artist chooses.

Although near the end of his life John Marin worked nonobjectively, he is best known for his very personal reconstructions of nature. Figure 173 shows him with a cityscape of New York. The Manhattan skyline is in the background. This provides an especially dramatic example of the synthesizing transformation wrought by the artist. As you look at the actual skyline, you are aware of the concentration of buildings which Marin has indicated in an effective way merely by suggesting a complex of building shapes. The oval and triangular shapes in his sky are provided to define visually that area of the painting and to bring it into visual consistency with the portion having building shapes. The painting is further organized by the washed-in colors, both below and above, to a portion of which the artist's brush happens to be pointing. In the simplest way the artist has unified his picture plane, suggested the visual look of the skyscrapers, and, in the verve of his brushwork and the simplicity of his characterization, revealed his own energy and capacity for a personal reorientation to the world. This seems to be implicit even in the photograph of the man, whom we see as neat but nonconformist, sensitive but also defiant, independent, confident.

173. John Marin and painting. 1950. (Bernard Hoffman photo, courtesy LIFE Magazine)

Josef Albers has spent nearly a lifetime perfecting his orphist-suprematist paintings. A work of his like *Study for an Early Diary* [IV], requiring many hours of preparation, is the antithesis of Pollock's, where spontaneity and chance play the leading role. Albers leaves nothing to chance. The usual method of the painter is to build up his design in an increasingly complex unity, creating the needed additional subtleties of color by new tones mixed on the palette. Albers found this too hazardous, because color is perceived only in relation to other color and to add a new tone to a painting which is approaching completion causes a certain alteration of effect among the relationships previously established. He wanted a system which would allow him to try out total arrangements in a flexible way. His solution was to limit himself to standard colors from the tube and to work with preliminary designs using painted paper, which could be trimmed with scissors to try different size relationships. Once the right design had been found, it could easily be duplicated in a final painting, using the same proportions and the prepared color.

Albers has favored the square as a basic shape, partly for the visual reason that it is more amenable to adjustment than complex shapes (it always retains its squareness, being easily trimmed to a new size) and partly for psychological reasons. Among geometric shapes the square is the simplest which also suggests no common object beyond itself. A rectangle horizontally placed might suggest a wall panel or a house. A vertical rectangle might suggest a window or a tall building or even a man. A circle suggests a wheel. The true square—or its three-dimensional form, the cube—is in less common usage and is less likely to evoke object-associations. This enhances the purity of the work as a nonobjective creation. Furthermore, the square is the most stable shape. It does not roll like the circle, nor point elsewhere, like the triangle, lie down or balance upward, like the rectangle. It is self-contained, existential in its squareness.

The inflexibility of the square as a shape renders it correspondingly less adaptable than other shapes to expressive use as a symbol of personal feelings. It is only in size, coloring, and placement that it can be the vehicle for self-expressive differences in handling. Albers likes the tendency of the square to seem only itself and he consciously seeks a pure effect, yet by this careful placement, and by judicious relation of color-area to an ensemble, he inevitably achieves a personal expression. We will return to this at another point.

Perfect color matching in reproduction is not yet commercially practicable, and the tone relationships in our Plate IV are slightly different from those of the original; although giving a very good idea of it. The outer border has a little blue in it, which establishes a subtle relationship to the blue at the center and gives the border itself a red-violet or pinky rose tone. The second border—or call it a square—has a little red in it which relates to the outer border and makes the tone of this inner border slightly orange—that is, more pumpkin than mustard. The inner square is a soft blue. The warm, mixed tones occupy the greater area, balancing against the smaller, cooler, but purer blue. The result is visual equilibrium.

You may test this for yourself by holding your hand above the blue square, shutting off the top part of the picture. Immediately the blue seems too large. If next the blue is cut off with the hand, the pink and orange tones clash and are jarring. The lowered location of the orange and blue, in relation to top and bottom, is also important, giving greater "weight" and stability to the design and an unfolding, soaring effect above. Note that the top edges are in line, and the bottom, which further stabilizes the relationship. The design is all right upside down or on its side (try it!) but is definitely best as intended.

The detachment of Albers' work may seem to remove it from any connection with contemporary tensions, but it is still a protest in its way. It is uncompromisingly aloof and in the main is accessible only to the small group who regularly follow the advanced arts and to those like my reader who make the effort to understand. The measure of such a work's inaccessibility is the incredulity which often greets the information that Albers, a sophisticated man who taught at the Bauhaus and is now at Yale, spent a lifetime developing this kind of statement.

If Albers' painting represents a near ultimate in independence of expression, Naum Gabo's *Linear Construction in Space* [174] is not far behind; but with this difference, that Gabo experiments with materials—here, plastic with nylon thread—which are both contemporary and generally admired. Plastics of all kind have had a tremendous popular acceptance and, in their various guises, are liked for appearance as well as utility. Hence Gabo is touching something close to the contemporary taste and then transforming it through his independent vision into a nonobjective visual expression.

Although not emphasizing the accidental, Gabo shows a certain kinship with Pollock and Calder in the importance accorded to shifting patterns—here of light—in the total effect. A similar stress of change is seen in the strongly curving contours of the shape and its rich blend of detailed parts (the fine threads) in a complex three-dimensional unity. It is possible to see through the work to other parts of it and to its surrounding space, which adds other shifting effects, as one moves about. Here is a three-dimensional expression of the modern accent on change, realized with modern materials in a smoothly wrought, sophisticated unity. This is truly an abstract construction of our time. Yet it is this very element of sophistication which removes Gabo's construction from the common touch which its materials would encourage. While it is a positive statement, it is still for the elect.

As one looks over the "advanced" art of our time, among which I have tried to pick representative types, one sees increasing evidence that it is in conflict with many generally accepted values. In an age when an ever greater premium is placed on conformity, it is resolutely nonconformist. Where television and the photograph have made of visual realism a widespread means of popular communication, much advanced art turns away from visual realism entirely. Where popular opinion is carefully surveyed and generally followed by other makers of visual products, the advanced artist ignores it. And in an age when communication has been over simplified or made diverting or charming by the animated cartoon, comic book, and singing commercial, the artist remains relentlessly obscure and uncommunicative. It is commercial art, popular music, and the popular theater which speak for the public and form the artistic level to which the public responds understandingly. We must remember, too, that the "best" achievements in these areas are recognized as valid and of fine quality even by the avant-garde.

What function, then, does the advanced artist have? As one who revolts against the values of his age or subtitutes values of his own, how can he justify his place in it?

IV. Josef Albers: *Study for an Early Diary*. Winnetka, Ill.: Mr. and Mrs. J. W. Alsdorf Collection.

174. Naum Gabo: *Linear Construction in Space, No. 2.* 1949. Plastic and nylon thread. Collection the artist.

I believe that the separation of the advanced artist from the general culture, while real, is more evident than ever before mainly because of the larger part played by the general public today in the formation of taste. In the Renaissance and in most other periods the public had little to say about art, and while the general interest in art may have been greater, one wonders if a then advanced work, such as Botticelli's *Birth of Venus* or the even more advanced *Expulsion* by Masaccio, would have had any general understanding. Today the division is made clearer by the presence of an actively competing commercial art.

A sensitive minority is always more acutely aware of the imbalances of its age than is the majority. The strikingly divergent character of popular and advanced art today, in my opinion, is not a criticism of the positive aspects of our culture so much as a violent reaction to its negative aspects, such as our conformity and passive materialism in a time of world-wide upheaval. We have seen how the advanced artist's reaction may range from the violent expression of independence to a tranquil assertion of independent values.

Whatever the nature of their statement or protest, the avant garde are always experimental as artists. And the best of the artists in the popular field generally know what the fine artists are doing and are often experimental themselves. From the fine artists they draw new principles of design, new ways of seeing and organizing which are applied to their commercial products. Commercial art today would certainly not be the same without Alexander Calder, Brancusi, Mondrian, Matisse, Picasso, and even Kandinsky.

Most of us are too occupied with the specifics and external requirements of our daily lives to engage for ourselves in the free-ranging exploration of the artist. Whatever his subject, the artist performs a service that should be as vital in jarring loose the crystallizations of society as the bookkeeper's service is in helping to conserve and stabilize. If ours is an age of crisis, which in many ways it manifestly is, it would be a betrayal of our culture for the artist to reassert forms appropriate to the serene humanism of fifteenth-century Florence, or harmonies appropriate to Joseph Haydn's Vienna. That would be artistic whistling in the dark, as reflected in the typical *Saturday Evening Post* cover. If the artist achieves a modern tranquillity, it will have to be through modern symbols, or through old symbols reinterpreted. We may admire the great art of the past, learn from it, refresh and inspire ourselves with it, envy the security and coherence a particular culture appears to represent, and yet see the more clearly that the art of our time has its exciting qualities and, above all, is ours and of us. The advanced artist is performing a valuable function in his culture by symbolizing some of its deeper levels. He also supplies it with new and contemporary ways of seeing. The sound commercial artist is translating these discoveries functionally into an expression that can be understood and produced in our democratic society. But advanced art helps to shock us into being more contemporary—into greater awareness of what the contemporary means.

18-Criteria of Judgment

For many, figure skating is perhaps the easiest of all art forms to enjoy. The speed of the motion heightens its rhythmic effect and the gliding gives it smoothness and flow. Our response to the figures, whether they are simple or intricate, is essentially esthetic, although skating of any kind is likely to give a sense of freedom and of the joyous extension of the physical powers. The success of figure skating rests on the accomplished performance of a very few disciplined movements, which may be combined in different ways.

The reason we enjoy the trained performance more than that ordinarily seen on the country pond is that the trained performance makes fuller and visually more effective use of the medium. Figure skating is controlled movement of the body according to a pattern or design, and the trained skater has better control and more or better design than the untrained. Thus, control and design become criteria of good skating and combine to constitute what we call good form in it. They provide a basis for judgment of skating quality. Yet it is apparent at once that this is a relative standard. The state champion will have better "form" than the local, the national better than the state, and the Olympic champion—supposedly—best of all. Yet we may well enjoy seeing any of them perform, for the quality of form is also enjoyable at modest levels of intensity and refinement.

Anyone can make a stab at judging relative quality of skating, if given several performances to compare. But such judgment is much more difficult in the fine arts, for each of the fine arts includes so many more elements. Skating is essentially a pure art "form" and has relatively little "content." This immediately eliminates a vast range of complex and subjective overtones. Again, skating has one basic aspect of form—organized, rhythmic movement, while painting, for example, has size, shape, texture, hue, brightness, placement, *and* rhythm, with each of these elements subject to nuances of treatment and all combining in a final unified effect.

265

Establishing criteria of excellence for the execution of a forward circle on the skate, therefore, might seem relatively easy, because the position of the arms and hands, the bend of knees, and the angle of the body are the only variables, with each of these resulting from the natural adjustment of the body to the movement required. Even here, however, we cannot confidently speak of an absolute standard. It is currently considered good form for the skater executing such a turn to extend arms at about waist height with palms down and fingers together. His free leg, extended naturally and not far from the ice, in the course of the circle is swung from behind to a position ahead of the other foot. Flawlessly executed according to these criteria, the turn is undoubtedly a unified, flowing movement which brings esthetic satisfaction to the onlooker as well as to the participant.

However, it would be perfectly possible to execute this turn in a way which would still produce a unified visual effect, although involving different criteria. The free leg, for example, could be held higher at the start and be made to execute a greater swing. The palms of the hands could be held, initially, toward the body—in a plane vertical to the ground—and then be allowed to swing out, always in this plane. Other refinements would be easy to devise. Flawless execution of such a turn could again be a unified movement, bringing esthetic satisfaction to onlooker and executor. Is there any reason why such an alternative standard or set of criteria should not be equally acceptable to that currently followed? It may be argued that it would appear less "natural" and more stylized, but to insist on naturalness as a basic criterion of the art of movement is equally arbitrary. Some of the longest lasting dance forms, like those of the Javanese, are highly "unnatural," and the same could be true for skating.

It is thus apparent that even for as restricted and impersonal an art form as the skating of a circle, it is impossible to establish criteria of excellence which are not arbitrary. Fortunately, this need not disturb us. The presence of art quality in any degree implies arbitrariness. "Natural" movement tends not to be unified or at least not distinctively so, and it is the unifying element which marks the dance as distinct from ordinary movement. It may not matter so much, therefore, what the criteria of the particular skating turn are so long as there *are* criteria—or so long as there is the quality of form for which criteria can be devised.

Is this to suggest that *any* criteria will do, or that one set of criteria is as good as another? What if we required our skater to look up and wave at the audience when he was halfway around his circle? Would this be as "good" as the present concentration, and if so, why so? Certainly such an innovation would look grotesque or hilarious to a contemporary audience, but suppose it originated in the experience of some great champion. Such a gesture might subsequently become a stylized adjunct of the turn which audiences would be delighted to accept. It is conceivable that a turn without the salute could even come to be regarded as sacrilegious or outrageous to succeeding spectators. Many people do not know that the modern courtesy of tipping the hat originated in the medieval knight's practice of raising the visor of his helmet as a sign of peaceful approach. Original purpose may become lost or changed with time, while its formal embodiment continues.

Purpose (content) and form always exist in the art work, and their appearing absurd or great depends upon shifting criteria of excellence. Once it becomes accepted as a criterion that the skater salutes in the course of his turn, it is possible to compare performances and establish levels of excellence *on this basis,* just as in the turn under its present convention. The nature of art depends greatly upon underlying conventions of purpose and the accepted nature of form. They become ingrained in the culture, and this is why the experimental artist—the artist of the future —has such a difficult time. Without realizing it, perhaps, he is shifting the underlying premises.

If no single, absolute, and permanent standard exists for a perfect skating turn, the same is even more evident in the case of the infinitely richer and more complex expression of the fine arts. The fine arts are so much more complex that it is difficult to grasp the underlying current assumptions on which they are based or the criteria which reflect the specific working out of those assumptions.

The magnitude of the complexities involved may be revealed by comparing monuments of contrasting periods. Suppose that we seek to determine which is the "better" façade design, that of the Church of the Fourteen Saints [31] or that of the Tabernacle Church of Christ [32]. We may see this problem more clearly by trying to imagine the eighteenth-century church to be located in Columbus, Indiana, today, and the Columbus church in Germany in the eighteenth century. The very least reaction we could be sure of, in such case, would be confusion on the part of the local populace. Even in our relatively eclectic age, the baroque church would be too florid for a contemporary design and it would seem a reasonable assumption that the modern church would look far too plain, severe, and downright strange to those of the rococo taste. Yet each church was "modern" in its day and summed up tendencies that were then current. Clearly, one criterion of excellence in the fine arts would seem to be the fitness or promise of an art work for its particular time and place.

But what of those artists whose works were not appreciated until a later age? Fitness in the age, we see, is no absolute criterion, but is one *possible* criterion. We may inquire as to whether a work effectively expresses the style of its age and conclude that it is outstanding *in that respect.* We may investigate which works held the most portent for the future at a given time and conclude that such and such were outstanding in *that* respect. In short we are adapting the criteria to the nature of the achievement. For how can we say which is better, that an achievement sum up the best of its time, or that it speak for the future? We will return later to this concept of a changing basis of judgment, which I will call the *functional criterion.*

Meanwhile, let us look at the problem in the fine arts not in its complicated wholeness but in a deliberately narrowed range. Let us compare two very similar works by the same artist, Cranach's *Venus* [122] and his *Lucretia* [175] and let us compare them only as to quality of form. Which is the better? What we have previously noted relative to the *Venus* holds true for the *Lucretia,* that the artist's feeling for form is based on sensuously undulating contour and on a balanced arrangement of the light figure in its dark field. In these respects the two works are remarkably similar; yet there are differences. Notice the posture, for example. The *Venus* is standing with both feet on the ground, where the other has the weight mainly on one foot. The difference of effect this creates is that the body of the *Venus,* from the hips down, looks relatively static and at rest, while the torso seems to be swinging and to have movement. Lucretia's body is entirely in movement, or is exquisitely poised for it. Although her weight is on the right foot and her right hip swings out, the effect of movement to the left is marvelously countered by the extension of her left arm in the other direction and by the sweeping action of the veil. In the *Venus,* the veil is a rhythmically curving and flat shape which takes its place on the picture plane in a diagonal and side-paralleling sense. It looks static, almost "pinned" in place, in contrast to the free-moving arms and torso.

Notice, next, that Lucretia's right leg swells out more at the knee, and below it. This makes a rhythm of the outer contour of hip and leg, a wonderful, continuous, and repeating flow from ankle to breast. In the *Venus,* this curve is continuous only from the knee up; from the knee down it becomes straighter, stiffer. Venus's back is seen to be sharply in-curving, offering no counterrhythm to the swelling of the belly on the other side. Lucretia's left side is straighter, which helps to make of chest and hip a more continuous shape. In fact, the *Lucretia* is altogether a more unified shape, which tapers towards the hips from both head and foot. In the *Venus,* the arms, veil, head, headdress, necklace, torso, and thigh area all come closer to having independent design interest rather than being subordinate to a total shape having a visual climax.

From the foregoing it will be apparent why I consider *Lucretia* to have the better design of the two paintings. Within the terms which Cranach set for himself he achieved in it a more unified visual effect, less an assemblage of decorative parts. Nevertheless, the more exotic, distorted, and flatly modeled *Venus* will appeal to some tastes and, in ways, is closer to our contemporary orientation. It is more primitive and abstract, in contrast to the more classically graceful *Lucretia.* Have we no final standard then, even in such an "easy" problem as deciding between two similar works by the same artist and in respect only to form? Apparently not, for who is to say that the more primitive direction of the earlier work, the *Venus,* is any less valid than the more classical direction of the later? This discussion may show, rather, that through such careful analysis and comparison we discover *the nature of our own taste* and its specific referent in particular features of artistic organization. Armed with this knowledge, which we may designate as our own bias, we may approach art with more awareness and with a greater likelihood of enlarging and maturing our understanding of it.

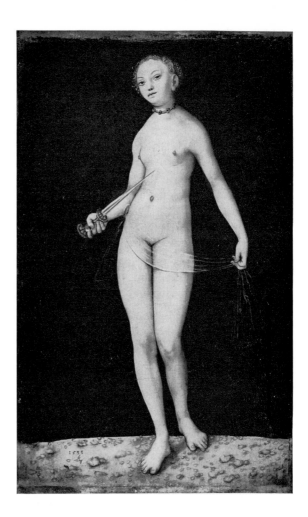

175. Lucas Cranach the Elder: *Lucretia.*
German. 1533. West Germany: National
Collection.

Thus, in judging between Cranach's two nudes, today's critic may
clash with Cranach's own taste and development. It is very important to
see this, for it presents the insoluble problem and the pathos of art evaluation. We approach not only one another but also art as strangers, whom
and which we cannot entirely understand; for as every artist likes his art,
so should we like it, if we could wholly understand him through it. There
exist then, varying sets of criteria of good art—those of the artist, those of
the observer, those of the era, of the nation, of the region, and so on. These
criteria may be understood as such or may be implicit only.

We shall understand the significance of this multiplicity of criteria
better if we turn next to the problem of relative excellence of content. It
can be a revealing experience to look from Cranach's *Lucretia* to Rembrandt's [176]. Although there are many other contrasts, these two paintings reveal in strikingly different emphasis the two great polarities of art
which are also its two great unities—form and content. In a way the whole
of the pictorial arts' tendencies is summed up in these two paintings.

To understand Rembrandt's more fully, we need to recall the story of
Lucretia. She was a Roman matron, renowned for her beauty and domes-

176. Rembrandt van Rijn: *Lucretia*. Dutch. 1664. Washington: National Gallery of Art, Andrew W. Mellon Collection.

tic virtue. A rival of her husband forced his attention upon her and for this she took her life with a dagger. It is a tragedy having a foundation in fact—one which Shakespeare himself used for its dramatic power. Indeed, Rembrandt, who was nearly a contemporary of Shakespeare, approaches the theme with a Shakespearean breadth. It is apparent that for Cranach

Lucretia was no more than the subject for a nude figure study. The dagger has a menacing sharpness, but the bland expression of the face and the handling of the pose suggest no concern whatever with the possible emotional realities of the situation.

Rembrandt's painting is another demonstration that the power of art goes beyond its subject. Lucretia's problem of feminine honor is not one which symbolizes a central or abiding concern, at least of our time; it is not a culturally fundamental issue whose solution would affect the direction of men's and women's lives and so that of their culture. Yet Rembrandt has brought to it a tenderness and delicacy, a warmth and passion which surpass the theme and invest it with a deep humanity. By comparison the Cranach appears, at most, knowing and sophisticated. In short, we have evidence again of what we have previously seen, that content becomes, ultimately, an expression of the values of the artist, of which his personality—revealed between the "lines" of his art—is an outpicturing. The theme itself may be misleading; it is only in the manner of its treatment that we come to grips with the inner significance of the work.

Can we speak of one value-level as superior to another? Is Rembrandt's humanity more desirable, more universal, ultimately more significant, than Cranach's sophistication, which is barely gracious and verges on hardness and the cynical? Many would feel so. Yet to make a final judgment, here, is to suppose a security as to ultimate values which the changing values of man through the ages would hardly support.

Imagine a man of superb physical coordination stabbing an innocent victim. We may conceive of the actual stabbing as being done with athletic grace, like a modern dance having a horrible reality. The murderer might even relish the act and impart a certain grim, stunning flourish to his efficient thrust. It is possible to consider this as a purely visualized action of the body, entirely apart from its consequences and apart from any question of morality. It is also possible to consider it solely on moral grounds. If we were trained dancers or connoisseurs of the dance, however, it might be difficult to put aside an instant recognition of the esthetic aspect of the act, even if we were appalled by its consequences. Form and content *may* be considered separately and one or the other ignored—except where we deal with the content of form itself. But if we are aware of both elements, it is impossible to avoid a total impression, *and this may involve mixed, even conflicting reactions.*

The above conception has an important bearing on our judgment of art. A man may have the power of visual coordination but in other aspects of his life be disorganized, frustrated, confused, bitter, even neurotic or psychotic. And through form symbolism these various aspects of his personality will leave more or less of a mark on his creation. When we look at an art work, we are confronting not only a creation of visual unity but a way of life. Cranach's refined and sensitive feeling for form is clear, whether we prefer it in its primitive or classical tendency, but the man Cranach as well as the artist Cranach is silently present in the *character* of his form. In any final choice between Rembrandt's and Cranach's versions of Lucretia, the hidden statements of the artists' nature and outlook are present, adding their coloration to the total effect, and influencing our judgment.

Art is a Gestalt, a final expression of countless interlocking factors of which the esthetic sensibility, the power to create visual unity and to make it intense, is but one aspect. It is this esthetic sensibility which motivates the artist, as such, but he cannot avoid symbolizing the rest of him—he is not just a dehumanized esthetic machine. And the "rest," in turn, causes him to give his organization its particular character. *The ultimate root variable is not form but content. Form is the root constant.* Form in any case will be expressive organization, but the particular character of its organization will be inexorably colored by other factors. Only the spider's web, the sea shell, the microscopic crystal, the enormous swirl of a spiral nebula, and the myriad other "designs" of nature lack these overtones. That is exactly why we do not speak of them as art, although we clearly see their "form." Amazing, awe-inspiring, or miraculous though they may seem, they yet lack human identification. They have certain *elements* of form in common with the artistic expression of man and so something mysteriously related to him, but they are impersonal. The smooth and weathered driftwood, the exquisite blue of the gentians on a rocky shore can never have the peculiar quality of a sculpture or painting; they have form alone.

The criteria of good art, accordingly, must relate to the expressions of individuals and of the time and place in which they live. To try to establish an ultimate standard is Utopian—implies determining ultimate values and the ultimate in human development. On the other hand, through intelligent examination of the art of the past or present, we may gain insight into the criteria that have existed and turn them to account in developing our own standards. We may discover ultimately to what extent our own criteria are part of the current stream and to what extent they may have independence and a personal character.

Within limits, moreover, we can reach conclusions as to quality *based on the evidence which art itself reveals*—the functional criteria, again. Study of contemporary experimental domestic architecture reveals, as we have previously seen, that it may be based on a close relation of house and site, on an intimate but practicable relation of interior and exterior, on the incorporation of functional structure into the design, on the design-use of the natural textures of material, on a flowing, open conception of space and plan—and so on. Once acquainted with these characteristics we can see how well a specific contemporary house embodies them, and which of two or more houses embodies them better. By noting variations or deviations we also achieve a growing awareness of the nature of the contemporary architectural esthetic.

In painting, where the emphasis is so strongly on form, often approached, today, with a reliance on spontaneity, how can we establish such a set of working criteria? In a sense, spontaneity contains within itself and implies a denial of standards. It is anarchic in tendency. If this is entirely inimical to what may be our particular orderly and perhaps traditional orientation, then we will simply not like such art. But if we see its cultural basis and approach it with the sympathy born of a contemporary fellowship, we may well find that many works, spontaneous or not, do achieve expressive unity. And then it becomes a case of testing their expressive content against our own values.

How does the brooding introspection of Mark Tobey [160] check with our own individual tendencies? Does the "organized chance" of Jackson Pollock [III] represent something positive and hopeful, or is it nihilistic, making unity only out of despair? Is Willem De Kooning's tortured personal experience [172] something which carries positive values for outsiders like ourselves? Are Josef Albers' serene squares [IV] a way to a poised coping with life, or are they only an escape from life into an unrelated but self-created and isolated inner security? The answers to these questions must be individually tested by the observer against his own needs and the perceptions of our time. The general answer will develop as succeeding generations achieve the perspective of their contrasting insights. Meanwhile we can do our best to see the underlying character of what is going on in art and, having considered the evidence, make our own tentative judgments.

Are there any criteria of good form which may be applied rather generally to the painting and sculpture of our time and yet allow them to be the flexible vehicle for expressing the current bewildering variety of underlying influences? A few such criteria might be these: respect for the material of art; exploitation of its texture and working qualities; de-emphasis of presentational elements; emphasis of visual elements; and finally, a concern for total organization in which the part may or may not retain individual interest—usually not. Beyond this is a splitting into subcriteria: spontaneity of form versus rational construction, adherence to a flat plane in painting versus maintenance of both plane and depth, and so on through countless refinements.

The above criteria may be applied regardless of the work's content or purpose, but it should be remembered that these latter factors may still influence our final judgment. A mural painting which has contemporary appeal as to form in the artist's studio may be completely out of scale when placed in its architectural setting. Thus we might judge it to be good in form but a bad mural. Another work may seem a success in a museum but a failure in a home or public building. Another work may have brilliant form but be repellent in content—De Kooning's *Woman* [172] may serve as an example.

In any age there are first-class artists and second or third. How are we to distinguish among them? Rembrandt's early work was thought better than his later by most of his contemporaries. Today the judgment is reversed. Rembrandt's late paintings are considered both more "modern" and greater. Johann Sebastian Bach was thought inferior to his sons by many contemporaries and followers. Today, the sons are recognized as more "modern" than their father, but they are not considered as great composers. In short, newness or modernity in a given period is no guarantee of ultimate esteem.

And how are we to distinguish in quality among experimental works? Can we tell a good nonobjective work from a less good, or from a bad? The answer to these questions is that we can make such judgments if willing to establish arbitrary—and therefore preferably tentative and hypothetical—criteria. Rest assured that the museum director, the connoisseur, and the professional critic are all operating from such criteria. No one has found the key to infallibility in the judgment of art.

However, some criteria may be more fruitful and dynamic than others. The evidence of the centuries—which may be displaced eventually but is as good evidence as we have—even indicates that some criteria are dead wrong. An example would be a judgment based on excellence of imitation alone, or on a lofty theme alone. But even assuming the need for some unifying organization before the work can be considered to have art quality, how can we identify superiority of such form? Criteria of excellence in this regard, as we have earlier seen, have been historically varied and are more likely to reflect their period and the nature of the individual making them than any stable criteria. In the tendency of the art of a period, lies the tendency of its criticism.

One standard which may be tentatively applied to the art of any period is that the particular form of the art work must have *expressive qualities as well as organization.* It must not only appeal to our sense of order—a floor pattern or wallpaper design may do that—but heighten our perception in so doing, either intellectually, emotionally, or both. This distinction will be brought out by comparing two contemporary works of the same type—mobiles, one by Alexander Calder [138] and one in a fine midwestern restaurant [177].

Whereas Calder's shapes form a cluster that gives definition to the area in which they move, the shapes in the other mobile appear too crowded for their size, an effect exaggerated by the inept placement of the small shape at the left, which seems almost to be flying away from the others and to have little to do with them spatially. Compare, also, the look of the individual shapes in the two works. Calder's are considerably more varied and daring—in the sense of departing from the conventional geometric. The ultimate virtue and test of comparative quality, however, lies not in variety, subtlety, or daring but in the expressiveness with which they are wrought. It is the intensity and wholeness of Calder's perception which make the other mobile look comparatively pedestrian and clumsy. There are no exact standards for such comparisons, and the basis for them may have to be derived from extensive personal experience.

Even though it is influenced by a myriad of underlying factors and is not the only aspect of quality in art, form is and will always be the great unifier. The construction of a discriminating personal taste does not call for liking every work of art in all its aspects, but does call for recognizing the positive qualities in art, whatever they may be. Form is their vehicle and is itself positive because it is unifying.

177. Restaurant mobile.

This may be evident in a comparison of Seymour Lipton's *Sanctuary* and Max Bill's *Rhythm in Space* [178 and 179]. Here we see such contrasting positive approaches to design. Bill makes the most of his smooth material's potential for purity of surface and sheerness of flow. Lipton produces a textured, more emotional surface and handles the curving forms, not with the continuous flowing ease of Bill's work, but in stages, giving an organic look, a sense of every part having its own character and of being in touch with a thoughtful and ardent hand. Bill's is cooler and less troubled.

I showed photographs of these two works to a young boy and asked him which he liked better. "I like them both," he said, "but they are different because the one on the left [it was Lipton's] has some meaning," a precocious comment for a youth, but certainly revealing that he responded positively and with insight to the sculptures. Lipton's work *is* thoughtful, directed inward in the clumsily tender protection of its great folds. Bill's is more open and outgoing, free, and joyous.

Whether we prefer the introspective richness of Lipton's work or the spirited freedom of the other is a matter of personal values. It is quite possible to respond to both; and indeed, these works may be taken as examples of the positive variety and power of abstract art and of its capability of combining form and content in a significant contemporary statement.

The art work may have its weaknesses of content and its strength of form, or vice versa. But the question of what constitutes weakness or strength of *content* is relative to the *values* of the observer, whereas the question of what constitutes weakness or strength of *form* is relative to his

178. Seymour Lipton: *Sanctuary*. 1953. Nickel-silver. New York: The Museum of Modern Art.

powers and experience of *esthetic integration.* Through the centuries man's attitude toward the content which an art work represents may change more than his appraisal of its esthetic worth. We can no longer accept, or at least not entirely, the values of primitive society which produced the "primitive's" particular form of art, yet we can enjoy that art.

The problem of developing criteria of judgment in art is an extension of one's development as a person. By analysis we may discover the nature of art criteria in the past and present, but those we finally prefer will be a projection of ourselves. There are no finalities among such judgments, and ours is only a part of the great mosaic which constitutes the taste and culture of a period. Every growing insight, every developing point of view contributes its glint to the luster of the whole. A house like the one architect Eduardo Catalano designed for himself [180 and 181] is a contribution to the culture of a larger sort. Its enormous wooden roof, 87 feet across and only 2¼ inches thick, is a hyperbolic paraboloid supported

179. Max Bill: *Form in Space*. Swiss. 1947–1948. Plaster. Private collection.

180. Eduardo F. Catalano, architect: Eduardo F. Catalano residence. 1955. Raleigh, N. C. (Ezra Stoller photo)

structurally at only two points. In effect it is all shell, with structural members eliminated. The inside is arranged so that areas requiring privacy are screened from the outside by the points where the roof-wall dips down to earth. But the living area [181] is placed where the shell opens out, inviting, with its sweep, a soaring vista. This house is profoundly experimental and may or may not be developed further as a type or have any general application in domestic housing. Yet it is encouraging that our culture leaves room for imaginative experiments, and that such daring construction as this is taking place. These are positive elements on which the future may build.

Form remains, in art, the great factor of cultural continuity. However achieved, it has the power to heighten our sensibilities. This may range from pure esthetic delight in a flowing abstract form [179, 180] to the more complex appeal of Rembrandt's works [4 and 130], but however manifest, it is a two-way experience, requiring both artist and observer. Certainly as observer you are engaging in a creative, form-making, and interpretive act as you, like Cézanne, "realize" the art work.

Changing cultures give form a new guise and different personalities permit it thousands of variations, but all these outer differences still represent a common and deep unifying impulse in man. It is present from the very beginning in art. The cave painting at Font-de-Gaume in France [182] was made many thousands of years ago, yet today we recognize it as a work of art of high quality. What is it about art that gives it such continuity over the millennia? Could it be that in the unifying impulse manifesting itself as form we are reaching close to the divine in man? Or is it no more than a neuro-integrative response to a changing environment? Whatever it is, it brings us close to that prehistoric brute, so close that we know he had a deep core of refinement, the equal of ours, however outwardly crude his ways. The art of succeeding millennia reveals countless addi-

181. Catalano residence, interior at screen wall. (Ezra Stoller photo)

tional or different elements, but the sustaining, unifying impulse at the root of all is unchanging. In looking at a contemporary abstract form [179] and the prehistoric painting, we are struck both with how man changes and with the constancy of his creative source. It is the marvel of art to be able to encompass both elements.

According to our own values we will find admirable or repellent the particular culture or personality manifest in art, but form seems to touch something more fundamental: deeper than culture, prior to the personality. Perhaps it is this fundamental creative and unifying impulse in man that is art's most constructive aspect, that makes it most refreshing and renewing to our spirit, that suggests our continuing human kinship as far back as the Font-de-Gaume cave painter and so with all mankind. At the core of all art, it may move us to compassion even in a manifestation we otherwise condemn or despise. It is as though through form we were putting to our own use the creative wellspring of nature.

The oak tree pushes out its branches in some adjustment to its environment as it develops, but it must still remain oaklike. The shaping force in the chromosomes of all living things controls the basic form of their growth. Man's physical embodiment, too, is so controlled; but only he can generate new forms—forms which hide in their outer appearance man's inner appearance.

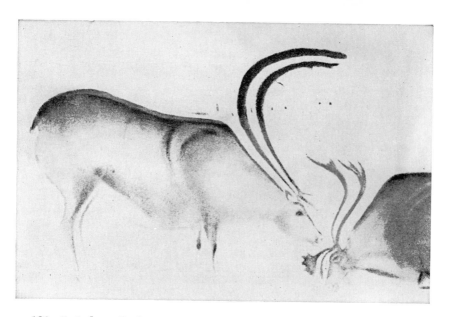

182. *Reindeer*. Prehistoric cave painting. Font-de-Gaume, France. (Photo after Breuil)

Even the uncertain, the transitional, the tragic may be dignified with form—and indeed often have been in the history of man. In this way the great artist has contributed an integrative beauty even to somber or unpleasant reality. If every age has large numbers of artists whose level of achievement is inconsiderable or overrated, the prophets of art and the men of high general competence have all too often been depreciated. Here is the more reason for looking into art not only with a keen eye, but with an open heart and mind.

Styles in Brief and Some Additional Concepts

Introduction

The vast majority of words have variable meanings. We assign meanings to them. And we may not assign the same meaning that an author has or thinks he has. These assignations of meaning depend partly on our knowledge of past and present usage and partly on our predilections. The use of words is a form of self-expression, as well as of communication.

The hazards involved in exactly comprehending individual words are compounded when the words are used to define. If I say, "*Art* is expressive organization in terms of a medium," one has to know what is meant by "expressive," "organization," and "medium"—all of which are open to a variety of assignations. And, even knowing the intended meanings, one still has to accept the statement as a personal projection, as a hypothesis.

The function of definitions in art, therefore, is to derive an understanding of usage and to facilitate communication, rather than to reveal ultimates. Some of the terms that have been used in this book and that follow are reasonably objective and beyond dispute. Others—like that just given of *art*—are only the statements of a working hypothesis, based on some evidence. Taken any other way, definitions are a block to the enlargement of awareness, rather than a source of enlightenment.

Generally speaking, the more abstract the word, the more difficult it is to assign meanings—through usage or definition—which will be understood clearly. This occurs especially when words or thoughts are rich in connotative potential. For example, what do we mean by *classic art?* The art of a certain period in time? The art expressing a certain style? The works of certain key individuals? All the works of a particular period? The art revealing a certain philosophy? The art of a certain period emphasizing certain materials? The theater, dance, and literature as well as the fine arts, or only the latter? A generic style applicable in any period, as the "classic" design of a refrigerator?

When the term *classic art* is used, it immediately arouses in the hearer or reader a composite awareness influenced by the possibilities indicated above and by others, including reactions of an emotional sort, predispositions for or against it, opinions of it held by people whom one respects or dislikes, and the general interaction of all these associations with the nature of one's personality. Small wonder that no single definition of *classic art* can be adequate! Even to define its period is arbitrary. To some people, it includes both Greek and Roman art. Others think of it as primarily the art of the fourth and fifth centuries, B.C., and for a long time many considered it primarily in its Roman phase.

This points to the advantage of usage over definition—or of definition enriched by usage. What follows is in some instances specific, limited, and reliable. In others it is hypothetical, suggestive, and arbitrarily selective. In our reading in any field we have the sometimes deceptive choice between the reliable and the unreliable, deceptive because the unreliable often is the more fruitful, as the objective phenomenon may also have provocative and "unreliable" overtones. For the reader who hopes to continue looking into art, vocabulary beyond that employed in the text of this book will be needed, and as many writers assume a background in this respect which is not easy to acquire, a few of the more important words and terms follow. Books have been written about some of them and they are presented here only as an introduction or, if you will, as a challenge to a broader approach to art.

Beauty and Ugliness

Beauty is an extremely difficult concept, concerning which opposite views may logically be taken, depending on the underlying assumptions. If we seek a general definition, a key question is the "location" of beauty. Is the beauty in the object or is it only fancied to be there—a projection by the person seeing it? Plato took the position that Beauty is an absolute, eternal thing, of which material manifestations are but imperfect hints or shadows. Moreover, in its transcendental state, Beauty is synonymous, for Plato, with the True and the Good—a position taken again over two thousand years later by John Keats.

It is clear that to adopt such a position one must assume the existence of transcendental reality; yet despite logical attempts since the beginning of man's speculation to demonstrate such Reality, it finally becomes a matter of belief or of faith. Believers in earthly beauty as the shadow or aspect of a transcendental Beauty have difficulty in accounting for different opinions as to beauty. Why do the artificially distended lips of some African tribeswomen seem beautiful, or at least attractive, to their men, but queer, or even ugly, to us? If beauty resides in the object as a reflection of a higher Beauty, how are we to determine who is right in perceiving or not perceiving it? If we decide that our judgment should be better than that of the native—a very tenuous presumption—we place ourselves in the position of granting that a point of view, the native's, can be projective. If we assume the native is right, then we admit that our interpretation of unattractiveness is an erroneous projection.

Believers in an ultimate Beauty have tried various ways of solving this dilemma. Clearly, if there is an absolute Beauty, the native woman's appearance either reflects it or does not. If one sees beauty there, he is either right or wrong. The believer in absolute Beauty is thus forced to take the position that those having views opposite his own are simply unable to see the beauty that is truly there. But who is to be the final judge when such disputes occur? If it is argued that God is the final judge, the mortal believer in absolute Beauty is still left with the lack of assurance as to which is the projected, erroneous beauty and which is the reliable hint of the True and the Good. Beyond doubt, the transcendental Beauty theory is difficult to sustain in application.

On the other hand, suppose we assume the converse, that beauty is entirely projected by the observer. In this case we have to account for some things seeming more beautiful than others. Why is the average flower more "beautiful" to most people than, say, is the average stone of comparable size? If it is argued that the flower has more apparent visual organization, then this is an admission that the quality which evokes the sense of beauty is inherent in the flower and therefore is not entirely projected. It is only "realized" by projection, by interaction of certain features already in the object with the organizing sensitivity of the observer.

An alternative solution to the dilemma of such positions—of which the above are but two of many—is to take the new position that while it may be interesting and even enlightening to ponder the question "What is beauty?", in the end it is the wrong question to ask, that more fruitful questions would be, "What conception of beauty is evidenced by the contemporary esthetic? How does such a conception work for me in achieving a personal and meaningful sense of beauty in my own life?"

The contemporary esthetic at the level of commercial art has two main and overlapping conceptions. The first sees beauty as that which esthetically catches and holds the public eye, like a successful new automobile model. Beauty would thus be the projection of public taste, reached through commercial art by trial and error. The second conception sees beauty as the harmonious relation of function and appearance. Public acceptance is still important, but there is a canon or principle of beauty involved here. The contemporary esthetic at the cultivated level inclines toward the second of the commercial directions and, generally, toward regarding beauty as expressive form.

Finally, we come to the approach which seeks neither to arrive at an ultimate definition of beauty nor at a definition related to cultural manifestation but sees beauty as *that which, through form, evokes a deeply satisfying awareness or feeling in the individual.* This would make beauty broader in its application than art, if by art is meant not form alone, but expressive form. If a sunset evoked a deeply satisfying awareness through its colors and cloud shapes, it would qualify as beautiful under the above arbitrary premise; yet it would not be art, for it is non-expressive. The same sunset might have no such appeal for another person and, clearly, would not be beautiful to him. According to this conception, the beauty does not reside, at least not primarily, in the sunset but is an individual projection; and the question of whether it is entirely projective is considered irrelevant, because the test of beauty is in the reaction of the observer.

The qualifying words "deeply satisfying" would distinguish the beautiful from the *pretty,* the *handsome,* or the *attractive*—all aspects of satisfying form but in a less profoundly affective way. Hence the distinction between a beautiful woman and a pretty one—highly projective and personal, yet a distinction for which most people feel the need.

It will be apparent that beauty is a word the meaning of which has been approached in ways varying from the purely theoretical to the pragmatic, with complications in all approaches. A discussion like the foregoing can serve only to suggest the main directions and to provide a starting point for further exploration. In general, the trend has been to see beauty as a projection by the observer—that is, it is largely, if not entirely, added to the object by the observer. The trend is also toward the acceptance of beauty as an esthetic value—that is, related to a sense of form.

Ugliness, an equally difficult concept, is discussable, like beauty, in theoretical terms, as culturally defined, and as an individual reaction. One of the theoretical problems is the extent to which ugliness is merely the lack of beauty, and the extent to which it has positive characteristics, or antibeauty. In terms of individual projection, a good working hypothesis is that *ugliness is that which through form or its noticeable absence evokes an awareness or feeling of deep repulsion.* The ugly would be that which "painfully disturbs a previously accepted esthetic ideal."

A complication here, as in the individual interpretation of beauty, lies in the question of nonesthetic influences. The funnel of a tornado may seem beautiful or ugly, depending upon one's past associations, and it is possible to conceive of its appearing beautiful *and* ugly—that is, of its being conflictingly evocative. The storm-tossed ocean may be exhilaratingly beautiful to one person, menacingly ugly to another, or evoke both effects for a third.

The term "noticeable absence" of form was introduced in the definition to admit as ugly certain jukebox designs, the hodgepodge of crowded neon lights in a narrow commercial street, the confused appearance of a junkyard, and so on, although even these may appear attractive or even beautiful to certain perceptions. It is an irony of human reaction to the world that the seeming polarities of beauty and ugliness should on occasion be interchangeable.

The term "deep repulsion" was introduced to distinguish the ugly from the *homely,* the *garish,* the *unattractive,* and so on, which are other aspects of repellent form, but less potently affective.

Greatness in Art

Another concept left out of the main text for reasons of its debatability and projective breadth is that of *great art,* which may be defined for discussion purposes as expressive form which epitomizes its time or becomes importantly significant for a later time. The question of what epitomizes the time in art is itself so debatable that it leaves the definition perhaps too open-ended. That is, the word "epitomize" presupposes in the things epitomized a degree of unity which may not be present. The things abstracted may be too complex for inclusive representation. However, this very openness of terminology permits contrasting epitomes to be included. Thus Pennsylvania Station in New York, a modern derivative of the ancient Baths of Caracalla in Rome, epitomizes among other aspects of early twentieth-century America its eclecticism, love of size, and ingenuity (the vaulting in the station is actually plaster hung on wires), but ignores this country's tremendous industrialism, which, for example, might be epitomized architecturally by the Ford River Rouge plant at Detroit.

Perhaps it is not unreasonable to suggest that these contrasting monuments—the one still recognized as a superior example of industrial building—are both great monuments of their time, representing different facets of the culture. Whether they will stand the test of the ages, however, is another matter, and we must distinguish between "great art" that is outstandingly exemplary of its culture and "great art" that has a profound appeal for succeeding cultures.

Greatness may also be interpreted in terms of originality, either appreciated or unappreciated in its day. The houses Frank Lloyd Wright built at the turn of the century did not epitomize any particular aspect of American culture, but in terms of architectural design and a philosophy of architecture were strikingly fresh, if not completely new in principle. They and Wright's succeeding buildings undoubtedly influenced a whole generation of young architects, including many in Europe—with far-reaching consequences for modern architecture. Wright provides a particularly clear demonstration that the atypical avant-garde, who may even scorn and denounce their time, may yet have claim to greatness, possibly more so than the more obvious candidates. The buildings of McKim, Mead and White serviced more aspects of American life than Wright's, were more in keeping with the prevailing cultivated taste of the day, and also influenced a generation of architects. By the above terms they have their claim to greatness, but it is the nonconformist, Wright, who appears to have run away with the final honors.

Fortunately, not all terms used in art are as amorphous or open to different approaches as those just discussed. Those that follow have clearer boundaries.

Style and Styles

Style has been defined as a characteristic way of doing something. We speak of a tennis player who habitually swings the racquet close to his body as having a "cramped style" of play. A chess player who constantly attacks has a "forcing style." The definition is broad enough to cover such applications. In the arts, some writers have emphasized the distinction between style and technique, defining *technique* as the method of working with particular tools and media, and *style* as the distinctiveness of one formal expression as compared with another. Hence it would be improper to speak of a fresco style as such—that is a technique—but proper to speak of Piero della Francesca's fresco style. This is a useful distinction because it emphasizes the difference between the peculiar demands, opportunities, or limitations of tool and medium and the liberating insight of form.

It must be conceded, however, that in practice many writers tend to blur this distinction because of the extraordinarily forceful effect of medium on the formal outcome. The flat shapes of the typical woodcut, for example, although an aspect of the technique, give to woodcuts generally such a characteristic look that the term "woodcut style" does suggest formal qualities which relate strongly to a medium and the techniques of working it. But the distinction between style and technique should be kept in mind, for it marks the important difference between the technician on the one hand and the artist on the other, the special aptitudes of each not always being combined in the same person or revealed in a single work.

Style is also a concept having an extremely broad application. By clarifying what we mean in the given instance, we can speak of the style of a whole culture, even as we can speak of the style of a single artist during a brief period within that culture. By the style of a culture we would mean all those esthetic aspects of the culture having continuity through it. No single one of these—as the persistence of the Doric order in ancient art—but rather the total effect of many elements would mark the culture's style. Because of the tendency of stylistic elements to change or develop, however, the application of style to a whole culture must characterize it so broadly as to have relatively little use.

Stylistic movements of a shorter duration within the culture, on the other hand, may be quite distinct and, if recognized, make clearer the nature of that period. Some of the most important of these movements will now be characterized briefly. We will look first at those which relate to the classical past.

Classicism and Classical Revivals

Classicism is the application of knowledge gained from the ancient Greek or Roman cultures which spanned the period roughly from 1500 B.C. to 500 A.D. In its motivation, classicism comes from admiration for ancient art and literature, for the ancient, rational approach to philosophy and life, for the ancient emphasis on moderation and on the dignity of man, and for a legal system in which boundaries of power and the rights of citizens were codified. These various elements have not aroused equal interest in all succeeding ages, but the influence of the classical culture never entirely died out, and in certain periods it achieved the status of a pervasive revival.

In *classical or ancient art* is revealed a rich cultural development which took place in a liberal atmosphere, reasonably open to free expression and inquiry—in contrast to the rigidly autocratic and relatively less developing cultures of ancient Egypt and the ancient Near East. As a result, it is not easy to find stylistic qualities which were a unifying factor throughout the whole classical period, although admiration for the human figure and a concern with man and his manlike gods [14, 129, 141, 148] was continuous. Sculpture and architecture were the primary arts and on the whole were treated with a consistent respect for human scale and a subtle feeling for proportion and the visual relation of masses. Classical architecture developed the three orders—Doric, Ionic, Corinthian—the peripteral, columned temple and in Roman times, the dome. The Roman discovery of concrete opened new structural possibilities, and Roman engineering skill manifested itself in great public baths, stadiums, and aqueducts. All of these were developed in the typical classical style of their day.

Carolingian Classicism was the first classical revival, taking place under Charlemagne, after he became emperor of the Holy Roman Empire in 800 A.D. He supported research in classical writings, the copying of classical manuscripts, and a study of ancient monuments. The influence of his short-lived classicism was great, for it stimulated an enduring interest in classical scholarship in centers of learning all over Europe.

Renaissance Classicism had its heyday in the fifteenth and early sixteenth centuries in Italy, whence it spread throughout Europe. It was strongly influenced in philosophy by the idealism of Plato (Artistotle had a greater following in the period preceding), in architecture by the writings of Vitruvius, an ancient Roman engineer, and in both architecture and sculpture (and indirectly in painting) by the many ancient remains which were unearthed or were still standing. Although borrowing extensively from these sources, the Italian Renaissance [29, 115, 121] developed its own distinctive and creative expression which in turn was freely borrowed from and creatively developed by countries to the north [18, 120, 122].

Neoclassicism was the classical revival of the late eighteenth and early nineteenth centuries, particularly in France, Germany, and England. It was characterized by a more extensive study of classical texts and by more archeologically exact referral to ancient monuments, based on systematic excavations. Napoleon was an enthusiastic neoclassicist, and his particular style became known as *Empire*. Neoclassicism in architecture split into two directions, the *Roman Revival* (for example, the Capitol at Washington, D. C.), typically employing the dome, the Ionic or Corinthian order, and Roman columnar proportions; and the more restrained *Greek Revival* (Second Bank of the United States, Philadelphia), typically employing the Doric order and the façade proportions of such ancient Greek temples as the Theseum and Parthenon at Athens.

While neoclassicism is a distinct style, it lacked the creative freedom of Renaissance Classicism and tended toward the academic. In painting and sculpture, the best neoclassicists, like Louis David, Dominique Ingres, and Antonio Canova, achieved a clarity and refinement having individual expressiveness. The painters lacked original classic sources and so turned to Renaissance classicists, especially to Raphael, for inspiration. The restraints of neoclassicism in contrast to the license of Romanticism (see below) reflected the tensions of a transitional period.

Academicism (reflected in academic art), loosely related to neoclassicism, is the uncreative adherence to the canons of artistic excellence of the national academies of art. Founded in the seventeenth century in France, the national academy as an institution spread to other countries and has consistently had classicistic tendencies. In the nineteenth century, academic art became particularly sterile, adhering to canons which inhibited formal expressiveness. Even subject matter itself was limited, a moral theme drawn from history or mythology being considered the most proper. Although academic art was often technically competent, it was and remains the least creative manifestation of classicism.

The Early Christian and Byzantine Period

In our brief review of styles we now turn back to the period beginning with the political acceptance of Christianity under the Emperor Constantine, in 323. The consequent emergence of Christianity from the status of a persecuted, underground movement coincided with the continued growth of two seats of power within the Roman empire: Rome and Byzantium. The latter was renamed Constantinople and became the empire's capital, but rulers in the west were virtually independent. Thus the declining years of the empire witnessed the rise of its eastern branch as the more powerful element, having its own distinctive and orientalized art in the service of the Church. This is Byzantine art, which favored the dome and the central plan in architecture. In Italy, where church architecture was chiefly based on the basilica or long nave [21], other classical elements persisted—for example, in the sculpture on sarcophagi. The mosaic, a major art form in both east and west, shifted from classical tendencies to a flatter, more decorative treatment under influence from the east. The major influx of eastern influence, however, came in the sixth century, when Ravenna, which had been capital of the western branch of the empire for over a century, was conquered by the forces of Justinian, emperor of the Byzantine branch. Thus the classic tradition passed to our medieval period with both eastern and western elements.

The Medieval Period

The period from about 1000 to 1450 was that in which the most exclusively Western culture developed. Even here, as indicated, the classic past was an influence; the great scholar Thomas Aquinas spent a lifetime attempting to reconcile the wisdom of the ancients, particularly Aristotle, with the doctrines of the Church. Despite persisting classical elements, however, the medieval period traveled its own cultural and artistic way. In the arts, architecture [23, 24, 25]—richly adorned with sculpture [149, 150, 152]—was the leading expression. In the *Romanesque* period (*c.* 1000–*c.* 1200), the round arch predominated and vaulting was sustained by the inert mass of the outer walls. In the *Gothic* period (after 1200), the arch became pointed and the weight was supported by a system of balanced thrusts, a dynamic principle. This made possible an enormously high nave and glassed-over clerestories such as we saw in Regensburg [23].

The Baroque

Baroque art flourished in the seventeenth century and in the first half of the eighteenth. It combined some elements of classicism and some of medieval mysticism in a creative and complex synthesis. Empirical science and ardent piety flourished simultaneously in a period of absolute monarchies and of the growth of capitalism and world trade. The Baroque style is based upon painterly treatment of surface, emphasis on spatial depth and on over-all unity at the expense of the part. It is emotionally complex, ardent, and difficult to grasp [20, 92, 130, 176].

Rococo art is the eighteenth-century phase of the Baroque, tending on the one hand towards the simplicity and clarity which became Neo-classicism [123], and on the other hand toward an even more complex expression of Baroque principles. In this phase, which flourished in Southern Germany, asymmetrical forms, particularly the wave and the shell, were joyously combined with architecture, sculpture, and painting in highly complex and rich effects [30, 26].

Romanticism

Romanticism is not a style but a philosophy or an attitude toward life which may strongly influence style. It is exclusive to no epoch but was an important facet of the mood of the late eighteenth and early nineteenth centuries. It was in part a reaction to the insecurity created by the political unrest in Europe, by the rapid growth of a new industrial social order having no cultural tradition, by the mixed religious disillusion and social optimism occasioned by the discoveries of science, and by the individual's sense of loneliness in a world of transition, secured much less than formerly by group solidarity and a common faith.

As a philosophy, romanticism is related to late-eighteenth-century idealism, which maintained that all reality is ultimately spiritual, that the Absolute is Spirit and is approached not by reason but creatively, by intuition and self-expression. Hence nature is the great source of romantic inspiration, the way to discovery of the Absolute, for it is untainted with the limitations of man. This love of the "natural" accounts for the abandonment of the formal garden and the rise of the "English" garden with its natural, winding paths. Man wanders in this world and surrenders to it instead of subjecting it to his confident will. Romanticism abjured formalism generally, opposed rules, conventions, and a rational approach to life. Hence it is in definite opposition to classicism. Romanticism favored, rather, the values of sincerity, spontaneity, and passion. This points to romantic tendencies in contemporary art.

In nineteenth-century art, the romantic attitude tended toward realism—thus permitting nature to speak for itself—or toward a coloristic and textural treatment of surface to create an emotional effect. The landscape and natural subjects became very popular.

Among the romantic philosophers were Jean Jacques Rousseau, Friedrich von Schelling, and Ralph Waldo Emerson (whose philosophy of transcendentalism is essentially romantic). Among writers and poets were Victor Hugo, William Wordsworth, and Lord Byron. Among artists were Eugene Delacroix, Thomas Cole, and Camille Corot.

Architecture's contribution to romanticism was the *Gothic Revival*, the richness, mystery, and emotional tension of Gothic decoration and space having a natural appeal for the unsettled, idealistic, and yearning romantic spirit.

Its lack of systematic doctrine gives Romanticism—as initially indicated—the quality of a mood or feeling toward life. It may evolve in any situation or time where the individual feels himself isolated in a hostile or inhospitable society. According to one viewpoint, idealism of any sort is a form of romanticism, and hence neoclassicism would be merely a rational attempt, rather than a typically intuitive or emotional one, to satisfy a romantic longing for a better world. Perhaps a new term, like rational romanticism, might be employed for such expressions. In any case, romanticism's typical manifestation was personal, emotional, idealistic, intuitive, nostalgic, and nature-loving.

Realism and Naturalism

Romanticism is not a style of art but a cultural condition, mood, and philosophy which affected art. Realism is both an art movement and a philosophy. Naturalism is a philosophy, and its connection or lack of connection with the arts should be understood.

Philosophically, *realism* holds that there are realities independent of the mind and also independent of and superior to any physical embodiment. That is, the idea of a chair has a higher reality than the actual chair and already existed as Reality before anyone thought of it. This is the position of Plato.

One also hears of Platonic *idealism*. Plato's emphasis on the higher reality of idea does make him in certain respects an idealist. However, the idealists do not agree with Plato that ideas may exist independent of mind. That is a central tenet of realism.

In contrast, *realism in art* (*c.* 1830–1860) holds 1) that any subject matter in the external world is suitable material for the artist, and 2) that the subject matter should be rendered in a presentational or imitative way.

Realism in art is thus closer in its implications to *naturalism*, which holds, as a philosophy, that it is not necessary to predicate a supernatural cause of the universe, that the universe is self-contained, self-operating, purposeless, and deterministic. According to this belief, human life and behavior are in all respects the product of natural events, and man's highest good should be pursued under natural conditions without expectation of a supernatural destiny. Hence in art, the naturalist artist or writer would not look for hidden meanings or a supernatural "essence" but would serve as a simple reporter. Since, according to naturalism, all judgments of good and bad are conventional, the artist should avoid approving or disapproving, merely revealing environment and circumstance as he sees them. It is through a better knowledge of these that man can achieve a more intelligently "natural" place in his world.

It is clear that realism in art has nothing to do with realism in philosophy but is close to philosophical naturalism. Great modern naturalist writers were Gustave Flaubert and, above all, Emile Zola; the greatest avowed realist in art was Gustave Courbet. Although Courbet said that anything was fit subject for the artist and boasted of his realism, he was not able to escape entirely from the romantic tendencies against which he reacted. Nevertheless, the trend away from meaning which realism and naturalism represented eventually helped to free the artist for the experiments with form that came at the end of the century. Realism in art *as a movement* should be thought of in the above connection, under Courbet, culminating in impressionism and close in spirit to naturalism. On the other hand, realism *as an illusionistic technique* served both romanticism and neoclassicism.

Some writers have tried to distinguish between realism and naturalism in art in such a way as to bring them into closer approximation with the distinction of the same terms in philosophy. Thus realism and naturalism in art would both employ imitative, rather presentational techniques, but naturalism would be satisfied with this and nothing more, whereas realism would seek, additionally, a "higher" or more ultimate significance. The Roman senator [148] would be an example of naturalism and the Caesar Augustus [129], with its larger aim of epitomizing, an example of realism.

While this distinction has interesting possibilities, it is very hard to apply precisely. Accordingly, the term naturalism is not used very much in art literature, most writers letting realism double for both meanings.

More recent offshots of realism are *American regionalism,* the recording of regional countryside and events in this country during the 1920's and 1930's (Grant Wood and John Steuart Curry); *social realism* (Jack Levine, Ben Shahn, and Reginald Marsh), inspired partly by the experience of the artists during the depression of the 1930's; and *magic realism,* exaggeratedly presentational and related to surrealism and the subconscious (Dali and Howard).

A form of realism which is not so remote from Courbet's general acceptance of the world as subject matter is *genre,* the recording of everyday life. Genre is almost as old as art itself, but it did not always employ a presentational technique. Ancient Egyptian, Mesopotamian, and Assyrian genre scenes are all highly stylized and are "realistic" in the psychological sense of suggesting a group, event, or situation. Thus, the Egyptian pharoah's wives are sometimes depicted in much smaller proportion than the pharoah himself, indicating their lesser importance; yet they may be still included as part of a scene [116]. Genre scenes appear in certain late medieval manuscripts in northern Europe and are an important part of northern art thereafter. A genre-realism was the leading art of seventeenth-century Holland, and certain artists, like Jan Steen, came even closer than Courbet to a complete acceptance of everyday subject matter, although they employed a more abstract lighting. Eakins' ring scene [2] is a modern genre scene, but Bellows' [1] is a more expressionistic genre.

Expressionism

Expressionism is both a way of approaching art which could occur in any period and a particular art movement.

1. *As an approach to art,* expressionism makes form itself evoke strong or deep feeling. It is simply a strong emphasis of the expressive aspect of art discussed in Chapter 15. It may be argued that all fine art worthy of the name is expressive and essentially self-sufficient, in contrast to applied art, which has uses other than esthetic. Unfortunately, this can be taken only as a generalization to which there are exceptions; if we do accept as a hypothesis that worthy fine art is expressive, it would still not be universally expressionistic. *Expressionism is present when feeling or emotion assumes a major emphasis or intensity* and is evoked by the form itself. Thus in Levine's *Feast of Pure Reason* [169] the artist's violent feelings are expressed by distortion of subject matter, by harsh lighting, by heavy agitated surface texture, and by acridity of color. The picture becomes not so much a picture of three men as of the artist's feelings about them—or the evil they represent. The Breisach Altar [17] is an expressionistic manifestation of an ardent spirit.

In *abstract expressionism*, the presence of strong feeling is even more apparent, because the subject is either absent altogether or highly distorted. Hence the subject does not carry so many meanings independent of form, as in the Breisach Altar, where the subject may be regarded as a man, as Christ, as a king, as the Savior of man, and so forth. Pollock's painting [III] is a typical example of abstract expressionism, where form alone carries the evocation of feeling.

2. *As a movement*, expressionism began in Germany in the early twentieth century and collectively represented several groups and some independent artists of expressionistic tendency. The most prominent German groups were *Die Brücke* (The Bridge)—Emil Nolde, E. L. Kirchner [100], Max Pechstein—and *Der Blaue Reiter* (The Blue Rider)—Wassily Kandinsky [7], Franz Marc, Paul Klee. Among prominent independents were Oskar Kokoschka, Hans Barlach, and Käthe Kollwitz [106].

German expressionism lost much of its cohesiveness after World War I, but even the anti-artistic, nihilistic *Da-Da* movement—Tristan Tzara, Max Ernst, Marcel Duchamp—and the supposedly impersonal *New Objectivity* (Neue Sachlichkeit)—Otto Dix, George Grosz—which followed the war had an exuberance or fierce clarity born of strong feelings and related to expressionism. The new objectivity, however, was a reaction against what was felt to be the submissiveness and emotionalism of expressionism. The current abstract expressionism is something of a revival of expressionism as a widespread tendency. Expressionism's relation to the dissatisfactions of romanticism should also be clear.

Primitive Art

One of the influences on the expressionist movement, both in Germany and in France, was *primitive art*, by which is meant the art of people having a tribal social order. The available primitive artifacts, coming chiefly from equatoral Africa and from islands in the Pacific, were first observed in ethnological collections. The reason for the influence on modern art of these primitive forms is complex. They provided examples of creative endeavor in which the creative element—the form—was starkly revealed. They seemed to offer clues to the formal "essence" of art, a heightened emphasis of texture, color, material, and of related masses or shapes. Primitive art, moreover, of which masks and figurines were the most numerous examples, often suggested great vehemence of feeling, even though the exact nature of the feeling might remain inscrutable. The implication was inevitable that through the use of analagous abstractive devices the modern artist could achieve a greater vehemence and self-expression in his own work. Again, the publications of Freud at the end of the nineteenth century stimulated an interest in such concepts as that of the *id*, an underlying, primitive subconsciousness, an elemental force which the primitive art seemed also to express. Again, primitive art suggested ways of revolting against what many artists considered the hypocrisy and philistinism of the ruling middle class. That is, primitive art was bizarre, shocking, and therefore opened ways of stirring up the complacency of society. Finally, primitive art was attractive to those who saw good in the "natural" man and who felt that this art provided an esthetic approach to a more fundamental human state.

We must distinguish primitive art in the above form and attractions from the primitive art of such artists as Henri Rousseau and Grandma Moses. Such modern "primitives" are artists whose way of creating has an apparent naïveté. This is closely related to *folk art*, which is the same thing at an impersonal or group level. And we must distinguish all these forms from the art which is primitive in the sense of being inept or untutored, because the primitive art that attracted the artists did so because of its esthetic competence.

Abstract Art

It may be cogently argued that all art worthy of the name has some element of organized abstraction—form—and that all art, accordingly, should be regarded as abstract. *Abstract art*, as a term, however, is conventionally applied today only to that art, produced from about 1910, in which form is the exclusive, or nearly exclusive, concern.

Abstract art developed two distinct tendencies: 1) an emotional, baroque, expressionistic tendency, beginning, approximately, with Kandinsky [7] and culminating in abstract expressionism [159, 160]; 2) a detached, classical, rational tendency beginning approximately with *Suprematism* in 1913—Kasimir Malevitch—continuing under *De Stijl* in 1917—Van Doesburg and Mondrian [8]—and culminating in such contemporary artists as Josef Albers [IV]. In its works emphasizing spontaneity, movement, or "kinesthetic response," abstract expressionism is also called *action painting*.

Fauvism, 1904—Henri Matisse, Maurice de Vlaminck—may be regarded as precursor of the expressionistic, baroque, direction of abstract art; and *Cubism*, 1908—Pablo Picasso, Georges Braque—as precursor of its rational, classical direction.

Currently, there is a trend towards applying the term abstract expressionism only to nonobjective art (that is, art based on an equilibrium of dynamic or shifting visual effects—a kind of stable instability which stirs one's feelings) and the term abstract art to all other art having a strong de-emphasis of subject matter.

May it be apparent from the foregoing that terminology is a referent, only, to hypotheses or understandings concerning meaning! Terminology is a tool of communication. In a few scientific fields some terms may continue indefinitely to convey precisely the same meanings. In art, terms often carry an admixture of value judgments ("Gothic," "baroque," and "impressionism," for example, have been used as terms of derision) and their meanings shift with the changing insights of each generation. Investigation of terms is only a convenient device for knowing more precisely what we and the other fellow think, feel, and mean.

SELECTED READINGS

THIS BOOK is not meant to be more than an introduction to the vast, difficult, and fascinating subject of the nature of art. But a bibliography large enough to reflect fully the dimensions of the problem would only dismay the hopeful reader. For this reason only a few references have been selected from among the many worthy possibilities, in the hope of enticing the reader along his way. One thing leads to another until the chain is broken or interrupted, and the books that follow contain their own particular challenges and supplementary reading lists.

One thing seldom taken into account by authors is that new writers are to follow them. A bibliography is an invitation to thinking that is past, pertinent though it may be. The thinking of the future will not of necessity be better, but it will have relevance to the character and insights of our ever-shifting culture. The reader who has been interested by this book, therefore, might well join at least one of the professional organizations which contribute to the literature of the arts.

Among these are the College Art Association, 432 Fourth Avenue, New York 16, New York, and The American Society for Aesthetics, Mr. George E. Danforth, Secretary-Treasurer, Department of Architecture, Western Reserve University, Cleveland 6, Ohio. Membership in the College Art Association includes a subscription to two periodicals, the *Art Bulletin,* typically publishing specialized research, and the *College Art Journal,* which contains articles of a high level on serious current topics. Membership in the Society for Aesthetics includes a subscription to *The Journal of Aesthetics and Art Criticism,* which, as the title implies, is less concerned with art historical matters than the previously mentioned periodicals, although inevitably the fields overlap. Of the three, the *College Art Journal* comes closest to being a popular, high-level journal of the arts.

Subscription either to *Art News,* 32 East 57th Street, New York 22, New York, or to *The Arts,* 116 East 59th Street, New York 22, New York, is also recommended. These are popular commercial magazines containing reviews of current exhibitions, articles, and good quality reproductions. They deal mostly with the pictorial arts and sculpture.

If your interest has been challenged by architecture, you might consider the *Architectural Forum*, 9 Rockefeller Plaza, New York 20, New York, or the *Architectural Record*, 10 Ferry Street, Concord, New Hampshire.

These seven periodicals cover a wide range of levels of approach; if they are unfamiliar to you, you might well examine them at your library prior to the commitment of subscription.

While a few works cited below have bibliographies and extended discussion, some symposia are also included. Individual contributions in these will vary in quality, but the symposium is still a good device for a rapid introduction to the range of discussion in a field and good complement for lengthier systematic coverages. The list is in a suggested order of reading, although the reader should consult his own preferences of subject matter.

Bernard C. Heyl: *New Bearings in Esthetics and Art Criticism*, 1952. Wellesley College and Yale University Press.
An introduction to semantics in the arts, with a plea for relativism.
R. J. Goldwater and Marco Treves, editors: *The Artist on Art*, 1945. Pantheon Books.
An anthology of writings by artists.
Morris Weitz: *Problems in Aesthetics*, 1959. The Macmillan Company.
Another anthology of writings on esthetics, grouped around central problems.
R. M. MacIver, editor: *New Horizons in Creative Thinking*, 1954. Harper and Brothers.
A symposium which covers poetry, music, literature, and social problems, as well as the visual arts.
Lancelot Law Whyte: *Aspects of Form*, 1951. Humphries (London).
An anthology, revealing surprising parallels of form in various fields. Related, also, another anthology:
Gyorgy Kepes: The *New Landscape in Art and Science*, 1956. Paul Theobald.
Gyorgy Kepes: *The Language of Vision*, 1944. Paul Theobald.
Interesting discussion of formal principles plus a very personal philosophy of contemporary art.
Ben Shahn: *The Shape of Content*, 1957. Harvard University Press.
As above, but with the emphasis on content.
Norman T. Newman: *An Approach to Design*, 1949. Addison-Wesley Press.
An esthetic based on the primacy of the creative process in the service of social and humanistic ends. Written for the practicing designer, but of importance to the layman as well.

The next ten books in some respects are more nearly related to the history of art than to esthetics, but their strong esthetic concern or emphasis gives them their place here.

Siegfried Giedion: *Space, Time and Architecture*, 1954. Harvard University Press.

A masterly survey of modern architecture and its origins.

Lewis Mumford, editor: *Roots of Contemporary American Architecture*, 1952. Reinhold Publishing Company.

A series of essays on architecture, dating from the mid-nineteenth century to the present.

Lewis Mumford: *From the Ground Up*, 10th ed., 1956. Harvest Books.

Observations by this distinguished critic on contemporary architecture and also on such related fields as housing, highway building, and civic design.

Joseph Hudnut: *Architecture and the Spirit of Man*, 1949. Harvard University Press.

Urbane essays on a variety of architectural topics.

Bruno Zevi: *Architecture as Space*, 1957. Horizon Press.

Some provocative theories by one of Italy's leading architectural critics.

Edgar Kaufmann, editor: *An American Architecture, Frank Lloyd Wright*, 1955. Horizon Press.

Wright's own words, selectively paralleled with his works.

W. R. Valentiner: *Origins of Modern Sculpture*, 1946. Wittenborn, New York.

A concise, illuminating book, unfortunately out of print.

Charles Seymour: *Tradition and Experiment in Modern Sculpture*, 1949. American University Press.

A perceptive examination of contrasting tendencies.

Carola Giedion-Welcker: *Contemporary Sculpture; an Evolution in Volume and Space*, 1955. Wittenborn, New York.

Brief text, biographical notes and bibliography. Many illustrations.

Herbert Read: *The Philosophy of Modern Art*, 1955. Meridian Books (Horizon Press).

Not a philosophy in the formal sense, but a series of essays on the background and problems of modern art, with an emphasis on painting and painters.

Now we return to books of a more exclusive esthetic concern, and to one modern survey.

Thomas Munro: *The Arts and Their Interrelations*, 1951. The Liberal Arts Press.

A clearly written and comprehensive survey of some of the main problems in esthetics. These are supplemented by additional problems in:

Thomas Munro: *Toward Science in Aesthetics; Selected Essays*, 1956, Revision of Work Published in 1928. The Liberal Arts Press.

Arnold Hauser: *The Philosophy of Art History*, 1959. Alfred A. Knopf.

This fresh and stimulating book deals with such basic problems as the tension between the momentum of form and the potentially contrasting force of social influences. Background knowledge, on the reader's part, of literature in the field of art history and criticism is highly desirable.

Iredell Jenkins: *Art and the Human Enterprise,* 1958. Harvard University Press.

Not easy reading, but a provocative book which cuts across all the arts and sees art as an agent of life.

Katherine Gilbert and Helmert Kuhn: *A History of Esthetics,* 1953. Indiana University Press.

Ingratiatingly written thumbnail sketches of the leading theories from Plato to our time. A reference work.

Charles L. McCurdy, editor: *Modern Art, a Pictorial Anthology,* 1958. The Macmillan Company.

Over a thousand illustrations, mostly in snapshot size, with brief text and a good bibliography. A useful reference book and survey.

INDEX

The Index is divided into three parts. The first, *Illustrations*, appears at the front of the book, organized according to figure number and listing page location of illustration and textual references. *To refer to an illustration according to artist or location of building*, see the section below, *Persons, Places, Things*. The titles and page numbers of illustrations are italicized.

The third section, *Materials, Processes, Concepts*, brings together those references having esthetic implication or meaning. This final section may serve as a broad check list of terms and words related to the meaning of art. Subheadings of the words *art* and *architecture* generally appear according to the letter of the subheading: thus, *primitive art*, rather than *art, primitive*.

PERSONS, PLACES, THINGS

MATERIALS, PROCESSES, CONCEPTS

clapboard, 123
classic (classical) art, 281f., 287
Classicism: academicism, 288; Carolingian, 287; Neoclassicism, 287; Renaissance, 287
color (hue), 20
commercial art, 246
complementary color, 21
composition (arrangement of parts), 36, 147
composition (closed and open), 24, 34; balanced arrangement, 31, 147; total unity of, 36
comprehensive design, 96
concrete: reinforced, 83; prestressed, 84
concrete art, 160
Conté, 136
content, 17, 43ff., 179, 204, 216f.; conflict with form, 217; criteria in judging, 269ff.; expressed with form, 220; variability of, in art, 272
context, visual, 47
contour, 26f.
cornice, 69
cottage, Cape Cod, 106
crayon, 133ff.
criteria of judgment: in skating, 265f.; functional, 267, 273; in art generally, 272f.; in relation to content, 269ff.; in relation to form, 268f.
culture, as controlling fundamental, 240
curve, catenary, 83
custom, 239

Dada, movement, 203
dance, 271
decoration (decorative), 67, 180
design: comprehensive, 96; industrial, 246; in nature, 272; organic, 104
definition, function of, in art, 281, 282
dome, 73, 93, 95
drawing, vs. painting, 129
drypoint, 145f.

emotion, esthetic, 240
empathy, 36
encaustic, 158
engraving (graphic medium), 145
esthetic, the: as decorative interest, 180; as experimental

vehicle, 196; as momentum of form, 254; as vehicle for experience, 41; as visual significance, 16
etching, 146f.; soft-ground, 148
experience (of art shared with artist), 212
expressionism, 292f.; abstract, 204, 293, 294
expressiveness, 212, 215f., 218; and beauty, 283; of content, 220, 223; of form, 227f., 230, 231ff.; as pervasive effect, 235; as requisite in form, 274, 281; of subject, 231
eyebrow (architectural), 85

façade, 69
fantasy, 40
Fauvism, 294
ferrocement, 84
field (of picture), 22ff.; integration of figures in, 181
figure-ground, 22ff., 226
fine artist, 247
folk art, 243, 294
form, 17, 25, 46, 204; conflict with content, 217; and criteria of judgment, 268f.; as essence of art, 240; as experimental influence, 250; expressing content, 220; as expressive goal, 226ff., 231ff.; root character of, 272, 278ff.; in skating, 256ff.
Francesca, Piero della, 286
fresco, 155
functionalism, 68ff.; in development planning, 107ff., 124ff., 153; in house planning, 97ff.

garish, vs. ugly, 285
genre, 292
geodesics, 91
gesso, 156
gestalt, 272
glass, modern usage, 115ff.; wall, 113
glaze: in ceramics, 161f.; in painting, 159
glue resist, 151
Gothic revival, 290
gouache, 158
greatness in art, 285f.
ground (of picture), 22

hall-type church, 63

hue (color), 20
hyperbolic paraboloid, 76, 276

impasto, 159
Impressionism (Impressionist), 30
intaglio (graphic process), 144
intensity (saturation), 20

levels of approach, 174, 242ff., 245ff.
lamination (architectural), 98
landscaping (architectural), 105
light (lighting), use of by Rembrandt, 190f.
lithography (lithograph), 137ff.; color, 139
levels, of approach to art, 174
lost-wax process, 165f.

mass production, 107
materials, functional approach to, 167f.
medieval (Gothic), 51, 63, 223, 289
medium, texture of, 30; definitions of, 159. 1. in architecture: as space, 58ff.; cantilever, 122; concrete, 76f., 83ff., 87; glass, 114ff.; laminated wood, 98; proportion of, 62f.; texture of, 63; wood, 112, 121. 2. in graphic arts: aquatint, 147; chalk, 133ff.; charcoal, 131; drawing, 129; engraving, 145f.; etching, 146; lithograph, 137ff.; pencil and pen, 134f.; silk screen, 149; wash drawing, 135; woodcut, 140ff. 3. in painting: gouache, 158; importance of binder, 159; pigment, 155; tempera, 156; water color, 157. 4. in sculpture: bronze, 165f.; ceramic, 161ff.; stone, 164, 166; welded wire, 166f.; wood, 164. 5. miscellaneous: as factor of form, 281, fiberglas, 247
mezzotint, 152
module (architectural), 117
mold, for bronze casting, 165f.; for concrete, 85
mosaic, 26
motif, 15
mural, ceiling, 155

naked, vs. nude, 179
nature, and romanticism, 290